Northwest Vista College
Learning Resource Center
3535 North Ellison Drive
San Antonio, Texas 78251

D1519370

MARTIAL ARTS IN THE MODERN WORLD

Edited by Thomas A. Green and Joseph R. Svinth

Westport, Connecticut
London

Library of Congress Cataloging-in-Publication Data

Martial arts in the modern world / edited by Thomas A. Green and Joseph R. Svinth.
   p. cm.
   Includes bibliographical references and index.
   ISBN 0–275–98153–3 (alk. paper)
   1. Martial arts—Anthropological aspects. 2. Martial arts—History. I. Green, Thomas A.,
1944– II. Svinth, Joseph R.
GV1102.7.A56M37   2003
796.8—dc21   2003051062

British Library Cataloguing in Publication Data is available.

Library of Congress Catalog Card Number: 2003051062
ISBN: 0–275–98153–3

First published in 2003

Praeger Publishers, 88 Post Road West, Westport, CT 06881
An imprint of Greenwood Publishing Group, Inc.
www.praeger.com

Printed in the United States of America

The paper used in this book complies with the
Permanent Paper Standard issued by the National
Information Standards Organization (Z39.48–1984).

10 9 8 7 6 5 4 3 2 1

To John F. Gilbey, who inadvertently showed us the way

CONTENTS

ACKNOWLEDGMENTS

All persons listed as personal correspondents have read the quotes attributed to them and were aware at the time of the correspondence or interview that these conversations were subject to eventual publication. Where requested, anonymity was provided.

Research involved with Joseph Svinth's chapters about Japanese boxing and kendo in North America was financially supported by grants from the Japanese American National Museum and King County Landmarks and Heritage Commission. The Melbern G. Glasscock Center for Humanities Research at Texas A&M University provided support through a fellowship awarded to Thomas A. Green.

Although they are in no way responsible for our conclusions (and indeed, would vehemently disagree with some of them), intellectual inspiration for this project included the pioneering efforts of Roger Abrahams, Donn Draeger, and Robert W. Smith. We also wish to thank the late Ubaldo Alcantara, whose graciousness and wisdom guided us on many occasions.

Colleagues who went far beyond the call of duty in providing ideas, information, and critiques included Jason Couch, Donna Fulford, Daniel Marks, Rory Miller, Ron Mottern, and Rachelle Saltzman. Earl Hartman and Valerie Green deserve special mention for their translation services. Others who provided invaluable assistance included Mick Antoine, Tom Bolling, Melissa Booth, John Clements, John Corcoran, David Cvet, Mark Feigenbaum, Jane Garry, Richard Strozzi Heckler, Mark Hewitt, Brian Kennedy, Deborah Klens-Bigman, Gary Kuris, Matt Larsen, Greg Mele, Tom

Militello, Curtis Narimatsu, Dennis Newsome, Kevin Plagman, Edward L. Powe, Guy Power, Dan Trembula, Doug Walker, Neil Yamamoto, and Homer Yasui. Obviously, errors are our own.

Finally, thanks are due to our contributors, who put up with a lot, and to our families, who put up with more. For Joseph Svinth, this includes Huldah and Giani, and for Thomas Green, Alexandra, Colin, and Valerie.

MARTIAL ARTS IN THE MODERN WORLD: INTRODUCTION

Thomas A. Green

Most works that carry the words "martial arts" in their titles contain instruction and describe purportedly ancient and unchanging Asian systems having vaguely spiritual overtones. This isn't one of those books.

The chapters of the present volume examine the forces and philosophies that shaped the fighting arts of the twentieth century. Because globalization is a phenomenon of the century, the events take place in diverse cultural settings. Thus, there are discussions of Western boxing in Japan, professional wrestling in Brazil, and street fights in New York City.

Moreover, rather than recording immutable, unchanging systems, this book documents change over time. Some of the arts described flourished in new physical, social, and psychological environments; others did not. Some remained martial in nature; others metamorphosed into sport, performance art, or discipline for self-fulfillment.

In this book are accounts of Asians adopting Western combative sports, while Westerners simultaneously turn to Asian martial disciplines. These descriptions coexist with armies using martial arts to teach self-actualization, movie stars advertised as the world's deadliest fighting men, and churches using martial arts to teach children not to fight. Such contradictions are the nature of martial arts in the modern world.

One of our themes is that martial arts are social tools. That is, they serve means other than individual fitness, self-defense, or self-improvement. We support the thesis by noting that martial art history is almost infinitely malleable, more often invented than faithfully recorded, made-up rather than

Corporal Arvin Lou Ghazlo, USMC, giving hand-to-hand combat instruction to Private Ernest C. Jones, USMCR, at Montford Point, North Carolina, during April 1943. Courtesy the National Archives and Record Administration. ARC identifier 532513. Online version downloaded October 16, 2002. Available through the online catalog at http://www.archives.gov/research_room/research_topics/african_ americans_during_wwii/african_americans_during_world_war_2.html.

passed down. Such manipulation is not unique to martial arts histories. However, while the cliché claims that the winners write history, the truth is that losers write histories, too, and how we interpret what happened may be of greater ultimate consequence than what actually happened.[1]

The reasons for such manipulation of history should be clear. As Richard Bowen has observed, "History is dangerous to authority because it holds up a mirror in which reflections of the past shine on present events" (personal communication, July 2002). Now, this is not to say that there is no such thing as an investigation made simply to try to make sense of the past. Nor are scientific investigations impossible. After all, as Nobel laureate Kary Mullis says, "It doesn't take a lot of education to check things out" (1998: 154). Nevertheless, most of the stories in this book show that the martial arts are what James C. Scott calls "weapons of the weak" (1985). That is, they are tools used by the dominated to get the upper hand, if only in the world of narrative. The youth outwitted bullies; the elderly master turned the tables on an ambitious underling; the people fought tyrants.

Another theme involves the almost neo-Luddite role that martial arts have played in a century of increasing technological sophistication. There are contradictions here, too. For example, although it still takes a teacher and a training partner to learn an art, e-communications are increasingly usurping the role of face-to-face interactions in the transmission of martial arts folklore. Meanwhile, just as some people look to the past to create their better future, others look to the computer screen.

Put another way, this book does not present martial arts as carvings in stone, but as reflections in mirrors. The goal of its chapters is to offer some insight into what is seen in those mirrors, and why.

A NOTE ON ROMANIZATION

In this book, romanizations of Asian words generally follow these systems:

- Chinese: Pinyin
- Japanese: Modified Hepburn
- Korean: McCune-Reischauer

However, there are inconsistencies. For example, because this book was intended for general readers, we omitted diacritical marks and macrons in transliterations. In addition, whenever a loanword appeared in *Webster's Ninth New Collegiate Dictionary* (1990), we used it. Finally, whenever we realized that this might lead to misunderstanding or confusion, then the correct interpretation is included parenthetically.

Personal names of Asians generally appear in the Asian order of family name first. Exceptions occur in direct quotations or when discussing people who became resident aliens or citizens of a foreign country.

SENSE IN NONSENSE: THE ROLE OF FOLK HISTORY IN THE MARTIAL ARTS

Thomas A. Green

INTRODUCTION

Whether by means of oral transmission or take-home handouts, novices learn about the origins and history of the martial art they study. Through these anecdotes, legends, and other traditional narratives, teachers recount the virtues of their predecessors and thereby establish the value (and *values*) of their martial discipline. Regardless of the means of transmission, these bodies of knowledge constitute what anthropologists call *folk history*.

At this point, I must emphasize that the accuracy of the claims made in folk histories is irrelevant to the following discussion. Clearly, some of the claims made about martial art systems are fraudulent, and a few stories are simply bad fiction composed by self-serving instructors. Although these hodge-podge "histories" are interesting (especially interesting is why otherwise rational people would accept them), the role played by these fantasies is beyond the scope of this essay. Instead, the focus is on the function of the folk narratives themselves.

WHAT IS FOLK HISTORY?

Although one could argue that history (of any sort) is infused with point of view and driven by special interests, most recent history is reasonably verifiable. Therefore, describing "what actually happened" using a mixture of contemporary documents, subsequent analysis, and interviews is the goal of "scientific history," or historiography.

Desire. Courtesy Joseph Svinth.

In a scientific history, narrative flow or story is not as important as clarity and accuracy. As the *Publication Manual of the American Psychological Association* (1994: 25) puts it,

> Scientific prose and creative writing serve different purposes. Devices that are often found in creative writing—for example, setting up ambiguity, inserting the unexpected, omitting the expected, and suddenly shifting the topic, tense, or person—can confuse or disturb readers of scientific prose. Therefore, you should avoid these devices and aim for clear and logical communication.

In addition, in scientific writing, it is essential to corroborate facts and support assertions. "Whether paraphrasing or quoting an author directly," says the *Publication Manual of the American Psychological Association* (1994: 97), "you must credit the source." The validity of a scientific argument rests entirely on its foundation of documentation.

At the other extreme are hagiographies, which are biographical accounts written for the sole purpose of glorifying some person. Hagiographies may have almost no basis in fact, but the author was motivated to glorify the subject by a tangible reward: by being paid, by being elevated in status within a social group, or by prestige through association. In brief, the author was told to say nice things, and so he did.

Here, however, we are looking at what the academic discipline of folklore terms "legends." Legends, folklorists maintain, are

- set in the historical reality of the group,
- populated by human characters, and
- accounts that focus on recurring issues of the group (origins, traditional enemies and allies, etc.).

In many cases, legends are grounded in the biographies of genuine historical characters (e.g., Wyatt Earp, Jesse James) or events (the spread of Ch'an [Zen] Buddhism through China). Although legends often incorporate extraordinary incidents, group members consider these events plausible. Indeed, group members often strenuously maintain the truth of the extraordinary account: You and I cannot dodge bullets, but the founder of our martial art could.

Labeling such narratives as folk histories does not devalue in any way these accounts or the group members themselves. Rather, the label designates a specific intent behind the accumulation and performance of the narratives. That purpose is to provide a lens through which members of the group view the present and past, and understand their own relationship to other groups.

While describing how folk histories provide a lens through which to view the world, anthropologist Charles Hudson (1966) has suggested that they are a fundamental means for interpreting experience and organizing behavior. Hudson furthermore notes that a group's belief system is consistent with current conditions and the group's folk history. The past is thus constructed as a means to understand the present.

This is not very different from the official histories promulgated by governments, churches, and school boards, except that the agendas being advanced are different, and that the folk histories tend to be oral rather than written.

HOW FOLK HISTORY IS TRANSMITTED

Unlike scientific histories, with their requirement for accurate citation, folk histories generally have multiple (and often anonymous) creators. As oral transmissions, these narratives are subject to modification by the ordinary people, as well as by the leaders of the group. Additionally, these narratives, like other forms of folklore, change in order to respond to the changing needs of the speaker or group. Therefore, while oral circulation does not automatically entail distortion, factual consistency over long periods is rare.

Because folk history is primarily an oral art form, it is heavily influenced by the art of storytelling. Thus, one commonly finds artistic clichés in plots, character types, and narrative episodes. Furthermore, folk history exists more to persuade (for example, we are entitled to x because of y) than to document. Therefore, events and personalities are sometimes manipulated or even reconstructed, sometimes in the face of quantifiable evidence. This nudging of the facts represents an effort to legitimize the priorities and point of view of the speaker (Green, 1997, p. 809).

As I have noted elsewhere (Green, 1997), the histories told to beginners in the martial arts often include ad-libbed remarks and anecdotes, the purpose of which is to flesh out the presentation. Of course, the choice of such narrative insertions (and the decision to include them at all) remains at the discretion of the often comparatively junior person charged with conducting the orientation. Obviously, this degree of latitude makes for great variation in what students learn about their art's history.

At any rate, the multiple versions of stories owe as much to dialogue and imagination as to documentation. Thus, while a rough consensus usually exists about basic facts (the forces of tradition limit variation), each story has uniqueness, and its telling often tells us as much about the teller's individual experiences, depth of understanding, and personality as it does about the subject of the tale.

HOW FOLK HISTORY IS USED

To Establish Credibility

Folk accounts of a martial art system's origins invariably seek to bring honor to the system and its founders. Either as individuals or as members

A martial art demonstration at the Shaolin Temple, from a version of Lin Qing, *Hongxue Yinyuan Tuji*, ca. 1880s. Lin Qing was a Chinese government official who visited Shaolin Monastery in 1828. He subsequently published an illustrated book describing his travels. According to Lin Qing, the head monk was uncomfortable showing him martial arts because of government decrees against such practices. Lin Qing described the demonstration using a phrase from *Zhuangzi*, namely, *"xiong jing niao shen,"* which describes movements of bears and birds. This in turn refers to physical exercises done during the fourth and third centuries B.C.E., when the *Zhuangzi* was recorded. Courtesy Stanley Henning.

of an esoteric tradition, people within this system were capable of extraordinary accomplishments, and therefore, modern lineage holders profit from the halo effect.

To serve this end, storytellers sometimes appropriate traditional narrative motifs. Examples include legends of the Shaolin Temple of Henan. The Temple is a widely accepted historical reference point, and traditional narratives linking systems to this point of origin are used to provide pedigrees for systems whose real origins have become obscured over time. In other cases, martial art folk histories reflect the desire of modern practitioners to establish credibility through association with a legendary past.

In these cases, ties to historical tradition may be claimed simply to appropriate the fame of the Temple for nontraditional systems.

Folk histories sometimes provide association with exceptional masters or events. For example, there may be stories about the founder's epic battles with foreigners or animals. (Bulls and tigers are particular favorites.) Sometimes this prowess is associated with physical discipline, and other times with mastery of esoteric knowledge. In either event, the assumption is that the master achieved his expertise through the acquisition of esoteric knowledge rather than native talent. Moreover, this esoteric knowledge still exists, to be revealed to the properly motivated student at some future time. In these stories, wandering Taoists, hermits, nature mystics, dreams, and even pointy-nosed goblins serve as vehicles for transmission of secrets. Thus, a triptych by Kunisada (ca. 1815) shows the Japanese hero Minamoto Yoshitsune being put through his paces by Sojobo, King of the Tengu (mountain goblins).

Martial legend draws from a common body of motifs, and entire narratives recur cross-culturally. The most common explanation among scholars for such replication is that there was an original creation and subsequent borrowing. Folk creativity enters the picture via the adoption of the original narrative plot and the adaptation of the tale to fit the needs of the borrowing group.

A common plot found in the creation myths of martial arts involves the founder witnessing a battle between a snake and a bird. For instance, in one of the origin legends circulating in the *taijiquan* (Wade-Giles: t'ai chi ch'uan) repertoire, one day Zhang Sanfeng witnessed a battle between a crane and a snake. From this experience, he created *taijiquan*. It is probably not coincidental that this snake and bird narrative is associated with more than one martial art. Similarly, Ng Mui is reputed in legends of the Triad society (originally an anti–Qing Dynasty secret society) to be one of the Five Elders who escaped a Qing attack on the Shaolin monastery. According to these stories, she created *yongchun* (Wade-Giles: wing chun) boxing after witnessing a battle between a snake and a crane. (Other versions have it as a battle between a snake and a fox.) From Sumatra comes the same tale of a fight between a snake and bird witnessed by a woman who was then inspired to create *pencak silat* (Henning and Green, 2001: 127–128).

Resistance Narratives

Resistance to oppressive (and usually foreign) governments or religions provides another common motif. For example, with the growth of the Chinese Triad societies in the early nineteenth century, some Triad martial art groups promoted a body of legend that attributed their origin to a second, southern Shaolin monastery located in Fujian Province. Given its self-serving goal, probably this tradition was consciously invented by Triad leadership rather than something that spontaneously originated within the group. Either way, the secret societies sought to gain the popular support needed to further their anti-Qing agenda by appropriating the heroic and patriotic image of Ming Dynasty Shaolin monks.

Histories linking religious havens, radical political resistance, and martial arts are not limited to Qing Dynasty China, but appear throughout time and across cultures. Some examples suggest that these traditions are probably the result of agendas shared by the politically oppressed rather than the result of cross-cultural diffusion. For example, some practitioners of the African Brazilian martial art of capoeira trace their art's origins to the seventeenth-century *quilombo* (runaway slave settlement) of Palmares and its legendary King, Zumbi. According to oral tradition and the songs sung during capoeira play, Zumbi nurtured capoeira and used it to fend off raids from the armed parties who pursued runaway slaves. The indigenous African religions that formed the basis for modern Candomblé and similar New World faiths also were nurtured in the bush. This pattern is consistent with the beliefs of the Shaolin origins of the Triads noted above and supports the argument of James C. Scott, who writes that tales of social bandits, outlaw heroes, tricksters, and peasant revolutionaries create a climate of opinion that furthers political resistance (Scott, 1985).

Parable

Despite practitioners frequently accepting the exploits of figures such as Zumbi and Ng Mui as givens, the historical records of these legendary founders are usually fragmentary. From the perspective of developing group identity, this fragmentary evidence is of course an advantage, as it means that the life histories of the founders remain malleable and, therefore, available to serve the changing needs of the group. In the process, biography becomes parable.

In parables, fictionalized accounts serve a higher truth. In other words, they describe what we should strive to be rather than what we are. That traditional patterns continue to emerge in contemporary martial biographies argues for continuing function.

For example, according to Peter Urban (Urban, 1967), the Goju Kai karate teacher Yamaguchi Gogen triumphed over a tiger in unarmed combat. This took place during Yamaguchi's confinement in a Soviet prison camp in Manchuria. Significantly, Urban labels this account a tale, thus signifying that this is an oral tradition and therefore subject to the qualifications of the genre. In Urban's account, guards tried to break Yamaguchi's spirit. They failed, but noticed the effect that his continued defiance had on his fellow prisoners. This was unacceptable, so they thrust him into a cage with a hungry tiger. However, to the guards' chagrin, Yamaguchi survived by killing the tiger in a matter of seconds. During the 1970s, Yamaguchi was personally asked through an interpreter about this event. Yamaguchi replied that he was indeed put into a cage with a tiger. However, he did not fight the animal. Instead, realizing there was nothing else to do, he sat down to meditate. Becoming bored, the tiger went to sleep, and eventually the guards removed Yamaguchi (Kregg Jorgenson, personal communication, January 2002). Nevertheless, Urban's version of the story persists. This is partly because he wrote it in a still-popular book, and mostly because of its consistency with traditional motifs. Among these are man's triumph over beast, the power of martial art as a tool to combat political oppression, the superhuman powers conveyed by martial art practice, and the deification of the founder. (Yamaguchi was head of the Goju karate organization to which Urban belonged at the time of his book's publication.)

Deification of the founders is an inevitable feature of martial art literature. Writing about Okinawan karate legend Motobu Choki, Graham

Motobu Choki, late 1920s. Courtesy Patrick McCarthy.

Noble (2000a) cites Peter Urban's description of Motobu as a massive man standing over 7 feet tall. Later, American Robert Trias corrected the account to reduce Motobu to a mere 6 feet 8 inches in height. On contacting karate historian Richard Kim, Noble reports that Kim stated that Motobu was "a little under 6 feet tall." Further investigation of the photographic and printed record led Noble to shrink Motobu to around 5 feet 3 inches. In this case, a martial legend was literally larger than life.

The impulse to exaggerate is so pervasive that Nagamine Shoshin in his *Tales of Okinawa's Great Masters* felt compelled to devote a chapter to "The Power of Myth," in which he debunked legends of the superhuman feats of the masters. Nagamine seeks to demystify without ridiculing, however, for he argues for the social function of these embellished historical narratives consistent with the current analysis.

CONCLUSION

To reiterate, the literal, documented, and historiographical accuracy of martial histories is not an issue in the present analysis. Neither is accuracy an issue to students of the martial systems in which these stories circulate, in part because questioning too rigorously can (and often does) lead to expulsion or resignation from the system.[1] At the same time, however, these stories serve quantifiable functions for group members. These functions range from encouraging a sense of group pride to demonstrating the proper procedures for doing something as straightforward as asking to get a drink of water.

Comparing folk histories to invented traditions (here defined as "instant formulations of new traditions") is instructive. Eric Hobsbawm and Terence Ranger (1983) contend that invented traditions serve the respective functions of establishing social cohesion, legitimizing institutions or "relations of authority," and socialization. Although the historical narratives of the martial arts should be viewed as consciously organized and utilized rather than invented,[2] they serve the same ends as invented traditions. For instance, martial art narratives provide a common ground for instructors and students. In addition, they perpetuate the manners and habits of foreign cultures. Finally, they improve group solidarity.[3]

At the same time, the stories and personal narratives suggest attitudes and strategies for dealing with persecution or violence (these are among the lessons of Shaolin resistance to foreign rule) and encourage a particular mind-set. This unitary worldview is conducive to extraordinary bonding and is one reason that the Marine Corps began stressing "warrior values."

Finally, the stories seek to minimize the stresses resulting from the physical and psychological demands of a rigorous curriculum. Virtually all systems develop narratives claiming a previously closed nature for their arts. In the "bad old days," training was far harder than it is today, or it was available only to a particular ethnic group, banned by authorities, or otherwise limited in circulation. The rhetoric of such narratives suggests that modern students should be grateful for any access at all: no price is too great to pay.

Because these constructed histories draw on traditional models found in both folklore and comic books (see Lewis, 1987), we give blatant charlatans too much credit when we accuse them of creating a martial art myth out of whole cloth. Returning to the observations of El-Shamy (in Green 1997), we note a set of central motifs:

- Childhood difficulties
- Early weakness being offset by emergence of mentor's or guardian figure's demonstration of superhuman strength and ability
- Rapid rise to prominence
- Struggles against representatives of evil
- Proneness to pride or other personality defects

Consequently, biographies of the founder often include the following features:

- Claims of mixed ethnic ancestry, typically resulting in the founder being bullied as a child
- The founder being taught an ancient, covert art by a family member in order to overcome illness, persecution, or personality defect (especially temper), or by a family friend in order to repay a debt to the founder's parent
- The founder's exceptional devotion to training leading to rapid advancement (typically a master's rank at a young age)
- A final lesson in humility from a mentor figure
- Finally, superhuman exploits against forces of evil

Thus, these accounts present us with a series of contradictions. While martial art practitioners continually modify their stories in response to contemporary events, their folk biographies remain remarkably consistent in their plots and presentation. While martial art stories seek to reassure the listener that the art he or she is learning has not changed in decades, the stories themselves are in a constant process of revision, reformulation, and mutation. Finally, although most recent history can be documented using newspaper articles, promotion certificates, photographs, and interviews, it remains almost impossible to set down a history of a martial art that both practitioners and nonpractitioners will accept.

On the other hand, we can attend to the relationships between martial folk histories and the group contexts in which they exist. Barring outright commercial exploitation, these histories are for the most part, to quote Nagamine (2000:116), "positive and serve to teach important lessons."

THE MARTIAL ARTS IN CHINESE PHYSICAL CULTURE, 1865–1965

Stanley E. Henning

INTRODUCTION

This essay is, in a sense, a groundbreaking effort. The subject is not new, but the approach and scope are.

The first Chinese-language book to attempt the history of Chinese physical culture was Guo Xifen's book (1919/1970), originally published in 1919. About half this book was devoted to martial arts. From the 1930s until his death in 1959, Tang Hao (b. 1897) published many excellent articles, booklets, and other research materials on specific issues in Chinese martial art history. In 1967, in Taiwan, Wu Wenzhong published *A History of Physical Culture in China during the Last 100 Years.* Finally, in 1985, Xi Yuntai published the first Chinese-language book dedicated purely to the history of the Chinese martial arts.

In languages other than Chinese, during the 1970s, Matsuda Ryuji published a Japanese-language *Short History of the Chinese Martial Arts.* This was translated into Chinese in 1984. In English, the first serious effort was Kang Gewu's *The Spring and Autumn of Chinese Martial Arts: 5000 Years* (1995). Unfortunately, this book is primarily a list of dates and facts, and it does not tie the information together in a coherent manner. Therefore, a more useful effort covering much of the period covered in this chapter is Andrew D. Morris's 1998 dissertation *Cultivating the National Body: A History of Physical Culture in Republican China.* This work is worth its weight in gold, and at 740 pages, that is a fair amount!

HISTORICAL CONTEXT

In some ways, Chinese physical culture in 1865 was similar to Chinese physical culture a thousand years earlier. In a society where the peasants worked hard from dawn to dusk, physical culture and one's work were essentially the same.

Next in importance to one's livelihood was group security. This meant military training. In traditional China, military training normally took place after the fall harvest. Military exercises included wrestling (basic hand-to-hand combat), archery, and the use of pole and edged weapons. Also considered military-related activities were forms of football, swimming, running, tile tossing, and weight lifting.

Exhibitions of Chinese martial physical culture also appeared in ceremonial dances and popular festival entertainment. Examples included the martial art exhibitions seen during opera performances, mystery plays, and trade fairs.

Individual exercises designed to maintain health were not directly associated with Chinese martial culture but were complementary to it. Among these were *qigong,* or energy cultivation techniques. Individuals throughout society, including Buddhist monks and Taoist recluses, practiced these methods of psychophysiological discipline.

In antiquity, some Chinese intellectuals practiced martial physical culture. For example, the six gentlemanly arts of early Confucian philosophy included charioteering and archery, and courtly music included both civil and martial ceremonial dances. This was similar to Plato's belief that a proper education combined a foundation in literature, mathematics, and music with military gymnastics. During the Qing Dynasty (1644–1911), however, intellectuals were discouraged from participating in martial pursuits. Nevertheless, some intellectuals still advocated martial arts training alongside book learning. Proponents of such practical learning included members of the Yan-Li School, established by Yan Yuan (1635–1704) and his disciple Li Gong (1659–1733).

MID– TO LATE NINETEENTH CENTURY

By the mid–nineteenth century, internal rebellions such as the Taiping Rebellion caused great upheaval and millions of deaths in China. Meanwhile, Europe, Russia, Japan, and the United States intruded from without.

During these traumatic times, Qing Imperial banner forces, local militias, bandits, and rebels continued practicing traditional forms of martial physical culture. For example, until 1902, imperial bodyguard units (Shanpu Ying) held annual wrestling matches on the grounds of the Great Buddha Temple in Beijing (*Dianshizhai Huabao,* 1884–1894). The justification was that, in spite of modern firearms, bare-handed fighting was still useful in some situations. Moreover, the display of sportsmanship demonstrated good discipline. Imperial displays included feats of strength, such as wielding a 120-pound iron halberd and lifting a 300-pound stone weight. In addition, there were demonstrations of archery and horsemanship (Zi, 1896/1971).

However, as more foreign weapons and military advisors entered China, foreign close-order drills and calisthenics came, too. For example, Li Hongzhang established a naval academy *(shuishi xuetang)* in Tianjin in 1880 and a military academy *(wubei xuetang)* in 1885. These schools used German, British, and Japanese advisors/instructors and taught Western-style military physical training or calisthenics (Wu, 1967: 21).

Foreign missionaries also established Western-style schools in various cities. Originally designed to educate the children of expatriates, gradually these mission schools opened to Chinese. The first of these, St. Johns University, was established in Shanghai in 1879. Additional mission schools soon followed in Beijing, Tianjin, and Hangzhou. Among the accomplishments of these schools was introducing Western biological sciences, anatomy, and physical training pedagogy into China (Hartnett, 1998: 37).

Outside the few big cities, the old martial culture continued to flourish. Reading the 1880s tabloid *Decorative Stone Studio Illustrated News (Dianshizhai Huabao),* one runs across a number of fascinating martial arts vignettes. These run the gamut from military and individual training to incidents of highway robbery, burglary, and just plain hooliganism.

One story describes four young women who trained strenuously in the courtyard of their home. They practiced balancing and jumping from one wooden stake (known as a plum flower stake) to another, meticulously avoiding falling on the sharp iron spikes in the space between the stakes. The story concludes with the remark that, although all four were attractive, no one dared to approach them for marriage because of their martial arts practice (*Dianshizhai Huabao,* 1884–1894).

Another story, titled "The Manly Woman," tells of a man held against his will for failure to pay his debts to an opium den owner. The man's wife boldly entered the opium den and confronted the owner. When he moved to manhandle her, she let loose a flying kick that sent him sprawling. Two others came at her from two directions, and she simultaneously knocked them both flat using a two-handed "bow draw" punch. Six others, seeing

The four plum-flower maidens, leaping from pole to pole. From *Decorative Stone Studio Illustrated News (Dianshizhai Huabao)*, 1880s. Courtesy Stanley Henning.

the commotion, rushed in at her from outside. Feigning a fall, she suddenly leapt up and caught one with another flying kick, then followed through and punched out three others. Sensibly, the remaining man did not challenge her. She then took her husband's hand and led him out the door (*Dianshizhai Huabao*, 1884–1894).

Yet another story describes an escort agent named Bai. An escort agent was a martial art practitioner who served as a bodyguard, or who escorted valuables in transit. One day, while en route with a consignment, Bai encountered a heavyset rogue Shaolin monk. The "monk" refused to let Bai pass, and said he would take the consignment away if Bai could not defeat him with three punches to his belly. Bai agreed, took aim, and punched him in the stomach. However, the monk did not budge an inch. Bai figured that the monk practiced *qigong,* so he flattered him for his prowess and asked if he could try again. The monk agreed, so Bai charged,

The manly woman. From *Decorative Stone Studio Illustrated News (Dianshizhai Huabao),* 1880s. Courtesy Stanley Henning.

and in the twinkling of an eye, the monk's testicles were in the palm of Bai's hand (*Dianshizhai Huabao,* 1884–1894).

In "The Cute Martial Prostitute," a young woman took a wooden staff and knocked the daylights out of hoodlums who came to wreck the bordello where she worked (*Dianshizhai Huabao,* 1884–1894).

Although fanciful, these colorful portraits together with 196 pages of examples in the *Qing Bai Lei Chao* (Qing unofficial history categorized extracts) paint a picture of the widespread practice of martial arts in Chinese society up to the twentieth century.

The stories also reflect the primary perception of these arts: self-defense. Martial arts were to late Qing China what the Colt and Winchester were to the American West.

ON THE EVE OF THE REVOLUTION OF 1911

During the late nineteenth century, Western military calisthenics were introduced into the Chinese military and the still-tiny Chinese public school system. Urban Chinese also were exposed to Western sports through the

A Chinese soldier ("Boxer"), 1900. U.S. Army Signal Corps photograph. National Archives and Record Administration, ARC identifier 530870.

activities of missionary groups such as the Young Men's Christian Association (YMCA).

Nonetheless, martial arts remained China's most widespread form of physical discipline. The pervasiveness of traditional martial arts in Chinese society was starkly revealed by the uprising of the Righteous and Harmonious Fists, or "Boxers," in 1900.

China's first popular physical culture and sports organization was established in Shanghai in 1909. In 1910, this organization took the name Jingwu Tiyu Hui, or Martial Excellence Physical Culture Association. Eventually it spread throughout China, and to this day, it maintains branches in various overseas communities.

In those days, Shanghai was organized into foreign concessions. Basically, the Europeans owned the city. The Jingwu Tiyu Hui was a patriotic organization, and it reportedly got its start after the Hebei martial art teacher Huo Yuanjia and his disciple Liu Zhensheng scared off a foreign roughneck who publicly challenged any Chinese "sick man of east Asia" to fight him.

Reflective of the changing times, to maintain its membership, the Jingwu Tiyu Hui offered Western sports alongside martial arts. Similarly, some YMCA branches offered martial arts alongside Western sports (Morris, 1998).

The Jingwu Tiyu Hui and the Shanghai YMCA apparently had an amicable relationship. An article in the *North China Herald* (May 8, 1920: 342–343) described the inauguration of the Ladies' Department of the Jingwu Tiyu Hui; the display was held on the premises of the Shanghai YMCA. Chinese boxing was the feature of the day, but when asked if they practiced any forms of foreign exercise, the young Chinese women replied:

> Yes. We play tennis, volleyball, basketball, rings, and other sorts of foreign gymnastics and games. Of course, you must understand that while we put Chinese boxing first, we do not preclude others from playing just as they please. If a girl wishes to play a certain game, she is at liberty to do so. However, we do not have calisthenics in our Club. ("Wushu: Chinese girl athletes," 2000)

EARLY REPUBLICAN CHINA: 1912–1927

In the wake of the Revolution of 1911, assorted physical culture associations were established throughout China. Many catered to the public. Some were privately run, but others were associated with provincial governments, and some served the military organizations of local warlords.

In Shandong Province, the Jinan garrison commander, Ma Liang (1878–1947), established one of the most famous military programs. As early as 1911, Ma gathered a group of martial art teachers and produced a training manual titled *Zhonghua Xin Wushu* (New Chinese Martial Arts, 1917). The manual provided easy-to-follow instructions for individual and group practice in Chinese wrestling, boxing, staff, and sword. Ma pushed his program, and by 1917, the national-level military and police training departments adopted it. In 1918, China's National Assembly also considered adopting it as the formal calisthenics regimen for the public schools.

Ma often used his troops to stage martial arts demonstrations. An Englishman living in China described one of these for the *Literary Digest* (May 29, 1920):

> Such shows begin gently enough, with a placid drill in calisthenics. After the calisthenics comes a sword-drill with straight swords, which is followed by a drill in the use of a quarter-staff about six feet long. Then comes the wrestling which is fast and furious, and which is no child's play. General

Ma Liang explains that it is much more completely developed than the "small part" which the Japanese have borrowed. In this phase of the drill the Japanese are, of course, intensely interested. General Ma Liang says that thousands of Japanese officers and men have come at one time or another to see the performances, and, according to creditable witnesses, one or two of the best wrestlers have thrown every jiu-jutsu champion whom the Japanese have been able to bring to Tsinan. Highly dramatic combats with lances and swords follow the wrestling. The layman sees in General Ma Liang's drill nothing but a highly diverting circus, but the military man sees in it a system of mental and muscular training which takes a loutish and stupid coolie and makes of him an alert, sensitive, highly disciplined man who can be readily trained in the use of any weapon and is prepared to undertake any amount of training, fatigue, and hardship. Military men who have seen the show have told the writer that there is scarcely any feature of it which could not be adopted to occidental uses. ("Strenuous Athletics," 1999)

New Chinese Martial Arts broke with tradition by offering simplified training in practical techniques. This was not revolutionary, as General Qi Jiguang had done the same when training his peasant volunteers to fight Japanese pirates in the mid–sixteenth century. However, as fate would have it, the New Chinese Martial Arts got lost in the New Cultural Movement debate of the 1920s. The New Cultural Movement debate was about how best to modernize China. It pitted tradition versus Western approaches, and in this debate, New Chinese Martial Arts was seen as traditionalist and anti-democratic. Therefore, it was relegated to the dustbin of history.

Of course, Ma's own actions did not help his cause. For example, following World War I, the Versailles Treaty gave former German territory in China to Japan. This sparked the May Fourth Incident of 1919, in which

Drawings used to illustrate late nineteenth-century copies of Qi Jiguang's military manuals. Courtesy Joseph Svinth.

Chinese students violently protested their government's impotence. At the time, Ma was responsible for martial law and enforcing curfew in Jinan. He went to the universities to lecture students on how to behave. When he met a negative response, he reportedly threatened the students with members of his martial arts–trained Broadsword Unit. At the same time, Ma also offended the Hui (Muslim) population. Although Muslim himself, Ma had Hui protesters arrested, and his toughs went through the Muslim quarter to beat up everyone involved with critical posters and cartoons (Peng, 1984).

Everyone joined the debate in one form or another. In 1917, the young Mao Zedong did not mention New Chinese Martial Arts, but he did advocate vigorous exercise and argue that the main purpose of physical culture was to instill martial boldness and fearlessness. Mao extolled what he called the civilized nations—Germany at the forefront with its nationwide practice of fencing, and Japan with its Bushido and jujutsu, the latter developed from Chinese precedents. On the other hand, another future Communist literary icon, Lu Xun, went on record in 1918 and 1919 as thoroughly opposing New Chinese Martial Arts, equating them to the "superstitious" practices of the disgraced "Boxers" of 1900 (Chengdu Tiyu Xueyuan Tiyushi Yanjiushi, 1981: 78–80).

To satisfy the growing interest in Chinese physical culture, Guo Xifen published the *History of Chinese Physical Culture* in 1919 (1919/1970). Over half the text was dedicated to martial arts. Although the proportion was correct, unfortunately the content was riddled with misinformation. For example, Guo uncritically repeated spurious material from an earlier work titled *Secrets of Shaolin Boxing* (Zun, 1971).[1] The most serious error popularized in these books was the story that Chinese boxing evolved from exercises introduced to the Shaolin monastery by the Indian monk Bodhidharma. This painted an exaggerated picture of the role of the Shaolin monastery in Chinese martial arts history that persists to this day (Zun, 1915/1971).

Although Chinese had an imperfect understanding of the history of their martial arts, the foreigners living among them did not have a clue. Witness, for example, this attempt to describe Chinese boxing in the *North China Herald* (May 10, 1924):

It is quite different from English boxing. In the latter, one's main object is to get at one's opponent and punch him out. But in China, the gentle art of self-defence is quite otherwise. Your main object is not to hurt your opponent, in the well-founded confidence that he will be equally careful not to hurt you. Hence a Chinese "boxing" contest between two people consists of a striking of attitudes, more or less threatening, a waving of arms and smiting of thighs (generally one's own), varied by certain kangaroo-like hops and flounders, sudden turns of the body, and alternate advances and retreats. ("Chinese Athletes," 1999)

NATIONALIST ERA: 1927–1949

In March 1927, Guomindang (Nationalist) forces sent to suppress warlords captured Nanjing. Afterward, they took steps to establish a central government there.

In the physical culture field, the Nationalists formed a Martial Arts Research Institute (*Guoshu Yanjiu Guan*) in Nanjing. To emphasize the Chinese nature of these arts (and tie them into the Nationalist ideology), they used the term *guoshu* (national arts) instead of *wushu* (martial arts). In 1928, with the unification of China essentially completed, the name of the institute was changed to Central Martial Arts Institute (*Zhongyang Guoshu Guan*). The former warlord Zhang Zhijiang was its director.

Unlike Ma, with his short-lived New Chinese Martial Arts, the Institute's objective was not the establishment of a universal, nationwide, standardized system of calisthenics and self-defense. Instead, its goal was to provide centralized control over traditional martial arts. Toward this end, the Institute funded research, publishing, and training. The following excerpt from the pronouncement made on the founding of the Institute reveal much about the nationalist sentiments of the times:

> Standing on this twentieth century stage where one cannot survive without competing, how can we prevent insults and gain respect?...The only path we can take to self-defense is to practice the martial arts....Comrades let us loudly affirm:...The spear and staff of the martial arts will strike down the Imperialism that has invaded us....The knife and sword of the martial arts will cut up all the unequal treaties!...Long live the martial arts of the Republic of China! (Jin, 1933/1970: addendum 3, 1–6)

In 1930, China's Ministry of Education ordered public schools to include martial arts in their physical education curricula. To satisfy the demands of such a widespread program, a Central Martial Arts Physical Culture Specialty School (later changed to National Martial Arts Physical Culture School) was established in 1933.

Martial arts examinations were scheduled annually in October at the national level, in April at province and city levels, and in December at the county level. Examination subjects were divided into two categories, aca-

Sun Lutang, headmaster of the Jiangsu Province Martial Arts Institute. Courtesy Joseph Svinth.

demic subjects and skill subjects. Academic subjects included Nationalist Party principles, literature, history, geography, physiology, hygiene, and origins of the martial arts. Skill subjects included traditional boxing and weapons (single-edged broadsword, double-edged straight sword, staff, and spear), Chinese wrestling, freestyle fighting, and military saber and bayonet techniques.

Martial art institutes were established in the provinces as well. Sun Lutang, a widely known proponent of *taijiquan, baguazhang,* and *xingyi-quan,* was head of one of these, the Jiangsu Province Martial Arts Institute. The core curriculum there was *xingyiquan.* Among those who trained at the Jiangsu Province Martial Arts Institute in 1929 was Ju Hao. Ju was assigned to the Jiangdu City police department at the time, and his subsequent recollection of the training he received provides insight into the program:

> I graduated from training at the Jiangsu Province Martial Arts Institute, where I studied Xingyiquan.... The training was divided into two parts, skill classes (in the field) and academic classes (in the classroom). There were six

hours of classes every day, four in the morning and two in the afternoon, one of which was an academic class. All the remaining classes were in skills. The academic classes included physiology and hygiene, infantry drill, the Three People's Principles, and the origins and important points of Xingyiquan. For the first month, we practiced the Santi Stance, because the basis of Xingyi-quan is the Santi Stance, and if this stance lacks a good foundation then one cannot hope to successfully master Xingyiquan. Beginning with the second month we learned one form a month, that is the "splitting," "crushing," "drilling," "pounding," and "crossing" five element forms....During the second six months, we learned the five element combined solo routine, the eight form solo routine, and five element duo routine...then we went on to the twelve animal forms and the mixed form solo routine. We graduated after a year of training. (Ju Hao, personal communication, April 11, 1976)

After graduating, Ju returned to Jiangdu. There he established the Jiangdu Martial Arts Institute and trained local youth for the purpose of "building health and strengthening the nation" (Ju Hao, personal communication, April 11, 1976).

In 1928, Huang Bonian, who taught at the Central Martial Arts Institute, published his own by-the-numbers training manuals. These were designed for military use, and taught the *xingyiquan* five elements form, the combined solo routine, and routines for saber and rifle-bayonet. The book was titled, *Xiezhen Quanjie Jiaofan* [Illustrated boxing and weapons instruction manual]. Although publication of "how to" manuals became common enough during the 1920s, with the possible single exception of *Record of Wrestling* (ca. 960 C.E.), research into the history of the Chinese martial arts only dates to the 1930s.

The pioneer historian was Tang Hao (Tang Fansheng, 1897–1959). Tang was supervisor of the Central Martial Arts Institute's publication section for a short time during its early years, and in 1930, the Institute published his famous *Shaolin-Wudang Kao* (Shaolin-Wudang research). This book exposed the myths surrounding the origins of both Shaolin boxing (the Bodhidharma myth) and *taijiquan* (the Zhang Sanfeng myth). This earned him the enmity of many in the professional martial arts community (especially people whose writings espoused these myths). The animosity was so strong that two highly respected martial art teachers, Zhu Guofu and Wang Ziping, had to stop some of the offended people from plotting against Tang.

Tang studied law in Japan shortly before his time at the Central Martial Arts Institute. While in Japan, he practiced *pici* (military saber and bayonet fighting with protective devices, what the Japanese called *jukendo*). Outspoken in his political views, the Nationalists accused him of being a

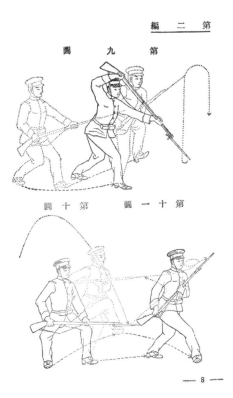

An illustration from Huang Jiexin (Bonian), *Xiezhen Quanxie Jiaofan* (Illustrated Boxing and Weapons Instruction), 1928. The book contains three main chapters: (1) Xingyiquan Five-Element Forms, (2) Rifle with Bayonet, and (3) Saber.

Communist, and later the Japanese regime in Shanghai had him arrested once as politically dangerous.

According to *taijiquan* historian Gu Liuxin, Tang wrote his booklet, *Critique of "Secrets of Shaolin Boxing,"* while hiding in a fellow martial art practitioner's rice store. He was constantly in financial straits, yet, through it all, he managed to publish many important works on martial arts history. On his copy of *Shaolin-Wudang Kao,* he wrote, "Draft finalized on the evening of my third son's death, sacrificed to homelessness and under-nourishment." At one point, he discovered that rats had chewed up many of his martial arts history materials. He hastily blamed his first wife for not caring for them. Distraught, she hung herself (Gu, 1982).

Another noteworthy writer on *taijiquan* was Xu Zhen (Zhedong). A professor of Chinese Studies at several universities, Xu studied martial arts under several teachers. His writings, along with Tang Hao's, are indispensable to our knowledge of early *taijiquan* manuals. Xu also contributed to comparative martial arts studies by editing a rare eighteenth-century family martial arts manual by Chang Naizhou, which Xu titled *Chang Family Martial Arts Book* (Ma, 1995).

These historical writings were the exception. During the 1930s, teachers were mostly the remnants of an older generation, and like most people, these men were more concerned with making a living than historical research. Nonetheless, Tang and Xu set a shining example for future martial arts scholars to emulate.

The foreign community's appreciation of the Chinese martial arts continued to be less than exemplary. In 1906, Herbert Giles made a breakthrough of sorts with his *Adversaria Sinica* article titled "The Home of Jiu Jitsu." From a twenty-first-century vantagepoint, it may appear that Giles stumbled in his assessment. However, given his limited selection of sources, he did a creditable job documenting that Japanese jujutsu evolved from Chinese boxing.

Three decades later, Julius Eigner apparently read Giles's article while researching a far less scholarly piece titled "The Ancient Art of Chinese Boxing." As can be seen, he gained little insight from either Giles's article or personal observation:

> Although Jiu-jitsu, the Japanese art of self-defense which originated from the Chinese boxing practices, is known practically all over the world, nothing more than the mere fact that there exists such an exercise as Chinese boxing is known to the West. Where this exercise, which justly may be termed strange and weird, comes from, what it means and what its aims are, seem to be still unknown.... Because Chinese boxing has so decidedly this Oriental touch which seems to defy all clear cut definitions and explanations it seems to be an impossible task for an outsider to unlock its mysteries. (Eigner, 1938)

Although the Chinese made some advances in developing a nationwide martial arts cadre before the war with Japan (1937–1945), the examination system was not so successful. The freestyle-fighting event proved particularly difficult to manage. Partly this was due to inadequate rules and safety measures. Thus, descriptions of bloodied faces and broken bones during the first examination in 1928 sound similar to descriptions of Tang Dynasty wrestling matches.

A bigger problem was rivalry between the different schools, styles, and teachers of boxing. The founders of the Central Martial Arts Institute initially only managed to aggravate matters by organizing the institute into Wudang and Shaolin branches. The Wudang branch included *taijiquan, xingyiquan,* and *baguazhang,* while the Shaolin branch included all other styles of boxing. This arrangement proved unsatisfactory from the beginning, contradicting as it did one of the founding goals of the Institute, and it was later quietly discarded. Nonetheless, it contributed to the mistaken belief that there were "internal" (Wudang) and "external" (Shaolin) schools of boxing.

In 1934, the Institute formed a martial art standardization committee. The task of standardization proved formidable indeed. A survey conducted in 1919 confirmed the existence of 110 different styles of boxing throughout the country (73 styles in the Yellow River region, 30 styles in the Yangtze River region, and 7 styles in the Pearl River region). Moreover, someone observed that the number of styles had increased since then (Guo, 1919/1970: 47–49).

Some Chinese advocated standardizing martial arts because they believed that this would help unify the country. Zhu Minyi, for example, combined elements of *taijiquan* with modern calisthenics *(ticao)* to produce an easily learned hybrid exercise called *taijicao* (taiji calisthenics). In 1933, Zhu published a book called *Taijicao Instructions and Commands,* trained a cadre of teachers, and then led 2,000 elementary students in a mass demonstration. In 1939, Zhu joined the "peace movement" espoused by his brother-in-law, Wang Jingwei, who founded a Nanjing puppet government under the Japanese. Zhu's "Citizen's Calisthenics" *(Guomin Ticao)* became the official form of calisthenics of the puppet regime. Zhu was executed as a traitor in 1946 (Morris, 1998: 493–511).

The high point for the Chinese martial arts during the Nationalist era came in 1936, when a nine-member troupe performed at the Eleventh Olympiad in Berlin. This was the first time the group had demonstrated outside China, and the high acclaim it received provided some consolation for a lackluster showing by the Chinese Olympic team. Ironically, Zhu Minyi's *taijicao* was the opening entry in the martial arts troupe's program (Morris, 1998: 509).

The low point came in 1937. With the beginning of the War of Resistance against Japan, an era ended.

IN THE COMMUNIST-CONTROLLED AREAS: 1928–1949

Following failed urban uprisings in 1927, China's Communists moved into to the countryside. There they ultimately established bases in Jiangxi,

Hunan, Shaanxi-Gansu, and other areas. In these Soviet areas, as they were originally called,[2] physical culture and sports were important activities. As might be expected, emphasis was on military-oriented exercises such as running, grenade tossing, and obstacle courses. Nonetheless, there were also team sports such as volleyball, basketball, and football (soccer).

Martial arts were usually included as individual or choreographed group demonstration entries. With the exception of wrestling, they were characterized more as an element of Chinese physical culture than sport. This was not a new development. As far back as Yuan period (1279–1368) opera, martial arts were used as a form of gymnastic entertainment. Modified martial arts were easily incorporated into propaganda shows intended to build troop morale. In addition, they were amenable to practice by both sexes. The following is a description of a performance by the Yan'an Women's Self-Defense Unit in 1940:

> Over 100 heroic, lively women, broadswords strapped across their backs, carrying red tasseled spears in their hands, followed the lead of a waving red flag and moved into fighting formation. They performed three broadsword dances, and amidst the bright flashes of the sword blades they would frequently let out a fierce shout—*sha* [kill]!—which reverberated afar in a great martial spirit. (Chengdu Tiyu Xueyuan Tiyushi Yanjiushi, 1981: 167)

TAIWAN AND HONG KONG: 1949–1965

When they moved to Taiwan in 1949, the Nationalists did not attempt to reestablish the Central Martial Arts Institute or any similar organization. Nonetheless, martial arts continued to be practiced and passed on by individuals. Noted martial art teachers who came to Taiwan included Chang Dongsheng (1908–1986; a former all-China champion wrestler), Zheng Manqing (1902–1975, a *taijiquan* master who later emigrated to the United States), and Fu Shuyun (a woman who had been a member of the team that performed in the 1936 Olympics).

In 1970, a group of martial art practitioners in Taiwan who were originally from mainland China formed the Chinese Martial Arts Press (Zhonghua Wushu Chubanshe), which began to publish reprints of martial arts books of the 1920s and 30s. The following is a partial translation of a preface to one of their texts (Zun, 1971):

> The martial arts are a brilliant part of our culture. They are also the best all-round body strengthener and self-defense art in the world. Now, though

The push hands exercise of *taijiquan*. The man on the left is the Shanghai teacher, Yang Cheng-fu. By Janet Bradley.

there is gradually nothing to see but outward forms, still the writings of past masters are not lacking in valuable material well worth studying and researching. If those interested in the martial arts will increase their studies and practice, they cannot but help to revive the martial arts and spread them. However, most of the published works on the market have been tampered with, titles of books have been changed as has content and even authors' names. Furthermore, there are false works claiming to be the works of past masters to cheat and take advantage of those who love the martial arts. Not only is it hard for beginners to distinguish between the real and the fake, but even those familiar with the martial arts are often fooled. Mistakes are passed on, to be studied afterwards, confusing researchers and hindering the revival of the martial arts.

Some well-known martial art teachers went to Hong Kong instead of Taiwan. Wu Kung-cho (1903–1983) was grandson of the originator of Wu style *taijiquan,* the Imperial Guard officer Wu Jianquan (1870–1942). Wu began teaching *taijiquan* in Hong Kong in 1937, the year the Sino-Japanese war broke out. When the Japanese occupied Hong Kong in December

1941, the family moved back into China, but it returned after the war. Another famous *taijiquan* teacher, Tung Ying-chieh (1886–1961), moved to Hong Kong about 1945. Tung was a former student of Yang Cheng-fu (1883–1936) in Shanghai. Finally, Yip Man (1893–1972), Bruce Lee's (1940–1973) *yongchun* (Wade-Giles: wing chun) teacher, moved to Hong Kong from Foshan, Guangdong, around 1950.

TRENDS IN THE PEOPLE'S REPUBLIC OF CHINA SINCE 1949

After the founding of the People's Republic of China in 1949, responsibility for the martial arts came under the Martial Arts Section in the Sports Directorate of the Physical Culture and Sports Commission. In 1953, the Commission organized a Traditional Physical Culture Research Committee to review the traditional sports of both the Han Chinese and the various minorities.[3] The result was an All-China Traditional Sports Festival held in Tianjin City. A documentary film recorded the event, and altogether, 139 styles of boxing were demonstrated on this occasion (All China Traditional Sports Festival, n.d.).

For the martial arts, 1955–1965 represented a period of unprecedented administrative developments. Publications included individual as well as group efforts, and articles in *New Sports* magazine recounted the martial arts practice of famous figures in Chinese history, to include Confucius.

In 1959, the book *Mianquan* (soft or continuous boxing) was published. The author, Lan Suzhen, had participated in the 1953 Tianjin sports festival. The preface noted that Lan developed her modified *mianquan* set according to exercise and dance principles as well as martial arts techniques. Although her performance was generally well received, some martial art practitioners expressed dissent. In their opinion, some of the movements contradicted traditional rules. The publisher admitted that the work of organizing the martial arts was in the beginning stage. He also said that the book was published for a dual purpose: one was to satisfy a real need for published martial arts material, and the other was the hope that the book would arouse constructive comments and ideas (Lan, 1959: editor's comments).

In 1959, *Rules for Martial Arts Competition* was published. This booklet established the competition standards for performing standardized *changquan* (long boxing), *nanquan* (southern boxing), and *taijiquan,* and straight sword, broadsword, spear, and staff sets. Other styles could only be performed for demonstration until such time as competition standards

The bright red cover of Lan Suzhen, *Mianquan* (Soft/Continuous Boxing), People's Physical Culture Publishers (1958 third printing). The booklet is a manual for the style of boxing that Lan demonstrated publicly in 1953, and its choreographed routines epitomize accepted martial arts practice in the People's Republic of China from 1949 to the present. Only in relatively recent years has much attention been given to developing contact competitions similar to those associated with karate and taekwondo. Courtesy Stanley Henning.

were developed for them. The following year, the Physical Culture and Sports Commission produced a series of booklets titled *Regulation Sets for Martial Arts Competition*. The popular *changquan* and its associated weapons sets took top priority for standardization.

In the process, traditional and new techniques were combined and each set went through various committees for testing and certification. Boxing and weapons sets were developed for three levels of proficiency: beginning, intermediate, and advanced. The advanced level introduced an extra female boxing routine to account for differing physical demands. All this was accomplished under the policy, "Let a hundred flowers bloom, weed through the old and bring forth the new."

The benefits of this policy for popularizing the martial arts seemed obvious at the time; however, it also resulted in rejection of traditional routines that failed to conform to the new standardized rules, and it forced many boxing styles to the brink of extinction. The bottom line in this system was that competition consisted of how well one performed the standardized routines—it emphasized perfection of technique and appearance. As in gymnastics, competition merely tested one's degree of perfection in the performance of standardized forms.

In 1965, radical political storm clouds began to form, and during the period known as the Great Proletarian Cultural Revolution of 1966–1976, these burst forth into a torrent of abuse. Articles in the April and May 1965 issues of *New Sports* magazine (Jing, 1965; Xiang, 1965; Zhao, 1965) directed attacks at undesirable practices characteristic of feudal martial arts. Undesirable practices described included the following:

- Segregating students according to loyalty to the teacher or length of time studied
- Relegating new students to the supervision of assistants or treating them like outsiders
- Ostracizing students who left one group to join another
- Glossing over important points, thereby extending the period of time required for learning
- Encouraging monetary gifts to the instructor and performance of domestic tasks for him
- Making false claims as to the effectiveness of *taijiquan* in curing ills
- Making false claims about the use of inner energy
- Using hazy philosophical terminology to explain basic principles
- A tendency toward elitism
- Misdirected loyalties (e.g., loyalty to a teacher rather than the State)

Taijiquan was a prime target of these attacks. *Taijiquan's* undesirable tendencies specifically included unwarranted glorification of past masters, retention of feudal customs, the spread of superstitious ideas, and deep-seated prejudiced views engendered by opposing styles. However, from a Party standpoint, the most important reason was probably that *taijiquan* teachers advocated nonconflict. This was in direct opposition to the concept of class

Ballet scene at the Great Hall of the People attended by President and Mrs. Nixon during their trip to Beijing, China, February 22, 1972. Photo by Byron Schumaker. White House Photo Office Collection, National Archives and Records Administration, ARC identifier 194416.

struggle advocated by Chairman Mao. However, from this perspective, the entire martial arts system established before the Cultural Revolution, which emphasized the performance of routines and ignored free-fighting skills, also contradicted the concept of class struggle. Moreover, it prematurely assumed the existence of a classless, conflict-free society.

In the opening salvoes, *taijiquan* historian Gu Liuxin was accused of attempting to glorify Chen clan ancestors in his book *Taijiquan Research.* With this, serious writing about the martial arts ceased for the duration of the Great Proletarian Cultural Revolution, and an unknown quantity of old manuals and other materials was destroyed.

In some cases, groups created new styles of boxing that were supposedly better suited to contemporary needs. One of these, Miner's Boxing, attempted to combine basic martial arts techniques with the daily physical demands of miners, such as digging, drilling, and pushing carts (Fushun Xilu Tian Meikuang Shenjing Dang Zongzhi, 1965). Consequently, officially sanctioned martial arts departed ever further from their traditional nature and purpose.

Meanwhile, as the Chinese sought to reconcile their martial arts with shifting political policies, foreigners were exposed to a media deluge on the subject of Chinese martial arts. Unfortunately, most of the reporting contained more myth than fact, particularly as it related to the role of the Shaolin monastery. A notable exception was the writings of Robert W. Smith, who, during the 1960s, began to make some sense of the Chinese martial arts (Draeger and Smith, 1969).

Because the Chinese mainland was essentially closed to Americans until 1972, Smith's descriptions were based on information made available to him in Taiwan. Although dated today, these descriptions were the best available in English at the time, and they still make good reading. His discussion of the history of *taijiquan, baguazhang,* and *xingyiquan,* in particular, benefited from the scrupulous scholarship of Zhou Jichun (Jian Nan), a member of a prominent group of older martial art teachers living in Taiwan (Smith, 1974: 113–121). However, even Smith strayed off the path in his early *Secrets of Shaolin Temple Boxing,* in which he claimed that Shaolin was "the father of all boxing forms in China" (Smith, 1964: 12; see also Henning, 1999: 330, note 29). While Smith's writings pointed the way out of the wilderness, the path remains long and arduous even today

CONCLUSION: SOME OBSERVATIONS ON LOOKING BACK

Attempting to put trends into periods is an arbitrary and risky affair. Still, looking at the martial arts in Chinese society during the period 1865–1965, one can discern some interesting contradictions.

For example, the martial arts, whose main premise is survival in a conflict-prone environment, were a widespread element of popular culture coexisting under a veneer of Confucian ideology that preached harmony. Harmony represented the ideal, while the martial arts reflected the reality. Their very necessity made martial arts the dominant form of physical culture in traditional Chinese society. Meanwhile, the insular, conservative nature of Chinese society ensured their survival well into the age of firearms and introduction of Western sports.

In China, martial arts were symbols of both repression and liberation. Thus, they were associated with righteous heroes *(xia)* in popular novels, and gangsters on the streets of big cities such as Shanghai and Tianjin. Consequently, they maintained credibility among the population but simultaneously demanded control and oversight by the authorities.

When the system in which they thrived collapsed in 1911, traditional martial arts became marginalized, especially in cities directly exposed to the combination of modernization and Western influences. Nonetheless, they adapted to become a form of recreation and physical fitness.

In the new order, martial arts continued to have contradictory attributes. Thus, one person could view their practice as a celebration of individualism. At the same time, another might see them a unifying force, as did the men responsible for establishing the Central Martial Arts Institute in Nanjing. Yet, the existence of this special institute was itself evidence of the marginalization of these arts, which now appeared to require special attention to survive.

For the Nationalists, it proved impossible to manage the task of maintaining the individual characteristics of the numerous styles of martial arts while testing their basic nature as fighting systems under standardized rules. Nonetheless, it was a brave experiment. For their part, the Communists initially emphasized a standardized, conflict-free, demonstration-oriented approach to the martial arts. In other words, they viewed them as similar to opera or propaganda team performances. However, this proved unsatisfactory as China began to open to the outside world after 1979. Since then, privately run martial arts associations, military/police-associated martial arts training centers, and even schools with a full curriculum and martial arts theme have sprung up throughout the country. In addition, martial arts faculty in the national physical culture and sports system have put increased emphasis on free fighting *(sanshou)* competition in hopes that the Chinese martial arts might somehow be recognized as an official Olympic sport.

All this gives the impression that Chinese martial art practitioners are seeking to return to their roots to face the future.

THE SPIRIT OF MANLINESS: BOXING IN IMPERIAL JAPAN, 1868–1945

Joseph R. Svinth

Although the advent of *bokushingu* (boxing) in Japan is commonly dated to the establishment of Watanabe Yujiro's Japan Boxing Club in February 1921, there were both boxers and boxing clubs in Japan before that date. For example, Sasaki Tokujiro, who worked as a cook aboard U.S.-flagged merchant ships, boxed in San Francisco and Seattle during the 1870s and 1880s (*Japanese-American Courier*, January 1, 1934: 6). Sasaki's East Coast contemporary was Uriu Sotokichi.[1] A samurai's son, Uriu was a midshipman at the U.S. Naval Academy who started boxing at the Annapolis YMCA in 1881. He evidently learned his lessons well, for many years later, while an instructor at Japan's Eta Jima Naval Academy, Uriu "literally silenced another officer's criticism of his [Christian] religion by a knock-out punch on the chin" (Sweetman, 1995: 156).

Likewise, around 1900, Sakurai Kojiro started a boxing club in Tokyo. While that club did not last long, in 1909, Kano Kenji (a relative of judo founder Kano Jigoro) started a longer-lived boxing club in Kobe.

Finally, *bokushingu* was not the first gloved boxing in modern Japan. Instead, that honor goes to a hybrid style known as *merikan*. In *merikan,* boxers in gloves fought against jujutsu practitioners in jackets. Elaborate rules provided a point scoring system, and so this was not submission fighting in the modern sense. For example, Harvey "Heinie" Miller[2] remembered a contest that took place in Manila in late 1908 or early 1909:

> The bout was to be two falls or knockdowns out of three. [The Japanese] was to wear a sort of jiu-jitsu shirt while the American was to wear gloves.

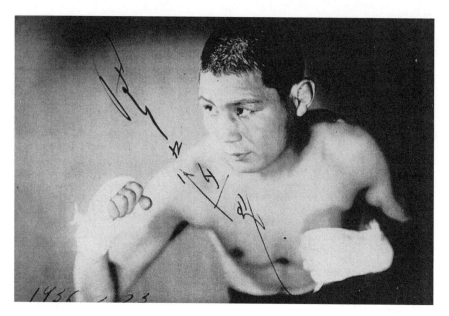

Japanese boxer Piston Horiguchi, circa 1935. Courtesy Paul Lou.

> [The Japanese] was not allowed to hit but all jiu-jitsu holds were permitted.
> The American was not allowed to wrestle or hold but all clean blows were
> permitted. (Miller, 1922: 5)

During these contests, sometimes the boxer won. For example, in the
contest described by Miller, the first fall went to the Japanese, via an arm
throw. The second fall went to the American, who landed a solid right
uppercut to the head just as the Japanese stepped in. The Japanese then
refused to go out for the final point. His excuse was "that he did not expect
to get hit, being under the impression that the gloves were only used as a
handicap for the difference in weight" (Miller, 1922: 5).

However, when the jujutsu practitioners had a better understanding of the
rules (or at least, more determination), then usually they were victorious.
For example, *Japan Times* (November 17, 1913: 1) had this to say about a
mixed match held in Yokohama:

> Seven times boxing champion Cally faced his jujitsu contestant Kawashima
> with vigor and enthusiasm only to be mercilessly defeated by the Japanese
> "boy." The English boxer showed his first class form, and thrice with his
> formidable left and right hooks to the stomach he made Kawashima hop in

the air as though he were on springs. But finally the English boxer had to surrender before the magic power of jujitsu with the score of 19 to 28.

Such mixed matches continued to be popular into the 1920s. However, as Japan's relations with the United States and Britain soured, such matches became less popular, mostly because both sides invested the bouts with great political significance. As the *Hilo Tribune-Herald* (December 16, 1925) put it:

A mixed match of this kind between a Japanese jiu jitsu expert and a white boxer is not a good thing for this community. It serves no good purpose and merely arouses useless race prejudices. A Japanese and a white man could box together and no hard feeling would arise. If the Japanese won, even the white fans would credit him with being good to win in a game that is practically new to the Japanese, and if he lost, the Japanese would not suffer any hurt of pride. The same would both be true of a jiu jitsu match. But on the other hand, jiu jitsu is something that the Japanese think undefeatable, while the Anglo-Saxon thinks the same of boxing, and both methods are practically rooted in each classes' national pride.

Now, all this said, Watanabe *was* Japan's first famous boxing promoter, and his Japan Boxing Club *was* home to several popular champions of the 1930s. Therefore, they deserve their subsequent fame.

Watanabe learned to box in California. According to *Japan Times,* "Watanabe has been active professionally in the ring for 20 years, his career commencing in 1901. He received his early training under a master trainer, the well-known R. Turner.[3] During the last 10 years he has engaged in 50 contests, 30 of which he won, 6 he lost, and the remainder being ties" (February 10, 1921: 5).

Watanabe's contemporaries included "Young Togo" Koriyama, who started a separate boxing club near Kobe in the summer of 1921. Like Watanabe, Koriyama had boxed professionally in the United States. He was "short, squat, barrel-shaped with a round, closely cropped bullet head and possessed of extraordinary strength. Of science he knows little or nothing, but his capacity to wade in, take all that comes his way and cripple an opponent in the clinches cannot be overestimated" (*Seattle Times,* March 10, 1912: 28). This reputation was deserved, too, as men Watanabe fought included the former world champions Harry Forbes, Oscar "Battling" Nelson, and Frankie Conley.[4]

Until 1952, Japan did not have a boxing commission. Instead, the Japan Boxing Association regulated the Japanese sport. Watanabe, Koriyama, and Kano Kenji established the Japan Boxing Association in 1922. It was

"MOOSE" TAUSSIG'S STABLE OF JAPANESE BOXERS.

Moose Taussig's stable of Japanese boxers in San Francisco, circa 1926. The arrow points to Taussig, who subsequently became a Honolulu bar owner. Courtesy Patrick Fukuda.

essentially a guild, and quite unsurprisingly, its chief purpose was to make money for Watanabe, Koriyama, Kano, and their financial patrons, who included both Japanese and California-based businessmen.[5]

The Japan Boxing Association organized its first card in Tokyo in May 1922. The boxers included Watanabe, Koriyama, and three Americans that San Francisco boxing promoter J.J. "Moose" Taussig had brought to Japan for the occasion. In 1934, Arthur Suzuki wrote that a Tokyo boxing card usually

> starts at 6 and continues till 11 p.m. A program consists of anywhere from 9 to 16 bouts, ranging from 4 to 10 rounds each.... The Japanese fighters insist on receiving their guarantees before the bout as they have no boxing commissions to protect their claims. But that does not keep them from doing their utmost in the ring. Although still crude boxers, the word quit is never introduced in their vocabulary and they are gluttons for punishment. (*Japanese-American Courier,* February 3, 1934: 2)

Club fights took place inside theaters. As Walter Cho told Don Watson of the *Honolulu Star-Bulletin,* "In Japan there isn't any fire regulation and standing room is sold for one yen. There were about 2,000 persons standing in the back and in the aisles" (Cho Scrapbook, n.d.). Meanwhile, championship bouts took place in baseball stadiums, sumo grounds, and Tokyo's Hibiya Amphitheater, which was an outdoor bandstand.

The style of attack that the Japanese fight promoters encouraged was the "piston attack." To Filipinos and Americans, the piston attack was hardly the apex of scientific boxing. Nonetheless, the method thrilled Japanese fans, who wanted nothing more than to see the fighters "rush madly against each other from the start, punching mechanically and make a quick end of the bout" (*Japan Times,* January 15, 1925: 4).

Details of how boxers learned the piston attack are scarce. An exception is the following statement by Alfred Pieres:

> The boxers [in Young Togo Koriyama's gym at Mikage, outside Kobe] keep on training all the time. Despite the occasional cold snaps that Kobe has been recently having, there they are, almost in their first birthday suit, with just a pair of very short drawers, doing their work.... [They] are good with their fists, but are still rather slow as regards footwork.... The boxers are working with a willing heart... [and] all appear to be in fine physical condition, muscular, well developed and hard as nails. (*Japan Times,* April 16, 1925: 4)

Unsurprisingly, injuries were common. Few careers lasted more than five years, and there were at least two fatalities.[6]

The emphasis on the piston attack suggests that Japanese martial culture was a primary influence on Imperial Japanese boxing ideology. After all, Bushido, the Way of the Warrior, was a popular (if misunderstood) concept in Japan during the 1920s and 1930s (Friday, 1994), and Young Togo Koriyama taught kendo and judo as well as boxing at his Mikage gym. On the other hand, it might be equally correct to say that parents wanted their sons to be manly, that boys wanted the tremendous punching power (and income) of Jack Dempsey, and that promoters used whatever vocabulary best suited local needs.

Certainly, the Japanese military patronized boxing. Japanese officers in Europe during World War I observed the British using boxing as an introduction to rifle-bayonet training, and subsequently, they sought someone to introduce boxing into their officer candidate schools. The person they found was Captain Warren J. Clear, a U.S. Army officer assigned to the American legation in Tokyo during the mid-1920s (Svinth, 2000b).

Furthermore, Watanabe Yujiro said, in so many words, that boxing developed "he-men." First, he said, the sport classified boxers according to weight. Consequently, stature was irrelevant and everyone competed equally. Second, participation taught boxers to face their fears and do their best. Thus, it built character (*Japan Times,* March 16, 1928: 8). Yet, ironically, when Japanese schoolboys did box, it was often politely. For example, Yado Kari wrote that whenever a collegiate boxer "delivered a hard blow, he would apologize by bowing his head slightly or by showing a friendly look in his eyes. There was no knockout in those days. When a boxer began bleeding in his nose, a cry of horror went up.... [Promoter] Watanabe had a hard time explaining to the student boxers that they need not and should not refrain from hitting a groggy opponent. 'You must cultivate the spirit of manliness,' he roared" (*Japan Times,* February 21, 1931: 2).

Finally, there is no doubt that Hollywood films "in which the hero knocks men right and left" (*Japan Times,* February 21, 1931: 2) were popular in Japan during the 1920s. For example, Jack Dempsey's *Fight and Win* played in Tokyo from late 1924 until the middle of 1925. Likewise, advertisements for Reginald Denny's *Fighting Blood* series described the films as "the biggest treat in the world for anybody who can get a kick out of a real 'go' between HE-MEN" (*The Ring,* January 1923: 21). "The hero of these wonderfully human stories is a lowly soda jerker," added an article in *The Ring* (January 1923: 20), "who becomes overnight a champion of the prize ring!" In other words, it was not Japanese martial culture, but a combination of military support, young men's desire to be manly, and the power of the movies that made boxing popular in Imperial Japan.

By 1924, Japanese colleges and universities were organizing their own varsity and intramural boxing clubs. For nationalistic reasons, however, some things needed to be changed. For example, the name *bokushingu* was changed to *kento* (fist fighting). In 1931, Watanabe Yujiro explained the reasoning behind this change:

> The game which was introduced in the market ten years ago, it was not a genuine one and it was a mixed up game of boxing versus jujitsu. Japanese thought the boxing game is made for "judo" and all the foreigners are champion boxers, especially the Americans. Therefore the boxing was called "merikan" in those times instead of "kentow," which we name the game now. (*Japan Times,* February 9, 1931: 4)

Nonetheless, most technical vocabulary continued to use English loanwords. "Middleweight," for example, became *midoryu-kyu.*

Japan's first intercollegiate boxing tournament took place at Tokyo's Yasukuni Shrine in November 1925. Six months later, in May 1926, another amateur tournament took place at the Yasukuni Shrine. The main event featured 18-year-old bantamweight Nakamura Kaneo versus 21-year-old featherweight Takahashi Kazuo. *Japan Times* said Nakamura "uses his left with good effect while Takahashi is noted for his wicked

Nakamura Kaneo, mid-1920s. Nakamura had about 40 fights in California, and according to Moose Taussig, 35 of these resulted in wins. However, according to Arthur Suzuki, writing in the *Japanese-American Courier* (October 21, 1933, p. 2), "We remember him [Nakamura] as a good-looking youngster with an appealing nature, fast and somewhat clever with his dukes but woefully weak on punches. He displayed flashes of brilliance but that was against second-raters and did not add to his prestige." Courtesy Patrick Fukuda.

right cross" (*Japan Times,* April 23, 1926: 8). Both men subsequently became professional boxers.

One month after that, in June 1926, Meiji and Waseda Universities organized a separate intercollegiate tournament. Together with the May bouts, these three Japanese collegiate tournaments exerted influence as far away as Hawaii. "When I was in Japan last year," the Hawaiian K. Oki told the

When this photo was taken in the mid-1930s, Korea's Jo Teiken was the sixth best featherweight in the world. The other man is Jo's manager, Frank Tabor. Courtesy Paul Lou.

Honolulu sportswriter Don Watson, "I noticed that many of the young boys were taking up boxing. In fact, several smokers were staged while I was there and they all drew big crowds. The Japanese like any competition between individuals and that is the reason they are taking up boxing" (*Honolulu Star-Bulletin,* April 5, 1927). Consequently, Oki, a leader of Honolulu's Asahi baseball organization, began promoting boxing among Americans of Japanese ancestry living in Hawaii.

In October 1927, boxing became part of the Meiji Shrine games, which were Imperial Japan's most internally prestigious amateur games. Abroad,

Korean boxer Gen Umio in Seattle, 1937. By Janet Bradley.

Japanese-trained boxers also competed in the U.S. Golden Gloves, the Far Eastern Championship Games, and the Olympics.

At first, these Japanese amateurs fought according to rules analogous to those of U.S. professional boxing. However, after the 1936 Olympics, the Japanese made their rules mirror Olympic rules. Initially, this mostly meant that boxers started wearing padded headgear while training and competing, but eventually it also meant a move toward the standup English style of point fighting rather than the crouching American style of knockout fighting.

In those days, Korea was a colony of Japan, and the boxing team at Seoul's Keijo Imperial University was international class. Its coach was

Kin Yeijutsu.[7] Several Koreans also boxed for home-island university teams. Their schools included Meiji and Chuo.

Examples of Korean collegiate boxers include Boku Ryushin. In college, Boku boxed for Keijo University, and in 1934, he participated in the Far Eastern Championship Games held in Manila. He turned pro in 1937, and by 1940, he was the undisputed Japanese featherweight champion. However, he was never a popular champion, apparently because he was content to win on points rather than rush in for a knockout (*Japan Times,* September 5, 1940: 5).

Varsity athletes were not the only Korean amateur boxers. For instance, in early 1945, Kim Jae Joon's father enrolled him in a Seoul boxing club. Young Kim was soon boxing in local smokers, and within a few months, he had amassed 11 wins and 4 losses. Then, following Kim's fifteenth bout, a win by knockout, his opponent remained unconscious for 20 minutes. "I thought that I had killed him," Kim recalled. Consequently, his father took him out of boxing and enrolled him in a karate *(tangsoodo)* class instead ("Who Is the Grandmaster?", n.d.).

By international standards, most Japanese professional boxers were a fizzle. Yes, Jo Teiken was ranked sixth in the world in 1934, but he was ethnically Korean and fought mostly in California (Svinth, 2001b). Therefore, most Japanese sources list Horiguchi "Piston" Tsuneo as the best Japanese professional boxer of the 1930s. While probably true, it is also true that the highest international ranking Horiguchi ever got was third best in Hawaii (Svinth, 2001c).

This apparent ineptness was partly the fault of the piston attack, but also the fault of the promoters. During the 1920s and 1930s, Japanese promoters brought various over-the-hill foreign champions to Tokyo, and as a rule these foreigners did not train (or fight) too hard. Thus, standards (and competition) were not high. There were of course exceptions. Sometimes the too-successful foreign boxer was not invited back; other times, Japanese judges publicly reversed unpopular decisions involving the foreign boxers. Probably the most notorious case of judges reversing a decision involved Piston Horiguchi and Joe Eagle in January 1937.[8]

To summarize, Yujiro Watanabe, who established the Japan Boxing Club in Tokyo in February 1921, was Japan's first famous boxing promoter. Japanese fans and promoters liked boxers who used the piston attack. However, the piston attack was not especially successful internationally, in part because international fighters were often content to win on points rather than rush in for the knockout. Finally, because promoters always cater to their customers' tastes, most Imperial Japanese professional champions were ethnically Japanese. Nonetheless, from a technical standpoint, some of the Empire's best boxers were ethnically Korean.

PROFESSOR YAMASHITA GOES TO WASHINGTON

Joseph R. Svinth

What if we made our judo known abroad? Wouldn't it be a great
thing which would allow us to get people to know Japan better?
—Yamashita Yoshiaki, circa 1887 (Tomita, 1962: 128)

In 1902, a wealthy Seattle businessman named Sam Hill was routinely
working ten hours a day, six days a week. This prolonged absence caused
his 9-year-old son to turn "sickly," as being spoiled and selfish was then
known. Rather than spend more time with the boy, Hill decided that judo,
which he had seen during a business trip to Japan, would be just the thing
to imbue young James Nathan "with the ideals of the Samurai class, for
that class of men is a noble, high-minded class. They look beyond the
modern commercial spirit" (Tuhy, 1983: 71).

Hill therefore asked a Japanese friend named Shibata to find him a good
judo teacher. In February 1903, Shibata told Hill of a Professor Yamashita
Yoshiaki of Tokyo.[1]

Yamashita was born in Kanazawa City, in Ishikawa Prefecture, on February 16, 1865. The son of a minor samurai, he received some martial art
training as a youth. In August 1884, he became the nineteenth member of
Kano Jigoro's Kodokan, where he began studying the jujutsu style subsequently known as judo.

An earlier version appeared in *Aikido Journal,* 25:2 (1998) (pp. 37–42). Copyright ©
2002 by Joseph R. Svinth. Adapted by permission.

"To Prof. Y. Yamashita with the regards of his pupil Theodore Roosevelt April 13th 1904." Courtesy Joseph Svinth.

Despite all the stories about how it took years to get rank in the old days, Yamashita earned his first *dan* ranking after just three months at Kano's school. Subsequent promotions continued apace, and he received his fourth *dan* after just two years. He received promotion to sixth *dan* in 1898, and, upon his death in October 1935, he became the first person to receive posthumous promotion to tenth *dan*.[2]

Yamashita's skill was not solely theoretical, either. He was a member of the Kodokan teams that wrestled the Tokyo police jujutsu club in 1883 and

Yamashita Yoshiaki, 1920s. Courtesy Joseph Svinth.

1884. Additionally, E. J. Harrison, who studied judo at the Kodokan before World War I, reported that 17 men once assaulted Yamashita and a friend in a restaurant. "The gang were dispersed in a twinkling, three of them with broken arms and all with bruised and battered faces," said Harrison. "As fast as one of the two experts artistically 'downed' his man the other would pick the victim up like an empty sack and dump him unceremoniously in the street" (Harrison, 1946: 16).

Finally, Yamashita was an excellent instructor. Highly educated and urbane (he spoke good English and wrote beautiful Japanese), his postings included the Imperial Japanese Naval Academy and Tokyo Imperial University.

Hill knew none of this. All he knew was that his friend in Connecticut said that Yamashita was a good judo teacher, that judo was supposed to build character in boys, and that his son James Nathan was in need of stronger character.

On July 21, 1903, Hill wrote Yamashita to invite him to Washington, D.C., where James Nathan was living with his mother. Yamashita agreed to come to America, and on September 23, 1903, the 38-year-old Yamashita, his 25-year-old wife Fude, and his 19-year-old assistant Kawaguchi Saburo boarded the SS *Shinano Maru* in Yokohama. Because Hill was paying his fare, Yamashita traveled first-class. For his part, Kawaguchi traveled second-class, doubtless because his father was paying his way. Still, neither man traveled steerage. Thus, when they arrived in Seattle 15 days later, Yamashita proudly told immigrations officials that he was a professor hired to teach "jujitsu" to the children of Mr. Hill. Kawaguchi just as proudly proclaimed himself Professor Yamashita's assistant ("List or Manifest," 1903).

On October 17, 1903, Yamashita and Kawaguchi gave a judo exhibition at the Seattle Theatre. This was a private show, not a public one; the theater was between shows, and Hill hired it for the evening. Guests included Sam Hill's mother-in-law Mary Hill (wife of railroad magnate James J. Hill, the man of whom it was said, "In the West there are many mountains, but only one Hill"), Senator Russell Alger (a Republican from Michigan, and a former Secretary of War), and several sportswriters.

During his show, Yamashita told the audience that judo was a word meaning "victory by pliancy or yielding." What this meant, the *Seattle Post-Intelligencer* quoted Yamashita as saying, was that

> When the opponent in a hand-to-hand conflict exerts the greatest muscular power he is easiest to overcome, for the expert in judo, by a subtle trick of yielding, converts the antagonist's momentum into his own destruction. The unfortunate leans too far, loses his balance, and swift as lightning the adept exerts one of his peculiar holds on the neck or arm. (*Post-Intelligencer,* October 25, 1903: 39)

Furthermore, judo was an exercise in Social Darwinism:

> Only the fittest survive, and the life of each master is a long struggle for supremacy. The devotees of the science and the art say that the same stern principles exhibited in the physical practice are carried into the moral precepts....Only a few reach that stage, the majority stopping at physical development and the lessons of honesty and sobriety. (ibid.)

Speeches done, Yamashita and Kawaguchi demonstrated throws and holds for the crowd. People seeing such demonstrations for the first time invariably thought that they were prearranged gymnastics rather than real wrestling. For instance, sportswriter Ed Hughes wrote, "Sam Hill years

Sam Hill, Professor Yamashita, and the Seattle Theater. By Janet Bradley.

ago brought over some jiu-jitsu experts from Japan and showed them at the Seattle Theatre.... The Japanese Mr. Hill brought over here used to give clever exhibitions, but it was exhibition stuff purely. It was not the real thing" (*Seattle Times,* January 27, 1912: 8).

Undoubtedly thinking the same thing, Hill arranged for Yamashita to meet someone who was not part of his personal troupe. After all, he wanted a jujutsu teacher, not an acrobat. Toward this end, Hill arranged a bout with some professional wrestlers in Seattle. When the wrestlers failed to appear, he substituted a guest named C. E. Radclyffe, a 210-pound Englishman who was a trained boxer. According to the British wrestling writer Percy Longhurst, here is what the boxer had to say about the encounter:

I confess I have never been up against such a slippery customer as the little Jap. To land him fairly on the head or body was impossible. He avoided punishment by falling backwards or forwards, and once even passed between my legs, almost throwing me as he did so, and recovering his feet behind me in time to avoid a vicious back-hand swing. I tried everything, from straight punches to "windmill" swings, but he was too good for me. Once he had come to close quarters a certain fall for me was the result. After taking three or four heavy tosses, I had had enough of it, having due regard to the fact that I had an hour or so before just got through a long and good dinner. (Longhurst, 1936: 200)

His worries about the Professor's abilities gone, Hill then took his Japanese to the District of Columbia to meet James Nathan. What James Nathan thought of the professor and his judo is unknown, but as James Nathan was notoriously lazy, what he had to say about it is probably better imagined than repeated.

However, Yamashita had no trouble finding employment teaching judo to the children of the Washington elite. Although his regular students were mostly rich men's, he didn't mind. According to an article in the *New York World* (Sunday Magazine, May 29, 1904:1), Yamashita's only requirement in his judo classes was "an absolute good temper." His wife was equally fortunate, and her students included the daughter of the Democratic vice-presidential candidate (Hallie Elkins) and another woman whose father was a former governor of Mississippi (Jessie Ames).

While in the District of Columbia, Professor Yamashita gave some lessons at the Japanese Legation. The Japanese naval attaché, Lieutenant Commander Isamu Takeshita, was from a samurai family, and he knew a good thing when he saw it. In 1926, he persuaded aikido founder Ueshiba Morihei to move to Tokyo, and in 1935, he introduced *aiki budo,* as aikido was then known, into the United States. Therefore, it is hardly surprising that in March 1904 he also arranged for Professor Yamashita to meet with President Theodore Roosevelt in the White House.

As Roosevelt put it in a letter to his sons, he believed in "rough, manly sports" so long as they did not "degenerate into the sole end of one's existence,...character counts for a great deal more than either intellect or body in winning success in life" (Bishop, 1919: 63).

Roosevelt also thought he knew all about jujutsu. After all, in 1902, a Philadelphia policeman named J. J. O'Brien had shown him some tricks he had learned in Japan. (O'Brien had been a constable at Nagasaki's Umegasaki Station from 1895 to 1899, so the instruction was legitimate.)

Maria Louise "Hallie" Davis Elkins. She and her socialite daughters were among Yamashita's first North American judo students. Courtesy Lee Norton.

According to an article published in *Literary Digest,* O'Brien began his demonstration by showing Roosevelt some technical illustrations. Suddenly Roosevelt stopped at a photo of a woman sticking her stiffened fingers into a man's eyes:

> A little worried lest this maneuver should make an unfavorable impression, the Captain [O'Brien] stammered:
> "Mr. President, a dangerous situation requires a desperate defense. That was invented to give a woman protection against a thug who suddenly attacked her."

Colonel Roosevelt's response, according to a writer in the *Philadelphia Public Ledger,* was reassuring.

"I think, Captain," he is reported to have said, "that this is the best thing in your repertory." ("Training," 1927: 47)

However, what Yamashita showed was a complete system rather than a few tricks. Moreover, despite what sportswriters believed, his acts were not prearranged: They *were* that good. Therefore, in the words of the *New York World* (March 13, 1904: 2). Yamashita and his partner "caused Mr. Roosevelt to quit winking and gasp. They showed him what jiu-jitsu really is and they were engaged on the spot."

Although *The World* reported that there were seven degrees in jiu-jitsu, and Roosevelt intended to have at least five of them, Roosevelt's true goal was not rank, but weight reduction. Since becoming President, his weight had soared to over 220 lbs., and he hoped to be down to 200 by the elections. Therefore, during March and April 1904, Roosevelt practiced judo three afternoons a week, using a ground floor office in the White House as his workout space. Then, for the rest of the summer, he practiced occasionally. He stopped training during the elections, and afterwards, there is no evidence that he ever seriously resumed.

The President's training partners included his sons, his private secretary, Commander Takeshita, Secretary of War William Howard Taft, and Secretary of the Interior Gifford Pinchot. When these people were unavailable, then Roosevelt tried his tricks on husky young visitors. The latter included Robert Johnstone Mooney, who with his brother visited the White House on the afternoon of August 18, 1904. Mooney's brother was a noted amateur boxer, and after doing a little sparring with the visitors, Roosevelt, "sprang to his feet and excitedly asked: 'By the way, do you boys understand jiu-jitsu?' "

We replied in the negative, and he continued, pounding the air with his arms, "You must promise me to learn that without delay. You are so good in other athletics that you must add jiu-jitsu to your other accomplishments. Every American athlete ought to understand the Japanese system thoroughly. You know"—and he smiled reminiscently—"I practically introduced it to the Americans. I had a young Japanese—now at Harvard—here for six months, and I tried jiu-jitsu with him day after day. But he always defeated me. It was not easy to learn. However, one day I got him—I got him—good and plenty! I threw him clear over my head on his belly, and I had it. I had it." (Mooney, 1923: 311)

To prove his point, Roosevelt demonstrated his techniques on the Mooneys using considerably more enthusiasm than control. Professor

Yamashita Yoshiaki, Kano Jigoro, Kermit Roosevelt, and Yamashita Fude in Japan, 1920s. Courtesy Joseph Svinth.

Yamashita remarked the same problem. According to an American journalist named Joseph Clarke, Yamashita said that while Roosevelt was his best pupil, he was also "very heavy and very impetuous, and it had cost the poor professor many bruisings, much worry and infinite pains during Theodore's rushes to avoid laming the President of the United States" (Clarke, 1920: 69).

If asked, the President probably would have agreed with these statements. For example, on March 5, 1904, he wrote his son Kermit, "My throat is a little sore, because once when one of them had a stranglehold I also got hold of his windpipe and thought I could perhaps choke him off before he could choke me. However, he got ahead" (Bishop, 1919: 93).

A month later, he wrote his son Theodore, Jr.:

I am very glad I have been doing this Japanese wrestling, but when I am through with it this time I am not at all sure I shall ever try it again. . . . I find the wrestling a trifle too vehement for mere rest. My right ankle and left wrist and one thumb and both great toes are swollen sufficiently to more or less impair their usefulness, and I am well mottled with bruises elsewhere. Still I have made good progress, and since you have left they have taught me three new throws that are perfect corkers. (Bishop, 1919, 94)

Yamashita left Washington around May 1904. Apparently someone (probably Hill or Roosevelt) had suggested that he teach judo to Harvard football players, thereby reducing their risk of death or serious injury. However, this never occurred, as at the insistence of President Roosevelt, Yamashita instead took a position teaching judo at the U.S. Naval Academy.

Yamashita started at Annapolis in January 1905. Training took place Monday, Wednesday, and Friday afternoons. He earned $1,666 for the semester, but had to pay his own assistants. The class had about 25 students.

While teaching these classes, Yamashita constantly stressed that what he taught was a gentlemanly art rather than something done by ruffians or professional wrestlers. Opinions regarding the quality of his instruction varied. According to the *Army and Navy Journal* for February 18, 1905 (677), some believed "it was the best possible means of physical training, while others regard it of little value, indeed, of positive harm as inculcating unfair and unsportsmanlike ideas of physical contests."

Such debates occurred throughout North America during 1905. Much of the debate was engendered by the Russo-Japanese War, in which Japanese propagandists routinely attributed their successes to military judo training. However, Irving Hancock and Robert Edgren, a pair of journalists who were touting the wrestling skills of a jujutsu man named Higashi Katsukuma, also contributed. Although the journalists exaggerated Higashi's ability (he lost in three straight falls to an American wrestler named George Bothner in April 1905, and in minutes to a British wrestler named Yukio Tani in November 1905), the hype generated much controversy. Wanting to know the answer for himself, on February 23, 1905, the President arranged a private match between Yamashita and a middleweight professional wrestler named Joseph Grant. In a letter to his son Kermit, Roosevelt described the outcome:

Grant did not know what to do except to put Yamashita on his back, and Yamashita was perfectly content to be on his back. Inside of a minute Yamashita had choked Grant, and inside of two minutes more he had got an elbow hold on him.... [Nonetheless,] Grant in the actual wrestling and throwing was about as good as the Japanese, and he was so much stronger that he evidently hurt and wore out the little Japanese. (Bishop, 1919: 116–117)

The U.S. Army also expressed interest in discovering if judo had as much merit in military training as the Japanese propagandists claimed. Toward answering this question, Brigadier General Albert L. Mills and Captain Frank W. Coe of the Military Academy and Captain Peyton C. March of the Army's Bayonet and Sword Committee visited Annapolis on March 4, 1905. After meeting with the Naval Academy's Commander William F. Halsey, Sr. and Surgeon Edward S. Bogert, Jr., the soldiers observed a demonstration given by Yamashita and his midshipmen. Afterward, their report said that "jiu-jitsu is not of great value as a means of physical development, but that the possession of a knowledge of this system would inspire the individual with a degree of self-confidence; hence it is recommended that jiu-jitsu be incorporated in the [physical training] course with boxing and wrestling" (*Army and Navy Journal,* March 25, 1905: 812).

As it turned out, the Military Academy hired a retired world champion wrestler named Tom Jenkins instead, and never once regretted the decision.

Three weeks later Yamashita, a Japanese assistant named Kitagaki, and Midshipmen McConnell, Piersol, Ghormley, and Heim gave their first public judo demonstration.[3] While the crowd watched politely, it greatly preferred the boxing and wrestling shows that followed. A second show given in May 1905 met an equally cool response. Said the *Army and Navy Journal* afterward:

> While some of the holds were undoubtedly serviceable if procured, the contestants worked together in such a way as to give no indication that the Americans had learned anything that would be of real use to them in a tight place. Exhibitions were given of how to stop an opponent who hit, kicked, or rushed, but it was noticeable that the man on the defense...[had an] understanding of the particular attack he had to meet and received his opponent as prearranged. (June 3, 1905: 1092)

Although disappointed by this response, Yamashita left Annapolis in June fully expecting to return in the fall. Thus, he was shocked to hear in October that the Naval Academy had no money for a judo program and that his services were no longer required.

Understandably upset, Yamashita complained to friends at the Japanese Legation that he had turned down several jobs during the summer, thinking that the Navy would be rehiring him in the fall. Now, without sufficient funds for another year in America, he began making plans to return to Japan.

While Yamashita was packing his bags, President Roosevelt asked the Japanese ambassador how his former judo teacher was doing. Upon hear-

Leaders of Kodokan judo outside the Dai Nippon Butokukai headquarters in Kyoto, July 1906. Front row, left to right: Yamashita Yoshiaki, Kano Jigoro, Yokoyama Sakujiro. Back row left to right: Samura Masaaki, Isogai Hajime, Nagaoka Hideichi. Courtesy Joseph Svinth.

ing the answer, the President asked the Secretary of the Navy if there was some reason that Yamashita should not be rehired for another year. Secretary Charles J. Bonaparte could not think of a reason that he cared to tell the President. Consequently, he sent a letter to the new Superintendent of the Naval Academy, Rear Admiral James H. Sands, asking him to "please take the necessary steps to comply with the wishes of the President" (Chief, 1905).

Admiral Sands wasted no time telling his staff to find a way of funding the President's judo program, and within two weeks the Naval Academy staff had designed a curriculum and moved $1,700 into the appropriate budget. Admiral Sands then asked Yamashita to please come by his office in Annapolis "to arrange for the course of instruction in Judo" (Superintendent, 1905).

On December 4, 1905, Admiral Sands signed a contract with Yamashita in which the latter agreed to give 50 one-hour lessons at $33.33 per lesson. On May 6, 1906, Admiral Sands wrote the Navy Department to say that the judo course had been completed, but asked that it not be repeated in 1907. He said that it was the opinion of both himself and his staff that "a knowledge of Jiu-jitsu is not of great value to those who are being prepared for a life on shipboard" (Superintendent, 1906). President Roosevelt again begged to differ, and so money was allocated to bringing Yamashita back for a third year. However, following the end of the 1906 academic year, Yamashita left the United States for Japan, and on July 24, he attended an important judo conference held in Kyoto. His absence was hardly remarked by the U.S. Navy, which did nothing more with judo until 1943.

Meanwhile, back in Seattle, Sam Hill was annoyed. He had brought Yamashita to America to teach judo to his son, and then the Professor had deserted James Nathan for that damned cowboy in the White House. So, for the rest of his life, Hill would complain to anyone who would listen that Roosevelt had "taken away from Harvard my judo man without my permission or even asking" (Tuhy, 1983: 160).

And with that proclamation, Kodokan judo quit being of much interest to Seattle's elite, and instead became something done mostly by Japanese immigrants and their sons.

THE CIRCLE AND THE OCTAGON: MAEDA'S JUDO AND GRACIE'S JIU-JITSU

Thomas A. Green and Joseph R. Svinth

INTRODUCTION

Among the major developments in martial arts during the late twentieth century was the development of Mixed Martial Arts (MMA). Although MMA had rules, generally practitioners eschewed forms *(kata)* practice during training, and during contests, they punched, kicked, or wrestled one another into submission.

Impetus for this development included the introduction of Ultimate Fighting Championships (UFC) in 1993. The UFC financier was Semaphore Entertainment Group, led by New York music promoter Robert Meyrowitz. However, the man who actually organized the original "no holds barred" pay-per-view spectacular (and designed its trademark Octagon arena) was Rorion Gracie, a Brazilian who had settled in California.

Some say that Gracie essentially invented the model for UFC tournaments (Pedreira, 2002). However, by 1993, the model for the UFC was already a century old. It had been established before 1900 by (among others) Japanese jujutsu practitioners and *sumotori* (sumo practitioners) who traveled to America and Europe in the decades after the opening of Japan by Commodore Perry in 1853–1854.

Sometimes the early jujutsu practitioners competed against boxers and wrestlers. In general, neither the Japanese nor the boxers were topflight, in part because the champions were unlikely to generate much income if they won and stood to lose reputation if they lost. For example, on November 7, 1913, *Japan Times* described such mixed matches in Japan, and throughout

Japanese professional wrestler Maeda Mitsuyo, circa 1910. Courtesy Joseph Svinth.

the twentieth century, there were contests featuring judo versus boxing or wrestling. Comparatively well-known examples include Danzan Ryu jujutsu's Henry Okazaki versus Carl "KO" Morris in Hilo in 1922, judo practitioner Masato Tamura versus professional wrestler Karl Pojello in Chicago in 1943, and judo practitioner Gene LeBell versus journeyman boxer Milo Savage in Salt Lake City in 1963. In most cases (and in all cases named), the judo practitioner won. (A farcical contest between Muhammad Ali and wrestler Antonio Inoki took place in Tokyo in 1976, but because both men were famous, the outcome of that match was a pre-arranged draw.)

In other words, the early success of the UFC was not due to its innovative sporting format, but to its commercial viability on pay-per-view cable television.

The outcome of the early matches was equally unsurprising. As in UFC I, Royce Gracie (Rorion's younger brother) used Gracie Jiu-Jitsu, a judo-based system that emphasized ground wrestling, to win by taking strikers to the ground and forcing them into submission. In subsequent UFC matches, Gracie Jiu-Jitsu proved successful against a variety of traditional and modern martial arts. Therefore, it was not until the development of a distinctive MMA style that combined wrestling and striking that the "invulnerability" of Gracie Jiu-Jitsu was revealed as a myth.

JAPANESE WRESTLERS GO OVERSEAS

The first Japanese wrestling ever seen by Americans was probably the sumo exhibition staged for Commodore Perry in 1854. Illustrations and descriptions of these contests appeared in *Harper's New Monthly Magazine* (May 1856) and *Ballou's Pictorial Drawing-Room Companion* (May 30, 1857).

Subsequently, Japanese served as cooks aboard U.S. merchant and naval vessels, and undoubtedly some of them wrestled with their shipmates. Along the way, some of these Japanese sailors reached San Francisco, and by 1884, pioneers such as Matsuda Sorakichi were working the U.S. professional wrestling circuit. The numbers of Japanese wrestlers working outside Japan increased during the next two decades, and in 1907 Japan's reigning sumo champion *(yokozuna)* Hitachiyama visited Theodore Roosevelt in the White House, and in 1914, another *yokozuna,* Tachiyama, took his entire entourage to Hawaii.

Some of these Japanese (notably Britain's Yukio Tani and France's Mikonosuke Kawaishi) gave up professional wrestling for leadership roles in community-based judo clubs. Others (notably Fujita Yasuji and Sakai Daisuke) returned home to become politicians. (Fujita became a mayor, while Sakai became a member of the Diet.) Finally, several enjoyed successful international wrestling careers. Examples include the following:

- Taro Miyake, who helped establish judo in Britain ca. 1904 (and was still wrestling main events in Madison Square Garden in 1932)
- Matty Matsuda, who became the "world lightweight champion" in 1925
- Tetsuro "Rubberman" Higami, whose career stretched from 1917 until the 1950s, at which time he was the trainer of Japanese and Japanese American wrestlers such as Hisao "Duke Keomuka" Tanaka, Harold "Oddjob" Sakata, Kimura Masahiko, and Robert "Kinji" Shibuya

Maeda Mitsuyo combined several of these roles. Because Maeda is considered the grandfather of Gracie Jiu-Jitsu, his life is worth exploring in detail, as the examination sheds light on the origins of Gracie Jiu-Jitsu and, by extension, the MMA of the late twentieth and early twenty-first centuries.

MAEDA MITSUYO: THE COUNT OF COMBAT

In November 1878, Maeda Mitsuyo was born in what is today Hirosaki City, Aomori Prefecture, Japan. As a child, Hideyo, as he was known, practiced sumo and possibly Tenshin Shinyo jujutsu.[1]

In 1896, Maeda went to Tokyo, where he attended Senmon Gakko, a prep school associated with Waseda University. Seeking to expand his martial skills, on June 6, 1897, he joined Kano Jigoro's 100-mat judo club, the Kodokan. At the Kodokan, his chief instructor was Yokoyama "Devil" Sakujiro. An exceptional learner, by 1903, Maeda advanced to fourth *dan,* winning several major judo tournaments in the process. These accomplishments got him jobs teaching judo at Waseda University, the Peers College, and other Tokyo academies.

In 1904, Maeda went to New York. This came about because in 1903, a Seattle businessman named Sam Hill had invited a Kodokan instructor, Yamashita Yoshiaki, to teach judo to Hill's son, James Nathan. For various reasons, Yamashita never taught judo to James Nathan Hill, but during 1904–1905, he did give lessons to President Theodore Roosevelt. This success encouraged another senior judo teacher, Tomita Tsunejiro, to try his chances in New York City. Like Yamashita, Tomita brought a younger man with him as an exhibition partner, and the younger man chosen was Maeda.[2]

Tomita and Maeda arrived in New York City on December 8, 1904, and in January 1905, they went with Counselor Uchida of the Imperial Japanese Legation to visit the U.S. Military Academy at West Point. Their intent was to give a lecture, presumably on the Russo-Japanese War, to cadets. As part of the presentation, Tomita and Maeda demonstrated forms *(kata),* with Maeda acting as *uke* (the party upon whom a technique such as a throw or strike is demonstrated). Following this presentation, Maeda wrestled a cadet from the crowd and threw him easily. However, because Tomita had demonstrated the techniques in the prearranged performance, the cadets wanted to wrestle him, too. Tomita threw his first challenger, but his second opponent, a varsity football player named Charles Daly, thwarted Tomita's attempts to throw him. Both the U.S. and Japanese press considered this as a defeat for Japan.

Despite this lackluster debut, Tomita and Maeda soon opened a judo club in New York City. According to an article published in the *New York World* in April 1905, there were perhaps 10 Japanese teaching judo in New York, Washington, and Boston, and most of them trained with Tomita. There may have been some American students, too, but nothing is known about them.

In 1906, to the embarrassment of the Kodokan, Maeda turned to professional wrestling. ("With Judo, we have no professionals in the same sense as other sports," Kano Jigoro once told Gunji Koizumi. "No one is allowed to take part in public entertainment for personal gain. Teachers certainly receive remuneration for their services but that is in no way degrading. The professional is held in high regard like offices of a religious organisation or professor in the educational world" [Koizumi, 1947]. Obviously, the status of American professional wrestler is not quite the same as that of minister or professor.) In fairness to Maeda, probably he needed the money.

One of his early matches was with John Piening, "The Butcher Boy." This match was held in the Catskills of New York in July 1906. Like most of Maeda's non-Japanese opponents, Piening, standing about 6 feet and weighing 170 pounds, dwarfed the 5-foot 6-inch, 155-pound Maeda. Nonetheless, Maeda won. Subsequently he toured the American South.

In early 1907, Maeda went to Britain, where he continued his wrestling career. First, he went to London, where he stayed with Ono Akitaro. Ono was a judo fourth *dan* turned professional wrestler, but because he weighed 225 pounds, he had a harder time finding work than did the 155-pound Maeda.

During the period 1907–1909, Maeda taught judo at the Naval Station at Whale Island and at Cambridge University. He also wrestled professionally. For example, in February 1908, he reached the finals of a wrestling tournament held in London (he lost to the heavyweight champion, Jimmy Esson) (*Health and Strength,* February 15, 1908: 152). In March 1908, he defeated middleweight wrestler Henry Irslinger in a match that *Health and Strength* (March 14, 1908: 257) described as "one of the squarest, straightest wrestling matches...seen in England for many years."

During 1908, Maeda also wrestled professionally in Belgium, Scotland, and Spain. The angles employed in those days would hardly seem out of place today. For example, when Maeda and Ono went to Spain in June 1908, their partners included Phoebe Roberts, a Welsh woman billed as the female judo champion of the world (Svinth, 2001a). The wrestlers also admitted whispering directions to one another during matches (Watt, 1995–2002, Part 8: 3). While in Spain, Maeda adopted the stage name Maeda Komaru. This meant "Troubled Maeda," and was an ironic allusion to his financial troubles. In time, this became Conde Koma, or Count Koma.

In December 1908, Maeda went to Cuba, and during the next seven months, he allegedly gave 400 public demonstrations.

In July 1909 and January 1910, Maeda went to Mexico City. As usual, he worked arranged matches designed to impress the crowds (Lundin, 1937: 93; Watt, 1995–2002, Part 15: 3). Subsequently, the Mexican promoters imported European champions to challenge the Foreign Menace. In other words, this was standard professional wrestling ballyhoo (Lundin, 1937: 93–94).

In 1910, Maeda was wrestling in bullfighting rings in Leon, Mexico (near Guadalajara). Perhaps to escape the tensions of the incipient Mexican Revolution, he then returned to Cuba, where he had matches in Havana and Guantanamo. During late 1911 and early 1912, Ono Akitaro, Satake Shinjiro, and Ito Tokugoro were with Maeda in Havana. All three men were very good at both wrestling and judo, and with Maeda, they became known as the Four Kings of Cuba.

On January 8, 1912, the Kodokan promoted Maeda to fifth *dan*. There was some resistance to this by a faction in Japan that did not approve of professional wrestling. Nonetheless, many Japanese viewed Maeda's pioneering efforts with pride. "The Cubans are taking fancy to our jujutsu," said *Japan Times* (November 1, 1912). "Indeed, this peculiar martial art of Nippon has become such a great fad among the islanders that three Japanese experts of jujutsu, all graduates of the Ko-do-kan of Tokyo, are at present in Cuba teaching the art to the wealthy classes of Cubans."

In Cuba, the professional wrestling hype continued as Maeda tried to arrange matches with wrestling and boxing champions Frank Gotch and Jack Johnson. Of course, both Gotch and Johnson ignored him. After all, a victory over Maeda would gain nothing for the Americans, whereas a loss would subject them to ridicule. In May 1912, there was a rebellion in Cuba. Marines landed, martial law was declared, thousands of black Cubans were killed, and interest in professional wrestling declined. Therefore, Maeda decided to visit Central America.

In El Salvador, the Salvadoran president[3] saw Maeda's demonstration, and this led to Maeda getting an invitation to teach judo to Salvadoran soldiers. However, after just a few months, the Salvadoran president was assassinated, and Maeda left for Costa Rica. Maeda may also have wrestled in the Canal Zone.

Around 1914, Maeda arrived in Brazil. He was not the first judo practitioner in that country. Instead, that honor appears to belong to a man named Miura, who was aboard *Kasato Maru,* the ship that brought the first Japanese immigrants to Brazil in 1908.

Carlos Bortole wrote in his summary of an interview with Rildo Heros Barbosa de Medeiros that Maeda gave his first exhibition in Brazil in Porto Alegre. Unfortunately, he did not name his source. It is documented, however, that Maeda wrestled in Rio de Janeiro, São Paulo, Salvador, Recife, São Luís, Belém, and finally Manaus, where he arrived on December 18, 1915. In Manaus, Maeda presented a show that featured both judo demonstrations and challenges from the crowd. This was followed on January 4–8, 1916, by a wrestling tournament. Because he was the promoter, Maeda did not participate, and Satake Shinjiro won the championship (Bortole, 1997).

Following the show, Maeda reportedly went to Britain. However, his arrival in England has not been confirmed through incoming passenger lists at the Public Records Office in London. Therefore, it is possible that he stayed in Brazil.

MAEDA AND THE ORIGIN OF GRACIE JIU-JITSU

Wherever he was in 1916, Maeda was back in Brazil in 1917, where, according to Barbosa de Medeiros (Bartole, 1997), he got a job with the Queirolo Brothers' American Circus. If true, then this is probably where Maeda met the Gracie family, as in 1916 Gastão Gracie was reportedly managing an Italian boxer associated with that same circus. (Less plausibly but more grandly, the Gracies maintain that Maeda and Gastão met when both were representatives of their respective governments.) In any event, during late 1919 or early 1920, Maeda began teaching the rudiments of judo to Gastão's son, 17-year-old Carlos.[4]

In 1925, Carlos Gracie established his own school in Rio, and this marks the official birth of the system that developed into modern Gracie Jiu-Jitsu. There is agreement that Maeda's instruction played a pivotal role in the creation of the Gracie system, but the exact nature of his contribution is controversial.

For example, there is no doubt that one of the major differences between judo and Gracie Jiu-Jitsu is that in judo, you can win a match using a clean throw, whereas in Gracie Jiu-Jitsu you must win by submission. This probably reflects the influence of Brazilian professional wrestling. (Carlos Gracie's brother Hélio wrestled professionally from the 1930s to the 1950s.) However, perhaps to minimize Gracie Jiu-Jitsu's connections to professional wrestling, it sometimes alleged that this emphasis on ground-work is due to Maeda and Carlos Gracie not having *tatami* (judo mats) on which to practice throws. This is ludicrous, as there are many substitutes for *tatami*. Outdoors, carpets spread over grass work just fine, and indoors, the standard in Britain and North America into the 1950s was either a horsehair-filled wrestling mat or canvas stretched over sawdust.[5]

Others have conjectured that Maeda did not keep up with current trends in Japan, and therefore taught the kind of judo taught in Japan before the Russo-Japanese War. Proponents of this theory point to the remarks of Kimura Masahiko, who said in 1951 that the techniques of Hélio Gracie reminded him of the kind of judo done in Japan before World War II (Wang, 2002). Unfortunately for the premise, the judo that Kimura described was a collegiate style developed in Kyoto between 1914 and 1940. Therefore, there is no reason to think that Maeda would have been teaching it in Brazil in 1920.[6]

MAEDA: THE FINAL YEARS

Speculations aside, the Queirolo Brothers' circus folded around 1921. Afterward, Maeda reportedly traveled to Britain. In 1922, however, Maeda was teaching judo in Belém. He had a European wife named May Iris, and the couple had a daughter, but both wife and child died of malaria. Sometime afterward, Maeda married (or at least moved in with) a Scottish woman.

In 1925 Maeda became active in helping Japanese immigrants settle in Brazil, and in 1928 he moved to Tome-açú, a Japanese-owned company town in Pará. "The first Japanese settlers—43 families—arrived in [this part of] Brazil in 1929, lured by a settlement company's promises of cleared fields, roads, electrified houses, and stores" (Brown, 2002). Finding the promises unfilled, the immigrants followed the Brazilian slash and burn method of agriculture; the forest was cleared by hacking plant life as close to the ground as possible followed by burning and plowing under the stubble in order to fertilize the crops. These crops consisted not only of the standard local produce (corn, beans, manioc, and rice), but also tomatoes, cucumbers, bell peppers, radishes, and turnips. Most Brazilians refused to buy these exotic vegetables, and the Japanese ended up dumping, rather than selling, most of their surplus. Eventually the Japanese investors gave up on the project. Nonetheless, the settlers persevered, and in 1947, "Nanikosuke Ussei, who had arrived in 1935 with 20 seedlings of a black pepper vine variety from Singapore, discovered a way to profitably grow the spice" (Brown, 2002). However, this did Maeda no good, as in his day, the community was barely surviving.

In 1929, the Kodokan promoted Maeda to sixth *dan* in judo. About that time, he considered returning to Japan, but for his own reasons he stayed in Brazil instead, and in 1931 he took out Brazilian citizenship. In 1940, the Japanese government offered to pay for Maeda's trip back to Japan, but he refused, saying he still had things to do in Brazil; perhaps seeing the pepper crop grow to commercial viability was among them.

Maeda died in Belém on November 28, 1941, at the age of 63. The cause of death was listed as kidney disease. He had converted to Catholicism while in Brazil, and after a large funeral, he was buried at Saint Isabel Cemetery.

His promotion to seventh *dan* in judo was dated November 27, 1941, so the certificate arrived after his death. However, the Kodokan did not forget Maeda's contributions to spreading judo to Brazil, and in May 1956, it dedicated a stone memorial to him in Hirosaki City. Notables present at the dedication included Kano Risei, president of the Kodokan, and Samura Kaichiro, tenth *dan*.

GRACIE JIU-JITSU

From 1932 until the mid-1950s, Hélio Gracie (Carlos's brother) wrestled professionally in Brazil. Starting with techniques learned from Carlos and then perfected by himself, he wrestled in venues not unlike those in which Maeda had displayed his own skills. These matches were not always muscular theater, as was normal in North American professional wrestling; instead, some appear to have been reasonably legitimate challenge matches. Internationally, Gracie's most famous bout was probably the one with Kimura Masahiko in October 1951, during which Gracie lasted 13 minutes against the Japanese.

Nevertheless, outside Brazil, Gracie Jiu-Jitsu remained a little known and less appreciated art (Flores, 1960). Therefore, when Carlos's son Carley (who came to the United States in 1972) and Hélio's son Rorion (who joined Carley in the United States in 1979) began teaching their art to North American students, they did so in relative obscurity.

Hélio and Rorion Gracie, 1995. Courtesy Stanley Pranin and *Aikido Journal*.

The 1970s were a good time to bring Gracie Jiu-Jitsu to America, as it was the era of Bruce Lee, Billy Jack, and Kwai Chang Caine. Unfortunately, the market was more interested in flashy flying kicks than the slow, patient, maneuvering for position on the ground that is the hallmark of Gracie Jiu-Jitsu. Nonetheless, using ploys such as challenge matches magnified and hyped in the sports entertainment media, Rorion Gracie eventually developed the UFC model. (That marketing, as distinct from martial art, was foremost in his mind is demonstrated by his copyrighting both the Gracie Jiu-Jitsu name and logo.)

This brings us full circle, to the MMA events fought inside the Octagons of the 1990s. By 2002, these MMA events had evolved beyond the early UFC model, which gave Rorion's younger brother Royce victories in three of the first four UFC events. The arena devised to showcase Gracie Jiu-Jitsu as the ultimate fighting system grew from local challenge matches through televised Brazilian *vale tudo* (anything goes) events to extravaganzas in Las Vegas's MGM Grand, and then became the incubator for a new style altogether, the MMA designed specifically for use in the Octagon.

THE MYTH OF ZEN IN THE ART OF ARCHERY

Yamada Shoji

For most people, the term "Japanese archery" *(kyudo)* evokes thoughts of spiritual training or *kyudo's* close relationship with Zen. Commentators commonly assert that "*kyudo* resembles Zen." In examining the history of Japanese archery, however, it is no exaggeration to say that it was only after the Second World War that *kyudo* became particularly associated with Zen. More specifically, this occurred after 1956 when a book called *Zen in the Art of Archery* (originally, *Zen in der Kunst des Bogenschiessens,* 1948) by a German professor of philosophy, Eugen Herrigel (1884–1955), was translated and published in Japanese. This book has been translated into several foreign languages and continues to be a best-selling work on Japanese culture.

How did people approach Japanese archery before the appearance of this book? In the post-Meiji period (after 1868), most people practiced it either for physical education or pleasure. In pre-war texts about Japanese archery, with the exception of certain isolated sects, there is little or no

This article first appeared in *Nihon kenkyu: Kokusai Nihon bunka kenkyu senta kiyo* [Researching Japan: International Research Symposium Proceedings] 19 (1999, June) (pp. 15–34), under the title "Shinwa to shite no yumi to zen" [The myth of *Zen in the Art of Archery*]. It was subsequently translated into English by Earl Hartman and edited by William M. Bodiford for *Journal of Japanese Religious Studies,* 28: 1–2 (2001) (pp. 1–30). This version was edited further by Earl Hartman. Copyright © 2002 by Yamada Shoji. Adapted by permission.

Hiroshi Gosho doing Japanese archery in Seattle, 1935. Manuscripts, Special Collections, University Archives, University of Washington Libraries, UW 18495.

mention of *kyudo's* affinity with Zen.[1] Likewise, among modern *kyudo* practitioners, those who approach it as part of Zen training are extremely unusual in Japan. In spite of these facts, popular books and commentators emphasize the *kyudo*-Zen connection. This phenomenon deserves closer attention.

Many Japanese authors have discussed Herrigel (e.g., Nishio, 1978; Omori, 1982; Minamoto, 1995). All their essays basically repeat Herrigel's own account of the mystical episodes that occurred with his teacher, Awa Kenzo (1880–1939), affirming Herrigel's understanding and taking his interpretation as the starting point for their discussions of *kyudo* and, by extension, of Japanese arts. However, should Herrigel's work really be regarded as a reliable foundation for this?

It is a well-known fact among *kyudo* researchers that Awa Kenzo was an eccentric instructor. Authors who are not *kyudo* specialists, however, usually accept Herrigel's description of Japanese archery at face value. However, considering the disparity between actual *kyudo* and what Herrigel presented, it is impossible to uncritically accept his book as a reliable account of what he experienced and observed.

This essay will present a new reading of Herrigel's text and its associated sources and, by reconstructing his account, will clarify how the myth of *Zen in the Art of Archery* came to be propagated. Henceforth I will not use the term *kyudo* (literally "the way of the bow"), but will use the term *kyujutsu* (literally "the art/technique of the bow") because it is the term actually used by Herrigel. Before discussing Herrigel, though, it is useful to briefly review the history and techniques of Japanese archery so that we can be forearmed with some background knowledge and thus be better able to put Awa and Herrigel's relationship in the proper perspective.

THE HISTORY AND TECHNIQUES OF *KYUJUTSU*

Although there is archeological evidence of the existence of bows and arrows in Japan dating from much earlier periods, historians believe that the bow came to be used as a military weapon after the end of the Yayoi period (ca. 3rd century C.E.). They base this conclusion on evidence from Yayoi period archeological excavations, which have yielded arrow heads that are larger than those of previous periods and skeletons that show evidence of arrow wounds.

The Genpei War (1180–1185) saw bows and arrows come into full flower as military weapons. The organized lineages *(ryuha)* that have taught archery down to the present day, however, were not founded until the time of the Onin War (beginning 1467) when a man named Heki Danjo Masatsugu (ca. 1444–1502) supposedly taught the father and son pair of Yoshida Shigekata (1463–1543) and Yoshida Shigemasa (1485–1569) exquisite archery techniques (there is debate about Heki's historicity). From the time of the Yoshidas the transmission of this lineage can be historically documented. This lineage eventually became known as the Heki-ryu (a.k.a.,Yoshida-ryu) and it split into various branch lineages (ha), some of which still survive. In addition, a Shingon Buddhist priest named Chikurinbo Josei founded a separate lineage known as the Heki-ryu Chikurin-ha.

Technically speaking, Japanese archery can be divided into two main categories: ceremonial archery and military archery. Ceremonial archery is concerned with the ritual and thaumaturgic aspects of kyujutsu, and one can safely say that this is the exclusive domain of the Ogasawara-ryu, originally founded in the early Kamakura period (ca. 1185–1333) by Ogasawara Nagakiyo (1162–1242). This school taught methods of archery, horsemanship, and etiquette. (The early Ogasawara teachings, however, were lost during the Muromachi period (ca. 1336–1573), but were later revived by Ogasawara Heibei Tsuneharu (1666–1747), who thus became the direct founder of the Ogasawara-ryu that now exists in Tokyo.)

Military archery can be further divided into foot archery, equestrian archery, and what is called temple archery.

Foot archery refers to the archery used by foot soldiers on the battlefield. These archers must be able to accurately hit targets with sufficient force to penetrate traditional Japanese armor at a distance of approximately 30 m (the optimum killing range) in the heat of battle. The archery lineages that specialize in foot archery aim to develop an extremely accurate, subtle technique and to cultivate a death-defying spiritual fortitude.

Equestrian archery refers to the technique of shooting the bow from horseback. It emphasized the ability to skillfully manage a horse so that the archer could approach close enough to the target to shoot from a distance where it would not be too difficult to hit it. Consequently, in equestrian archery, training focuses on how to manage a horse while carrying and shooting a bow.

Temple archery refers to a competition where archers competed nonstop over the course of an entire day and night to see who can shoot the most arrows the entire length of the outside verandah of the Sanjusangendo (the Hall of 33 Bays) at the Rengeo-in temple in Kyoto, using only the space beneath the temple eaves, which measures 120 m (393.69 ft.) in length by 5 m (16.4 ft.) in height. Temple archery requires technique that

Archery target. Arthur E. Grix, *Japans Sport in Bild und Wort* (Berlin: Wilhelm Limpert, 1937).

allows the archer, with minimum fatigue, to shoot light arrows with a low trajectory.

Foot archery and equestrian archery are still practiced today: foot archery through the adoption of the 28 m (91.86 ft.) shooting distance as the basic layout of the *kyudo* archery range, and equestrian archery in the form of *yabusame* (where contestants ride down a straight course and shoot arrows at three separate targets). Temple archery, however, declined after the fall of the Tokugawa regime when competition at the Sanjusangendo ceased.

KENZO AWA AND *DAISHADOKYO* (THE GREAT DOCTRINE OF THE WAY OF SHOOTING)

Let us gradually bring the discussion closer to Herrigel. First, I will outline the life of Awa Kenzo, Herrigel's *kyujutsu* teacher. My principal source is a large commemorative volume by Sakurai Yasunosuke (1981). Because this work was published in commemoration of the one-hundredth anniversary of Awa's birth, it is not free of bias, but Sakurai cites a wealth of primary sources useful for understanding Awa. In this section, I will sum up Awa's life based on Sakurai's account.

Awa was born in 1880 in Kawakitamachi (Miyagi Prefecture) as the eldest son of the Sato family. At the age of 19, he married into the Awa family, and thereby acquired the Awa family name. The following year Awa began training in Heki-ryu Sekka-ha *kyujutsu* (a temple archery school) under the tutelage of Kimura Tatsugoro. After only two years he received his diploma of complete transmission *(menkyo kaiden),* the highest rank possible. Thus, when Awa was only 21, he established his own archery training hall.

In 1909 Awa opened a new archery training hall in Sendai City. In 1910 he began to study Heki-ryu Chikurin-ha *kyujutsu* (a temple archery school which had a strong Buddhist background) under Honda Toshizane. At about the same time, Awa became the archery instructor at the Number Two College in Sendai. It appears that Awa was an expert archer, being capable of hitting the mark nearly 100 times for every 100 shots. His instruction to his students also emphasized accuracy. Sometime around the beginning of the Taisho period (1912–1926), however, Awa began having doubts about his archery. A secret Heki-ryu Sekka-ha teaching "nothing is needed" *(nanni mo iranu),* resonated deeply with Awa, so deeply that he began to disavow *kyujutsu.*

This doctrine, "nothing is needed," is given as follows:

> As for the stance, the positioning of the body, the positioning of the bow, the grip on the bow, the grip on the string, the raising of the bow, the drawing of the bow, the draw length, the extension, the tension, the balance of hard and soft, the stretch, the rainfall release, and the morning storm release: I see that none are needed.[2]

On first reading it appears to assert that archery technique is unnecessary. Immediately following this, however, the text says, "'Not being needed' does not mean that they are unnecessary from the beginning. At the beginning when one knows nothing, if the beginner does not first completely learn the proper stance, then his torso and hips will not become settled." In short, in the beginning one must learn proper shooting technique, and then after sufficient skill is acquired, one will be able to shoot naturally without thinking about it.

Awa extended this concept to an extreme by interpreting it to mean that from the beginning no technique is necessary. On the basis of this misunderstanding, Awa began to call *kyujutsu* "a kind of hereditary disease that regards technical training as an art" and began to preach his own style of "*shado*" (the way of shooting), which he characterized as being "austere training in which one masters the study of humanity." As a result, the *kyujutsu* community treated him like a lunatic. Honda Toshitoki, the grandson of Honda Toshizane and the eventual headmaster of the Honda-ryu, harshly criticized Awa, saying that Awa shot merely as his whims and moods moved him. Concerning the doctrine of "putting an entire lifetime of exertion into each shot" (*issha zetsumei,* sometimes translated as "one shot, one life") which Awa later expounded, Ohira Zenzo, who was Awa's senior among the disciples of Honda, said that it was idiotic to tell people to just persevere until they dropped dead (Sakurai, 1981: 162). Honda's other disciples were equally merciless in their criticism of Awa.

It appears that Awa's advocacy that people convert from *kyujutsu* to *shado* was influenced by Kano Jigoro's successful conversion of jujutsu into judo. In one of the manuscripts that he left behind, Awa wrote, "To give the closest example, the reason why Kano Jigoro's Kodokan school of judo is praised not only in Japan but also in foreign countries is because, first of all, it is taught as a Way *(do* or *michi),* and rather than restricting its techniques to just one lineage or style alone it blends the strong points of all schools" (Sakurai, 1981: 145).

In 1920, when Awa was 40, he had a decisive eccentric experience. To quote Sakurai, Awa experienced a "great explosion." Sakurai, using some short compositions and drawings left by Awa as clues, describes this experience as follows:

> Late one evening, the family was fast asleep, all was wrapped in silence, and all that could be seen was the moon peacefully illuminating the evening darkness. Alone, Kenzo went to the archery range and with his beloved bow and arrows quietly faced the target. He was determined. Would his flesh perish first? Would his spirit live on?

No release. Total focus. He was determined that with this shot there would be no retreat, not even so much as a single step.

> The bitter struggle continued. His body had already passed its limit. His life would end here.
>
> Finally: "I have perished." Just as this thought passed through his mind, a marvelous sound reverberated from the heavens.
>
> He thought it must be from heaven since never before had he heard such a clear, high, strong sound from the twanging of the bowstring and from the arrow piercing the target. At the very instant when he thought he heard it, his self flew apart into infinite grains of dust, and, with his eyes dazzled by a myriad of colors, a great thunderous wave filled heaven and earth. (Sakurai, 1981: 159–160)

This kind of mystical experience very often forms the impetus for founding a new religion. For example, the story of the morning star flying into the mouth of Kuukai (774–835) during his religious austerities in Murotomisaki resembles Awa's experience.

After his "great explosion," Awa began to preach that one must "put an entire lifetime of exertion into each shot" and that one can "see true nature in the shot," the two ideas that later came to form the core of his teachings. Sakurai explains the essential point of these teachings as follows:

> Even though we are speaking of the power of Nature, one must train one's mental energy and generate spiritual energy [to unite with this power]. In this way one enters the Absolute Way that eliminates all relativity. Space is destroyed as one passes through it. Then for the first time one becomes wrapped in the radiance of the Buddha and can perceive the self which reflects the radiance of the Buddha. At this moment the self is both the self yet not the self. (Sakurai, 1981: 164)

Although "see true nature," meaning, attain awakening, is a Zen term, it is practically impossible to detect any Zen elements in Awa's teaching.

It appears that Awa never practiced Zen even once in his life. Sakurai (1981: 223) wrote, "No evidence can be found that Kenzo ever trained with a Zen priest." Moreover, Sakurai (1981: 266) states, "While Kenzo used the phrase 'the bow and Zen are one' and used the philosophical language of Mahayana Buddhism in particular to describe *shado,* he did not approve of Zen unconditionally."

Why, then, did Herrigel associate Awa's teachings with Zen? Before getting to that question, let us follow Awa's life to its conclusion. Herrigel became Awa's student one year after Awa's "great explosion" and one year before Awa began to talk about founding Daishadokyo (Great Doctrine of the Way of Shooting). Although this proposal provoked fierce opposition among Awa's students, he overruled them and formally established a new organization named Daishadokyo[3] in 1927. Awa's students at the Number Two College later testified that Daishadokyo consisted of "archery as a religion," that "the founder [of this religion] is Master Awa Kenzo," and that "the master described his rounds of travel to provide guidance in various regions, not as [archery] lessons or as instruction; he said that he was doing 'missionary work' "(Sakurai 1981: 210–11). Thus, it is clear that Awa's Daishadokyo possessed religious characteristics.

The year after Awa established Daishadokyo, he fell ill. Although at one point he appeared to recover, from that time on he remained in a partially incapacitated condition until he died of illness in 1939 during his sixtieth year. Today there are many *kyudo* practitioners who still follow the style of Awa's Daishadokyo. Nonetheless, as a religious organization, Daishadokyo died with Awa.

THE ENCOUNTER OF HERRIGEL AND AWA

We can now return to Eugen Herrigel. Herrigel was born near Heidelberg in 1884. At the University of Heidelberg he first studied theology but later switched to Neo-Kantian philosophy. At the same time Herrigel confessed: "Even as a student I had, as though propelled by some secret urge, been pre-occupied with mysticism" (Herrigel, 1953: 29; 1956: 56).[4] Because of his interest in mysticism, Herrigel became interested in Zen, which he thought to be the most mystical of religions, and through Zen, he developed an interest in Japanese culture.[5] In 1924, Herrigel obtained a position as a lecturer at Tohoku Imperial University in Sendai, where he taught philosophy until 1929.[6] After returning to Germany, he took a professorship at Erlangen University. He retired in 1951,[7] and died in 1955, in his 71st year.

In *Zen in the Art of Archery,* Herrigel explained how his interest in Zen prompted his decision to travel to Japan:

> For some considerable time it has been no secret, even to us Europeans, that the Japanese arts go back for their inner form to a common root, namely Buddhism.... I do not mean Buddhism in the ordinary sense, nor am I concerned with the decidedly speculative form of Buddhism, which, because of its allegedly accessible literature, is the only one we know in Europe and even claim to understand. I mean Dhyana Buddhism, which is known in Japan as "Zen." (Herrigel, 1953: 21; 1956: 44–45)

Today, I am sure that most people would object to the assertion that "all Japanese arts can be traced back to Zen." Herrigel acknowledged that his views on this matter resulted from the influence of D.T. Suzuki (1870–1966):

> In his *Essays in Zen Buddhism,* D.T. Suzuki has succeeded in showing that Japanese culture and Zen are intimately connected and that Japanese art, the spiritual attitude of the samurai, the Japanese way of life, the moral, aesthetic and to a certain extent even the intellectual life of the Japanese owe their peculiarities to this background of Zen and cannot be properly understood by anybody not acquainted with it. (Herrigel, 1953: 22–23; 1982: 16–17)[8]

We can divine from the above passages that Herrigel, influenced by Suzuki and driven by his own "preoccupation with mysticism," tried as hard as he could to detect Zen elements within Japanese culture.

Once in Japan, a Japanese colleague suggested that Herrigel "first choose an artistic endeavor that has been particularly strongly influenced by Zen and, while you are practicing that, approach Zen at your leisure in

Eugen Herrigel. Courtesy Universität Erlangen-Nürnberg.

a roundabout way" (Enoki, 1991: 202; cf. Herrigel, 1953: 31–32). Thus, Herrigel decided to learn *kyujutsu* and sought instruction from Awa. Although there is no evidence that Herrigel ever practiced Zen during his stay in Japan, a posthumous collection of Herrigel's essays entitled *Der Zen-Weg* (1958; translated into English as *The Method of Zen*, 1960) shows that Herrigel read extensively about Zen.

Herrigel relayed his request to be Awa's student through Komachiya Sozo (1893–1979), a colleague at the university who had studied *kyujutsu* under Awa at the Number Two College. Sakurai states, "Komachiya simply met Awa again for the first time in twelve years. At that moment there was no way that he could have been aware of the development and changes in Awa's state of mind since their last meeting" (Sakurai, 1981: 285). As a favor to Herrigel, Komachiya acted as his go-between with Awa. Looking back, in 1940 Komachiya wrote:

> I think it was the spring of 1926. Herrigel came to me and said, "I want to study the bow. Please introduce me to instructor Awa." The bow is difficult

to approach, even for Japanese. I wondered what had caused him to want to try his hand at it. When I asked him the reason, he replied: "It has been three years since I came to Japan. I have finally realized that there are many things in Japanese culture that should be studied. In particular, it appears to me that Buddhism, Zen most especially, has exerted a very strong influence on Japanese thought. I think that the most expedient way for me to get to know Zen is to study *kyudo*." (Komachiya, 1940/1982: 69–70)

Awa agreed to teach Herrigel on the condition that Komachiya act as interpreter. Thus, Herrigel began taking weekly *kyujutsu* lessons from Awa. While Herrigel struggled to understand *kyujutsu* rationally, Awa responded to him with words that transcended logic. Taken by itself, this conversation between Western culture and Japanese culture is extremely interesting and is a major reason why Herrigel's book was such a great success from a literary point of view. At the same time, however, it is probably more appropriate to see Herrigel not so much as a logician but as a mystic.

Consider these two protagonists. Awa was trying to make archery into a new religion, but Herrigel had no way of knowing about Awa's idiosyncratic nature. Herrigel ceaselessly searched for Zen, but Awa by no means affirmed Zen. What were the conversations between these two men actually like? Without analyzing this, it is impossible to properly evaluate Herrigel's account of his experiences. Therefore, I will analyze two of the most dramatic and inspiring mystical episodes redacted by Herrigel, "the target in darkness"[9] and Awa's doctrine of "*It* shoots," which Herrigel saw as the central pillar of Awa's teaching. I will cite the translations of both his first essay on Japanese archery, "*Die ritterliche Kunst des Bogenschiessens*" (The Chivalrous Art of Archery, 1936a), and of his later, expanded version that appeared as *Zen in der Kunst des Bogenschiessens* (Zen in the Art of Archery, 1948).

THE TARGET IN DARKNESS

The first incident, "the target in darkness," concerns the following event. In his 1936 account Herrigel explained how (after shooting at a close practice target for three years) when he was first permitted to shoot at a target on the archery range (which is 28 m long), his arrows did not reach the target no matter how many times he shot. Finally, Herrigel asked what he needed to do to hit the target. Awa told him, "Thinking about hitting the target is heresy. Do not aim at it." Herrigel could not accept this answer. He insisted that "If I do not aim at the target, I cannot hit it." At that point, Awa ordered Herrigel to come to the practice hall that evening. Herrigel explained what happened that night:

> We entered the spacious practice hall adjacent to the master's house. The master lit a stick of incense, which was as long and thin as a knitting needle, and placed it in the sand in front of the target, which was approximately in the center of the target bank. We then went to the shooting area. Since the master was standing directly in the light, he was dazzlingly illuminated.
>
> The target, however, was in complete darkness. The single, faintly glowing point of the incense was so small it was practically impossible to make out the light it shed. The master had said not a word for some time. Silently he took up his bow and two arrows. He shot the first arrow. From the sound I knew it hit the target. The second arrow also made a sound as it hit the target. The master motioned to me to verify the condition of the two arrows that had been shot. The first arrow was cleanly lodged in the center of the target. The second arrow had struck the nock of the first one and split it in two. I brought the arrows back to the shooting area. The master looked at the arrows as if in deep thought and after a short while said the following. (Herrigel, 1941/1982: 46–47; compare Herrigel, 1953: 84–85)

At a practice hall in the dark of night, before a solitary disciple, the master shoots an arrow at a target that is practically invisible and hits the mark. Then, his second arrow strikes the nock of the arrow that is in the center of the target and splits it. Anyone would be moved by this story.

Nonetheless, so as not to get carried away and lose sight of the true nature of the matter, I attempted to verify the rarity of this occurrence by quantifiable means, namely a computer simulation. Assuming that Awa's rate of accuracy was close to 100 percent, his hitting percentage would be a regular distribution of 99.7 percent, equal to what is called 3 sigma in statistical terms. The computer simulation yielded a 0.3 percent probability of the second arrow hitting the nock of the first one. Even viewed from a statistical perspective, the "target in darkness" incident was truly an unlikely occurrence.

However, Japanese *kyujutsu* practitioners believe that shattering the nock of one's arrow is a shameful failure, because the archer damages his own equipment. The "target in darkness" event was by no means something of which a *kyujutsu* practitioner would boast. In fact, Awa did not speak of this to anyone except one of his most senior disciples. Is it possible that Awa did not want to divulge that he had shattered the nock of his arrow because he was ashamed?

Regarding this episode, in 1940 Komachiya says: "After reading Herrigel's [1936] essay I asked Awa about this incident one day. Awa laughed and said, 'You know, sometimes really strange things happen. That was a coincidence'"(Komachiya, 1940/1982: 99). Also, Anzawa Heijiro (1888–1970), Awa's most senior disciple and the only person to whom Awa revealed this incident, said that Awa gave him the following account:

> The first arrow hit the target, and the second arrow made a sound like it had struck something. Herrigel went to retrieve the arrows, but after a long time he did not return. I called out, "Eugen! Oh, Eugen!" Then I said, "What is it? How come you do not answer?" Then, well, there was Herrigel sitting down directly in front of the target. I went up to him like this. [Awa imitated someone walking nonchalantly.] I said, "What is the matter?" Herrigel was speechless, sitting rooted to the spot...Awa said, "No, that was just a coincidence! I had no special intention to demonstrate such a thing." (quoted in Komachiya, 1965)

These are the words that Awa spoke to Anzawa. They are extremely simple and easy to understand. In short, it was a coincidence. There is not even the minutest whiff of mysticism.

The words that Herrigel attributes to Awa, however, have a completely different ambience:

> You probably think that since I have been practicing in this training hall for thirty years I must know where the target is even in the dark, so hitting the target in the center with the first shot was not a particularly great feat. If that was all, then perhaps what you think would be entirely true. But what do you make of the second shot? Since it did not come from *me,* it was not *me* who made the hit. Here, you must carefully consider: Is it possible to even aim in such darkness? Can you still maintain that you cannot hit the target without aiming? Well, let us stand in front of the target with the same attitude as when we bow before the Buddha. (Herrigel, 1941/1982: 47–48; emphasis in the original)

These are extremely mysterious words, very difficult to understand. What, exactly, accounts for the discrepancy between Herrigel's and Anzawa's accounts? This question hinges around the issue of interpreting. Ordinarily, Komachiya interpreted Awa's instructions for Herrigel. During the "target in darkness" incident, however, Awa and Herrigel were alone. In 1940, Komachiya testified as follows:

> Herrigel's [1936] essay describes an incident when, in pitch darkness, Awa lit a stick of incense, put it in front of the target, and shot two arrows, hitting the nock of the first arrow with the second. It also recounts what Awa said

at the time. Since I was not there to act as a translator that evening, I think that Herrigel, relying on his own ability to interpret the Japanese language, understood all of that by means of "mind-to-mind transmission" (*ishin den-shin*), as truly amazing as that is. (Komachiya, 1940/1982: 98)

Today, we cannot know what sort of conversation, in what language, took place between Awa and Herrigel on that night. Nonetheless, it is easy to imagine that Awa, speaking a language that Herrigel did not understand, experienced great difficulty in explaining this coincidental occurrence. The coincidence of the second arrow hitting the nock of the first produced a phenomenal space, an emptiness that needed to be given some kind of meaning. Here, the lack of an interpreter was crucial. Because an extremely rare incident occurred, perhaps it was only natural for Herrigel to imbue it with some kind of mystical significance. His introducing the Buddha into this story, however, merely amplified its mysterious quality to no purpose.

LANGUAGE DIFFICULTIES

Because my analysis of the doctrine of "*It* shoots" involves issues with Herrigel's understanding of Awa's language, before going further I wish to discuss Komachiya's interpreting in more detail. After Awa experienced his "great explosion," he fell into the habit of using many words that were difficult to understand. Komachiya offers the following reminiscence:

> At every lesson Awa would explain that *kyudo* is not a matter of technique but is a means of religious training and a method of attaining awakening. Indeed, like an improvisational poet, he would freely employ Zen-like adages at every turn. When he grew impatient, in an effort to get Herrigel to understand what he was saying, he would immediately draw various diagrams on the chalkboard that was hanging on the wall of the practice hall. One day, for instance, he drew a figure of a person standing on top of a circle in the act of drawing a bow and drew a line connecting the lower abdomen of the figure to the center of the circle. He explained that this figure, which represented Herrigel, must put his strength into his lower abdomen, enter the realm of no-self, and become one with the universe. (Komachiya, 1940/1982: 86–87)

Komachiya explicitly acknowledged that his interpreting frequently distorted the meaning of Awa's abstruse language:

> For that matter, in those days, there were many occasions when Awa would say something that seemed to contradict what he had taught previously. At

such times, I did not interpret for Herrigel but remained silent. When I did that, Herrigel would think it strange. He would insistently ask me about what Awa had just said, which left me feeling completely flummoxed. Even though I felt bad for doing so, I would say, "Oh, Awa is just extremely intent on his explanation, and he is repeating what he always says about putting an entire lifetime of exertion into each shot and that all shots are holy," and put a brave front on the situation. Essentially, as Awa expounded on the spirit of archery, he would become spontaneously excited, and, wanting desperately to express his feelings, he would use various Zen terms. Without realizing it he would say mutually contradictory things. Even today I think that both Awa and Herrigel knowingly let me get away with my translation strategy of "sitting on and smothering" [difficult sentences]. (Komachiya, 1940/1982: 87–88)

In reference to Awa's writings, Sakurai concluded that "Their logic is not rigorous, and long sentences, in particular, exhibit a lack of coherence" (Sakurai, 1981: 6–7).

It would be unjust, however, to criticize Komachiya alone for any misunderstandings. Herrigel quotes one of Awa's lectures as follows:

If the target and I become one, this means that I and the Buddha become one. Then, if I and the Buddha become one, this means that the arrow is in the center of an unmoved center, which is both existent and nonexistent, and thus in the center of the target. The arrow is in the center. If we interpret this with our awakened consciousness, then we see that the arrow issues from the center and enters the center. For this reason, you must not aim at the target but aim at yourself. If you do this, you will hit you yourself, the Buddha, and the target all at once. (Herrigel, 1941/1982: 43)

Awa frequently expressed himself with cryptic words like these. If we put ourselves in Komachiya's shoes, we can see that his free translation resulted from no malicious intent.

"*IT* SHOOTS"

Now, we can analyze the doctrine of "*It* shoots." In Herrigel's account this doctrine is introduced during a period when Herrigel had been unable to release the arrow skillfully no matter how hard he tried. He asked Awa for help, and the following dialogue ensued:

One day I asked the Master, "How can the shot be loosed if 'I' do not do it?"
  " 'It' shoots," he replied. . . .

"And who or what is this 'It'?"

"Once you have understood that you will have no further need of me. And if I tried to give you a clue at the cost of your own experience, I would be the worst of teachers and deserve to be sacked! So let's stop talking about it and go on practicing." (Herrigel, 1953: 76; 1956, 126–27)

Although troubled by this instruction, Herrigel continued training. Then, one day when Herrigel loosed an arrow, Awa bowed courteously and broke off the practice. As Herrigel stared at Awa in bewilderment, Awa exclaimed, "Just then 'It' shot!" Herrigel was thrilled. He wrote, "And when I at last understood what he meant I couldn't suppress a sudden whoop of delight" (Herrigel, 1953: 77; 1956: 128–29).

This dramatic event constitutes the central episode of *Zen in the Art of Archery*. Therefore, it should be evaluated very carefully. What, exactly, is meant by "*It* shoots"?

I have two reservations regarding this doctrine. First, there is no indication that Awa ever taught "*It* shoots" to any of his disciples other than Herrigel. Second, although "*Es*" abruptly appears in two passages in Herrigel's 1936 essay (which was the preliminary draft for *Zen in the Art of Archery*), there is no attempt to explain its meaning or to attribute special significance to it. In addition, it was not translated as "*It* shoots" in the Japanese language version.

The first reservation is based on a thorough reading of Sakurai's 1981 treatise, which is the definitive account of Awa's life and teachings. In this work, the doctrine of "*It* shoots" appears only in relation to Herrigel.

Concerning my second reservation, notice how Herrigel's two accounts of the "target in darkness" incident differ between his 1936 essay and his 1948 book. As noted previously, in his 1936 essay Herrigel quoted Awa as having said:

But what do you make of the second shot? Since it did not come from *me,* it was not *me* who made the hit. Here, you must carefully consider: Is it possible to even aim in such darkness? Can you still maintain that you cannot hit the target without aiming? Well, let us stand in front of the target with the same attitude as when we bow before the Buddha. (Herrigel, 1941/1982: 47–48; emphasis in the original)

In *Zen in the Art of Archery,* this was changed to the following:

But the second arrow which hit the first—what do you make of that? I at any rate know that it is not "I" who must be given credit for this shot. "It" shot and "It" made the hit. Let us bow down to the goal as before the Buddha! (Herrigel, 1953: 85; 1956: 141–42)

In response to these two reservations, the following hypotheses can be suggested:

1. Herrigel fabricated the doctrine of "*It* shoots" when he wrote *Zen in the Art of Archery.*
2. Miscommunication occurred between Awa and Herrigel concerning "*It* shoots."

Regarding the first hypothesis, if Herrigel created "*It* shoots," then he must have conceived of it during the 12 years that separated his 1936 essay and his 1948 book. The first hypothesis can be countered by saying that the essay format did not allow Herrigel to discuss archery in any great depth and detail, or that Herrigel himself was unable to completely solidify his understanding of "It" at that time. Moreover, Herrigel declared in his foreword to *Zen in the Art of Archery,* "The narration in this book contains not a single word that was not said directly by my teacher. I have not used any metaphors or comparisons that he did not use" (Herrigel, 1956: 37).[10] If this declaration is true, we can discard the first hypothesis. As I have already stated, I have doubts concerning the accuracy of Komachiya's interpreting. These considerations lead me to conclude that the words Herrigel remembers are not the words that Awa actually spoke. That was not Herrigel's responsibility, however.

Now let us consider the second hypothesis. Concerning "*It* shoots" (German, *Es geschossen;* Japanese, *sore ga iru*), Nishio Kanji (1982: 32) notes, "We do not really know whether Awa actually said the Japanese word 'it' *(sore)* or whether Herrigel merely inserted the German-language third person pronoun for some Japanese words that were spoken to him. The German-language third person pronoun *'es,'* which corresponds to 'it' *(sore),* is an impersonal pronoun that expresses something which transcends the self." Concerning this point, Feliks F. Hoff (1994), past President of the German Kyudo Federation, suggests that *"Es"* geschossen might have been used to translate the Japanese words *sore deshita* (that's it). In Japanese, when a student performs well, it is perfectly natural for the teacher to say, "That's it." It simply means "What you did just now was fine." Perhaps these Japanese words of approval were translated to Herrigel as *Es geschossen.* Hoff suggests that this allowed Herrigel to misinterpret the meaning of the original Japanese words along the lines of "something called 'it,' which transcends the self, shoots."

Although I support Hoff's thesis, I also believe that Herrigel must have anguished over the interpretation of "It." This anguish is suggested by the fact that it took 12 long years, even granting that a war intervened, before Herrigel was able to rewrite his initial 1936 essay on Japanese archery, in which "It" plays little or no role, and publish it as *Zen in the Art of Archery,* which has "It" as its centerpiece. This point is corroborated by the following statement, found in Herrigel's foreword to *Zen in the Art of Archery:*

> Over the past ten years—which for me were ten years of unremitting training—I made greater inner progress and even more improvement than before. From this condition of greater completeness, I acquired the conviction that I was now capable of explaining the "mystical" central issues of *kyudo,* and thereupon resolved to present this new composition to the public. (Herrigel, 1956: 36)

If the words that Awa cried out when Herrigel made a good shot were "that's it" *(sore deshita),* then they must have indicated a subjective quality that only a person accomplished in that art can understand. Judging from the context, the first time Awa praised Herrigel by saying *"It* shot" was when Herrigel was still practicing before the practice target and was not yet skilful enough to shoot at full distance. It is utterly inconceivable that "It," which indicates a spiritual condition sufficiently advanced to involve something that transcends the self, could have made its appearance at a time when Herrigel was still just a beginner. It is far more natural to conclude that Awa simply praised Herrigel by saying, "That was good."

Herrigel, however, came to the following conclusion regarding "It's" nature:

> Just as we say in archery that "It" takes aim and hits, so here [speaking of Japanese swordsmanship] "It" takes the place of ego, availing itself of a facility and a dexterity which the ego only acquires by conscious effort. And here too "It" is only a name for something which can neither be understood nor laid hold of, and which only reveals itself to those who have experienced it. (Herrigel, 1953: 104; 1956: 165)

Apparently, "That's it," was mistakenly translated as, "It shoots." Compounding this error, Herrigel understood "It" to indicate something that transcends the self. If that is what happened, then the doctrine of *"It* shoots" was born from the momentary slippage of meaning caused by the (mis-) translation of Japanese into German, which created an empty space that needed to be imbued with some kind of meaning.

Japanese archer, mid-1930s. From Arthur E. Grix, *Japans Sport in Bild und Wort* (Berlin: Wilhelm Limpert, 1937).

CONCLUSION

Although Herrigel lived in Japan for six years, he remained to the end a credulous enthusiast who glorified Japanese culture. For instance, his writings include exaggerations, such as "Japanese people, every one of them, have at least one art that they practice all of their lives" (Herrigel, 1941/1982: 61), and misinformation, such as "Japanese archers have the advantage of being able to rely on an old and venerable tradition that has not once been interrupted regarding the use of the bow and arrow" (Herrigel, 1941/1982: 9; compare Herrigel, 1953: 95).[11] Yet, at the same time, we can concur with Sakurai when he wrote:

Awa did use the expression "bow and Zen are one." Nonetheless, he did not expound *kyudo* or his *shado* as a way leading to Zen. Regardless of how Herrigel acquired that impression, today when many Japanese have the same misunderstanding we should not place the blame on Herrigel. Rather, the responsibility must be placed squarely on our own Japanese scholars who have failed to clarify the difference between the arts of Japan and Zen. (Sakurai, 1981: 238)

The two mystical episodes that lie at the core of Herrigel's *Zen in the Art of Archery* constitute empty signs. They emerged in the empty spaces created by a coincidental occurrence during "the target in darkness" episode and by the slippage of meaning in translating, "*It* shoots." In short, Herrigel, who ceaselessly searched for Zen-like elements in *kyujutsu,* created a modern myth.

I do not mean to suggest, however, that *kyujutsu* lacked any Zen influences. For example, there exists a seventeenth century archery catalog from the Heki-ryu Insai-ha which contains the following entry:

The Dead Bow and Living Bow: Refers to the same concept as the dead blade and living sword mentioned in the *Wumenguan.* "Dead blade" and "living sword" are Buddhist concepts taught in tantric (Shingon) lineages. We take this principle and merely rename it the "dead bow [and living bow]." It is the same principle as expressed by the saying "Rejoice in death and live, try to insure life and die." [In other words,] when one's mind is troubled by fear, one's bow is dead. When one is willing to sacrifice oneself and regards lightly the loss of one's own life, then one's bow comes alive.

This passage definitely shows a Zen influence. The *Wumenguan* (1229; Japanese, *Mumonkan*), of course, is a famous Zen text that is studied by all Zen monks. The way that it is appropriated by this archery catalog, however, refers to the mental attitude of warriors. There is nothing that can be connected to the teachings of Awa or Herrigel.

Boosted by the widespread popularity of D. T. Suzuki, *Zen in the Art of Archery* became an international bestseller soon after it appeared. Thus, the myth of *Zen in the Art of Archery* began its march around the world. Eventually, it reached back to its original source of inspiration.

Zen in the Art of Archery continues to be a bestseller. The Japanese language version, *Yumi to Zen* (1956), which represents the culmination of a circular translation process that rendered Awa's original Japanese words into German and, then, from German back into Japanese, has altered Awa's words to such an extent that it is impossible to ascertain his original expressions. Yet, in spite of this fact, many Japanese rely on it to acquire a certain fixed interpretation of Japanese archery. Faced with this situation, I have attempted to present a new reading of Herrigel and associated documents from a different perspective so as to clarify the mythic function that creates our conception of what constitutes "Japanese-ness." At the same time, I have attempted to counter the tendency that has prevailed up until now to read *Zen in the Art of Archery* with little or no critical awareness.

"THE LION OF THE PUNJAB": GAMA IN ENGLAND, 1910

Graham Noble

Wrestling in India[1] has a long tradition, but its early history is obscure, and probably lost. S. Muzumdar, in his classic *Strong Men over the Years* (1942: 13), wrote, "The great art of Indian wrestling has its legends but no history whatsoever." Consequently, he chose to start his account of wrestling and wrestlers in 1892, when the English champion Tom Cannon visited India and lost to the 21-year-old Kareem Buksh. That, it seems, was the first international contact between the Indian and western schools of professional wrestling.

The first great Indian wrestler to appear in the West was the 5 feet 9 inch, 280-pound Gulam, who wrestled in Paris in 1899 at the time of the Great Exposition. His manager put out an open challenge and a match made with Cour-Derelli, who was regarded as one of the strongest Turkish wrestlers in Europe. Gulam won the match, and evidently dominated the Turk (who was actually Bulgarian) throughout the match (Desbonnet, 1910: 150; Muzumdar, 1942: 18).

Afterwards, Gulam returned to India where he soon died from cholera. It was a century ago, and it's difficult to judge his real strength from that one bout with Cour-Derelli. Historians of Indian wrestling, however, often

This is an abridged version of a series of articles published at the *Journal of Combative Sport,* http://ejmas.com/jalt/jaltart_noble_0502.htm, in 2002. Copyright © 2002 by Graham Noble. Adapted by permission.

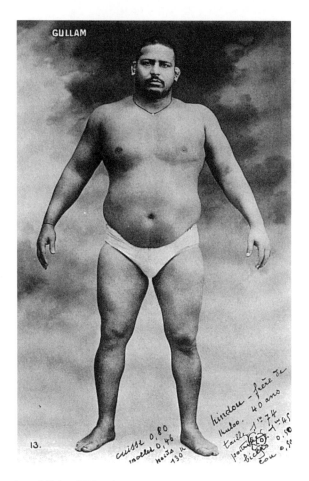

Gulam. Courtesy Michael Murphy.

look back to him as the greatest of champions. Certainly, those who saw him in Paris seemed to regard him as something special.

A few years after Gulam's death, a new prodigy came along. This was Gama (birth name, Mian Ghulam Muhammad) (Smith, 1963). Gama was born to a family of wrestlers in 1880 or so. I've never seen an exact birth date given for Gama, and calculations from references in books and magazines give variously 1878, 1880, or 1882. When he died in 1960, his age was given as 80, so the date of 1880 seems reasonable.

His father was a top wrestler and Gama is said to have started training at age five. When Gama was eight, his father died, but his training continued

The Great Gama, circa 1916. Courtesy Joseph Svinth.

under the direction of his grandfather. Then, when the grandfather died too, training resumed under his uncle, Ida Palahwan, who vowed that Gama would become the champion his father had wanted him to be. According to Joseph Alter (1995: 4), "Intent on impressing upon him the desire to be a great wrestler, he constantly pointed out to the young boy that this is what his father wanted above all else." From the time he was a child, wrestling seemed to be all that Gama knew. In time, as he reached maturity, he did become champion of India.

Gama first came to public attention at the age of 10, when he won a physical exercise competition held by the Rajah of Jodhpur. This was not a wrestling contest, but an endurance competition of *bethaks* (free squats), the fundamental conditioning exercise of Indian wrestling (Alter, 1995: 4).

That victory didn't necessarily show any wrestling ability, but it did demonstrate unusual qualities of physical robustness, willpower, and competitiveness in the young Gama. At that time, he was routinely doing 500 *bethaks* and 500 *dands* (stretching pushups) daily, and working on pit digging—turning over the earth of the wrestling area with a *pharsa* (hoe). He ate a special diet concentrating on milk, almonds, and fruit: he didn't begin eating meat until a few years later.

Gama began competing in wrestling matches when he was 15. "Very quickly, however, he proved to be virtually unbeatable, and formally became a wrestler to the court of Datiya soon thereafter" (Alter, 1995: 5). As he grew older, his training routine intensified and his diet upgraded to include meat, butter, clarified butter, and *yakhi*.[2]

The amounts eaten by the Indian champions were prodigious, and Barkat Ali gives, with what truth I don't know, the mature Gama's daily diet as six chickens or an extract of 11 pounds of mutton mixed with a quarter pound of clarified butter, 10 quarts of milk, a pint of clarified butter, a pound-and-a-half of crushed almond paste made into a tonic drink, along with fruit juice and other ingredients to promote good digestion. This expensive high fat, high energy, high everything diet helped to drive Gama's daily training, which in maturity consisted of grappling with 40 of his fellow wrestlers in the court, 5,000 *bethaks,* and 3,000 *dands.*

The figures may be exaggerated, but no one doubted Gama's dedication to his conditioning routine. In 1935, Percy Longhurst recalled seeing Gama training when he was in England:

> The morning he spent in going through a few hundred repetitions of the "dip"; this was followed by several bouts (no rests between) with his fellow Indians, Imam Bux and another. A two hours rest and a meal followed. The meal, by the way, was a quart of broth, concocted of a couple of fowls, with spices. The afternoon was given up to deep knee bending. Nude but for a loin cloth, out of doors in the warm September sunshine, Gama began his up-and-down motion. Methodically, rhythmically, his open hands on the top of a post standing about 4 feet out of the ground, Gama went on with his knee bending. There was nothing hurried about it; he started as though he meant keeping on forever; and after watching him for a long while, that, so I concluded, was his intention. I timed him by the watch for twenty minutes, and still he continued. (*Health and Strength,* May 4, 1935)

Gama first gained recognition as a wrestler in 1904, when he scored a series of impressive wins at a tournament organized by the Maharajah of

Rewa. In 1906, he won a tournament organized by the Maharajah Pratap Singh of Orchaz and got a position of wrestler at the Maharajah's court. Over the years, he defeated the champions of other states and cities—Govalior, Bhopal, Tikamargh, Datia, Indore, Baroda, Amritsar, Lahore—and around 1909 he gained recognition as Indian champion when he defeated Gulam Mohiuddin. Gulam Mohiuddin was regarded by some as Gama's equal, but when they met, he was defeated in only 8 minutes.

Ten minutes, 8 minutes, 2 minutes—when you read the accounts of Gama's Indian matches, such as they are, it seems that his opponents, some of them well-known champions, were simply brushed aside. However, there was one exception, the famous Rahim Sultaniwala. He was older than Gama, and was a one-time student of the great Gulam. He is described as standing 6 feet 11 inches and weighing 270 to 300 pounds— exaggerated figures, I would imagine, but still much bigger than Gama, who was around 5 feet 7 inches and 200 pounds.

There are discrepancies in the accounts, but it seems that Gama and Rahim Sultaniwala met two or three times before Gama went to England in 1910. Apparently, the two men first met at Junagarth, in the state of Lahore, when Gama was 19. Therefore, this would have been around 1900. Rahim took the offensive in that match and was somewhat taken back when his attacks failed to make much headway against his younger opponent. In the second half of the match, the advantage probably lay with Gama, but the action was stopped after 60 minutes by the Nawab of Junagarth and a draw given. The second time the two men met was around 1909, when they wrestled to a 2-hour draw.

S. Muzumdar gives a slightly different version of events, writing that the two men first wrestled a 20-minute draw at Datia. (Joseph Alter dates this as late 1907.) They met again at Indore in 1909, where the result was another draw, this time after a fight that lasted 3 hours. A few months later, Rahim and Gama wrestled yet another draw at Lahore, this time in a contest lasting 2 hours, 10 minutes.

How Gama's visit to England came about is not too clear, but the driving force behind it was R.B. Benjamin, an English wrestling promoter. According to one report, it was after seeing Gama defeat the well-known Chandra Singh Mudaliwala that Benjamin decided to bring Gama over to England (Haniff, n.d.:14). On Benjamin's part, presumably, it was a straight commercial venture, whereas for Gama it was a chance to test himself against Western champions and establish himself as the greatest wrestler in the world. For others, such as Sharat Kumar Mishra, the Bengali millionaire who sponsored the tour, it was a way of demonstrating the strength of Indian physical culture right in the heart of the British Empire.

Imam Bux. Courtesy Joseph Svinth.

At any rate, in early 1910, Gama, along with fellow wrestlers Imam Bux (his brother), Ahmed Bux, and Gamu, set sail for London.

They arrived in England in April. Some Indian writers have stated that Gama intended to take part in the John Bull wrestling tournament but was refused entry because of his relatively small size (Alter, 1995: 3). In fact, there was no John Bull Tournament. Moreover, it is unlikely that Gama's size would have been any problem. The much lighter Maeda Mitsuyo (as Yamato) competed successfully against heavyweights in the Alhambra Tournament, and Gama, at a little over 200 pounds, was not small by the standards of the day.

Anyway, by early May 1910, the Indians were settled in their training quarters, and *Health and Strength* announced "The Invasion of the Indian

Wrestlers" in its May 14 issue. The members of the troupe were listed as Gama, Champion of India; Imam Bux, Champion of Lahore; Ahmed Bux, Champion of Amritsar; and Gamu, Champion of Jullundhur. Their weights ranged from about 198 to 206 pounds, and the article noted that none of the wrestlers trained with dumbbells or barbells.

They would rise at 5:30 a.m., wrestle for two hours, and then drink two pints of milk with Indian spices. Breakfast at around 11:00 a.m. would consist of eggs, *dahl* (porridge), and rice, prepared by their own cook, who had traveled from India with them. A nap followed. Then, at 3:30 p.m., there were two hours of exercise. About 7:00 p.m., the main meal of chicken or mutton would be eaten. Finally, before retiring for the night at 9:30, another quart of milk with spices—the wrestlers had brought 20 varieties of spices with them.

Health and Strength (May 14, 1910: 521) also carried a challenge in which £5[3] was promised any "competitor, no matter what nationality, whom any member of the team fails to throw in five minutes." Additionally, any "man proving he has been refused the right to wrestle with the Indians will be presented with Five Sovereigns by the management from the Indians' salary."[4]

Doubtless the Indians were eager to meet the top professionals of the time. However, in issuing a genuine challenge, they were also intruding into a rather cozy world of pro wrestling, which operated largely as a music hall entertainment and was, as George Hackenschmidt explained (*Health and Strength,* March 20, 1909), a business. ("I am certainly very fond of the sporting element which enters into it," said Hackenschmidt, but "[I] should be absurdly careless if I allowed my tastes in that direction to interfere too seriously with my career in life.") So, if the Indians had expected to meet professionals willing to engage in genuine matches, then they were to be disappointed, as for quite a while, no challengers came forward.

By July, the lack of any response was becoming noticeable, so much so that *The Sporting Life* (July 8, 1910) carried a short article entitled "Gama's Hopeless Quest [to find a genuine opponent]." Around the same time, *Health and Strength* (July 9, 1910: 39) referred to the "apathy, cowardice, call it what you will" of the current crop of professional wrestlers. Interestingly, the same article mentioned that Gama had, in fact, many offers of "lucrative employment" if only he would be willing to "go down"—that is, take part in arranged matches. Then, the article went on, "He simply doesn't understand what that means."

A little later, the well-known American professional, Benjamin "Doc" Roller took up Gama's challenge. Ben Roller was a character in his own

Benjamin F. Roller, ca. 1905. Manuscripts, Special Collections, University Archives, University of Washington Libraries, UW13687.

right: a real medical doctor, apparently, who had gained his degree at Pennsylvania; a natural athlete who had excelled at football and heavy field events before turning to professional wrestling in 1906 at the rather late age of 30. It's difficult to say how skilled he really was, but Roller had worked with Frank Gotch and was a busy professional. He seemed a decent first test for Gama.

The contest between Gama and Roller took place at the Alhambra Theatre on the afternoon of August 8, 1910. It had been organized by *John Bull,* the popular magazine that seemed to support Gama's cause throughout his time in England, thus giving rise to the idea, strongly held by Indian writers, that there was a John Bull wrestling tournament that Gama entered and won. The contest was for £200 a side, the best of three falls, with the stranglehold and full nelson barred.

The Alhambra was "packed to the point of suffocation" (*Health and Strength,* August 13, 1910: 178), with hundreds turned away, and "the air was electric with excitement." When the men came together, it was clear that Roller was much taller than the "stocky native of the Punjab." The weights were announced as Roller, 234 pounds, and Gama, 200 pounds When the emcee declared that "no money in the world would ever buy him [Gama] for a fixed match, there was a perfect hurricane of approving shouts."

Upon the signal to start, Gama came out with his "curious kind of galloping action" and immediately dived for a leg hold that Roller only just managed to escape. The American tried to use his additional weight to stall, but an outside click almost had him over again. Gama then brought Roller down beyond the edge of the mat. After the referee ordered the men back to the middle of the wrestling area, he attacked again, taking Roller's leg and then applying "a lovely back heel" which sent Doc down to the mat with a crash. Gama immediately put on a half nelson with body roll and turned Roller over for the first fall. It had taken just 1 minute, 40 seconds.

As the second bout started, Roller was warier and spent a lot of time sparring for a favorable position. Roller seemed unsettled by Gama's feinting—and then the Indian dived for the leg and Roller was down, with Gama onto him immediately. The rest of the bout was a struggle for the pin-fall, Roller always on the defensive and Gama always on top, drawing favorable comment for his excellent legwork. Roller was in difficulties throughout (at one point he winced when Gama put on a powerful body hold) and although he broke free from holds several times, Gama was always quicker and would immediately apply another move. Eventually Roller, "trussed up on all sides," was turned over for the second fall after 9 minutes 10 seconds of wrestling (*Health and Strength,* August 13, 1910: 178).

The audience greeted Gama's victory with considerable enthusiasm. It was also well received by the press. Some commentators even thought (rather naively) that it could lead to a revival of real wrestling. The reporter for *Health and Strength* (August 13, 1910: 178) wrote: "I shall never forget the whirlwind swiftness of that first bout; the people gasped as they looked on, and they cried with one accord, 'There's no swank there!' "

Afterwards, it was reported that Roller was taken to Charing Cross Hospital and attended to by Dr. Edward B. Calthrop, who diagnosed fractures of the seventh and eighth ribs on the left side. In the evening, Roller was visited at his hotel by a reporter who found him with his body bandaged and "in excruciating pain." Roller was disappointed that the injury had handicapped him during the bout; he felt that he could have done better if he had been unhurt, but still considered Gama "a great wrestler" (*Sporting Life,* August 9, 1910).

At the end of the contest, while Gama was being cheered, Stanislaus Zbyszko came forward to shake the Indian's hand and congratulate him on his victory. An announcement was made that Zbyszko and Gama would meet in a month's time, September 10, at the Stadium (Shepherd's Bush). On behalf of Gama, a challenge was issued to the world, for £1,000 upwards. Frank Gotch was specifically named, and Gotch's agent, who happened to be present, said that Gotch would be happy to meet any wrestler who visited America.

First, however, another contest had to be decided. On September 5, a Monday afternoon, Imam Bux was meeting the well-known Swiss professional wrestler John Lemm at the Alhambra Theatre. The match was for £100 a side and a share of gate receipts, catch-as-catch-can style, the best of three falls.

Imam Bux was the second string of the five-man troupe, although some observers thought that he might actually be a better wrestler than was Gama himself. John Lemm was a leading professional who had won the Alhambra and Hengler's tournaments and who for the past couple of years had been trying to get a match with Hackenschmidt or Gotch. In 1908, when England's ill-fated Professional Wrestling Board of Control selected four men to wrestle for the Championship, John Lemm was one of the four (along with Gotch, Hackenschmidt, and Zbyszko). Lemm was short for a heavyweight, about 5 feet 7 inches, but he weighed 200 pounds. He was quick and strong, being known for a determined, rushing style. Moreover, he was powerfully built, particularly in the legs, and I think he may have claimed a world record performance in the squat at one time.

Again, the Alhambra was packed. As the two men stepped on the mat they presented a contrast in physique: Lemm short and heavily muscled, Imam Bux 6 feet tall, gangly and loose limbed. The weights were announced as Lemm, 196 pounds, Imam Bux, 204 pounds.

At the signal to start, Lemm rushed out and seized Bux in a waist hold. After a brief struggle, he used a back heel and Bux went down flat on his back. Recovering immediately, Bux escaped any follow up, and from that point on, Lemm was never in it.

Imam Bux's victory over Lemm in a little over 4 minutes of wrestling was a sensation. Lemm was crestfallen, but shook Imam's hand and congratulated him. The press too was full of praise for the Indian, and a fulsome summing up appeared in *Health and Strength* (September 17, 1910: 271), the writer stating that the match was "one mighty thrill from start to finish."

STANISLAUS ZBYSZKO
Champion Wrestler of Poland

Stanislaus Zbyszko. Reproduced from the original held by the Department of Special Collections of the University Libraries of Notre Dame.

During that five minutes I saw more actual wrestling, more variety of holds and locks and throws, more dramatic, soul-stirring incidents than I have witnessed for many a year.

Let us have a few more big matches like unto that, and I tell you straight that the grappling game will soon become the greatest game of all.

In the audience, watching all this, was Stanislaus Zbyszko, who was due to meet Gama in five days time. He didn't say anything, but he must have been thinking. In the last few weeks, he had seen Roller and Lemm, two well-known, solid professionals, blown away in a matter of minutes. As he wrote to Robert W. Smith (personal communication, no date, in Graham Noble collection) almost 50 years later, "I knew I had work on my hands."

Zbyszko was born Stanislaus Cyganiewicz, in Krakow, Poland, a city which was at the time part of the Austro-Hungarian Empire. The Social Security Death Index says that his date of birth was April 1, 1881. Zbyszko–the name he later took for his wrestling career—started training in his teens, and while attending college in Vienna, he joined the well known Vindobona Athletic Club. There he trained with weights and made rapid gains: Zbyszko was one of those rare people who are genetically disposed to put on muscle rapidly with exercise.

Early photos of Zbyszko show an impressive development of the upper body. He was still relatively trim at this time, but he soon put on additional size. The extra weight was useful for wrestling, and some of it may have been excess flesh by today's standards, but beneath, there was still massive muscular development.

To prepare for his match with Gama, Zbyszko went into training at Prinn's, the Rottingdean blacksmith, under the supervision of Bill Klein. He rose at 6:00 a.m., worked out for an hour with his younger brother Ladislaus (Wladek, I presume), then went for a walk and a swim before breakfast at 9:00. After an hour's rest, he took a long walk over the hills ("ten to fifteen miles") and the rest of his practice consisted of wrestling, skipping, boxing, and working out with the medicine ball. A thorough massage ended the day's training. Supper was at 8:00 p.m., and bed was at 9:00 (*Health and Strength,* September 10, 1910).

Klein had watched Zbyszko's diet, so that his weight was reported as down to 238 pounds, and he may even have gone below that. In a match with Gama, quickness and conditioning were important, and so Zbyszko was working on reducing his weight.

For his part, Gama was training at Surbiton, going through his usual routine of thousands of *dands* and *bethaks* and wrestling with his compatriots. Some of the initial enthusiasm for Gama's victory over Roller had worn off, particularly because it now seemed that he had had to work hard to pin a man who was suffering from two broken ribs. However, apart from one instance when Roller winced from a Gama waist hold, "The Doc" showed little sign of his injury during the match. I may be unfair and too cynical, but when you read the background of Benjamin Franklin Roller, you begin to question whether he actually had any ribs broken at all. After all, this was the same Doc Roller who told the *Seattle Times* in December 1910 that he was wrestling every night, and had had 21 matches in November (Svinth,

2000a). It's hard to reconcile that level of activity with someone who was injured (broken ribs take at least 4–6 weeks to heal). Instead, it sounds like the saga of the broken ribs was a story line Roller regularly trotted out for dramatic effect and to emphasize his gameness.

In the Gama contest, he may for once have actually suffered broken ribs, but there is an element of doubt, and that makes any judgment on Gama's performance problematical. Experts seemed to think that Gama would beat Zbyszko in their upcoming match, and some people may have been swayed by Gama's boastful promise to throw the Pole three times in an hour. Nonetheless, there was still quite a bit of uncertainty about the outcome.

The great wrestling match for £250 a side and the John Bull Belt started at 4:00 p.m. on September 10, 1910. The venue was the 68,000-seat stadium built for the 1908 Olympics at Shepherd's Bush, and the crowd, estimated at 12,000, was lost in the huge stadium, which looked empty. The referee was the well-known Jack Smith.

Within a minute of the match starting, Zbyszko was taken down. He then took up a defensive position, where he remained for the rest of the match. At intervals Gama would try a waist hold, a quarter nelson, a half nelson, but his efforts were futile and it seemed that, even in these early stages of the match, he had pretty much run out of ideas.

Gama tried hard but he was ineffective against an opponent who wouldn't wrestle in open play. Zbyszko remained strong, however, and at one point, "rearing up from the ground to his hands and knees he momentarily precipitated Gama into the air" (*Health and Strength,* September 17, 1910: 274). Then he returned to his passive defense, and the wrestling stopped once more.

On the 2-hour mark, Zbyszko sprang to his feet and managed to get a reverse waist hold on Gama. He lifted him slightly and both went down, but Gama got back on top and the monotony continued.

A little later, the two men were on their feet for a few seconds as Zbyszko tried for a waist hold. However, Gama was "strong and nimble" and evaded the attack. Gama attempted a crotch hold but Zbyszko was too heavy for him.

A halt was called after 2 hours, 35 minutes, with Zbyszko in that defensive position on all fours, and Gama on top trying to work some kind of a hold. Because, under the terms of the match, there had to be a result, it was announced that the men would wrestle to a finish at the Stadium the next Saturday, September 17.

The Sporting Life estimated that in the whole 2½ hours, there had been maybe 1½ minutes of wrestling. It headlined its report, "Fiasco at the Stadium," and described the bout as "a miserable farce" (September 12, 1910). Both *The Sporting Life* and *Health and Strength* called for a new rule to stop the passive methods used by Zbyszko. Both publications blamed Zbyszko for the way the match turned out. Writing in *Health and Strength,* "Half Nelson" described Zbyszko as "woefully lacking in enterprise," and added, "his caution exceeded all reasonable bounds" (September 17, 1910: 274). The editor of the magazine called him "a figure of ponderous, gawky, clumsy cowardice" (September 17, 1910: 235).

Gama did not escape criticism, either. Everyone recognized that he had tried honestly to overturn Zbyszko—it was just that his efforts had been ineffective. "Gama was frankly disappointing," said *The Sporting Life* (September 14, 1910). "He evinced a woeful ignorance of the technicalities of ground wrestling. His attack was all of one kind, and continued in spite of its non-success." There was general agreement that, although Gama was quick, he lacked skill and variety in groundwork, and Zbyszko was just too strong for him. In a letter to *The Sporting Life* (September 14, 1910), Henry Werner wrote that "Gama's knowledge of the mat is not far above that of a novice and his holds were broken with the greatest ease. Imam Bux would be a far superior opponent to Zbyszko than Gama as a match would very quickly prove."

On Saturday, September 17, at the appointed time, Gama turned up with his entourage, but—no Zbyszko. His name was called several times, but he had already left the country, supposedly because his mother was seriously ill, although there was a rumor that he was wrestling in Vienna. Again he was vilified and there were demands that he never be allowed to wrestle in England again. Gama was declared the winner by default, and Horatio Bottomley, the owner of *John Bull* magazine, presented him with the 100-guinea "John Bull" belt and the £250 stake. Bottomley praised Gama's sportsmanship and the beneficial influence of the Indians on British wrestling. He said that if Gama were to win two more championship matches the belt would become his personal property.

Then, almost before anyone realized, they had gone: packed their bags and returned to India. The reasons for the departure of Gama and the troupe were unclear, but it was said to be due to the problems in making matches and so on. Some reports implied that the Indians had been "driven home," although Herbert Turner was skeptical about that. He had heard that Benjamin, the group's manager, had accepted an offer of £1,000 for a

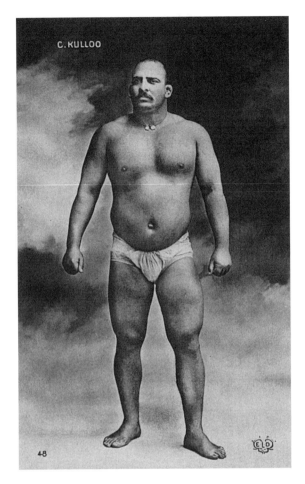

Kulloo. Courtesy Michael Murphy.

series of engagements in India, and that he would also be making money from the Eastern rights to the film of the Gama-Zbyszko match. Turner added the information that the gate receipts for that match amounted to £749, that Zbyszko received nothing, and "Gama did not receive a seventh part of this amount" (*Health and Strength,* October 8, 1910).

There is still one more chapter in this story. In April 1911, Benjamin brought over another group of wrestlers, including Ahmed Bux. Bux had two easy wins, over Maurice Deriaz on May 24, 1911, and Armand Cherpillod, on July 10, 1911.

In mid-July, a new batch of Indians arrived in England, including the highly respected Gulam Mohiuddin. Although weighing just over 180 pounds, he challenged all heavyweights. No matches occurred immediately, but a couple months later, Mohiuddin met French champion Maurice Gambier. This match took place in Bordeaux in a bullfight arena before a crowd of 5,000. It was in the French Greco-Roman style, and yet Gambier was thrown twice in 5 minutes. Gulam Mohiuddin had only a few days to accustom himself to Greco-Roman wrestling, so if this was a genuine match, his was a terrific performance, as good as any of the other Indians in their better known English victories.

As far as I know, that was the last significant competitive match fought by the Indians in their prewar incursion into British and European wrestling arenas. Others came later, but the days of legendary victories were gone and they made little real impact. That may have been due to a decline in the general standard of Indian wrestling, though a more important reason was that professional wrestling was now a totally worked environment. There was no longer a place for professional wrestlers who wanted real matches. Genuine wrestling bouts were (a) too short, (b) too long and boring, or (c) otherwise unsatisfactory. For the growth of professional wrestling in its modern form, the product had to be managed and its outcomes controlled.

Back in the early 1900s, you could still have genuine contests, though they were not frequent and the Indians had difficulty getting them. Gama, Imam Bux, and Ahmed Bux made an impact, but they often had to work against the vested interests of pro wrestling: the promoters, managers, wrestlers, theatre owners, and to some extent the public themselves, all of whom wanted "a show." That is not to say that the Indians were on some kind of crusade. Even Gama, in the later years of his career, showed little inclination to put up his own crown against new challengers. Nonetheless, they were dedicated wrestlers who trained hard; they wanted to wrestle; and Gama definitely aspired to be recognized as the greatest wrestler in the world.

In that respect, the visits of 1910 and 1911 didn't fulfill their promise: the Indians made waves, but mostly they were unable to get the major matches they wanted. Thus, their appearances had little long-term effect on professional wrestling. They were certainly respected for their abilities, and were given full credit for their victories over Roller, Lemm, and Deriaz. Still, an authority like Count Vivian Hollender could feel that they were not given the welcome they deserved:

Many people who swear by, and even applauded Hackenschmidt and other foreign wrestlers, will not even bestow a welcome to a British subject even if it is not a Britisher. I refer to the Indians. It is an extraordinary thing that an American negro, as a boxer [Jack Johnson, then world champion], should be more popular than an Indian, who is not only a British subject, but an entirely different class of man. (*Health and Strength,* May 27, 1911: 517)

Although there may have been indifference to the Indian wrestlers, there are few racist (in modern terms) comments about them in the reports of the time. Before Gama's match with Zbyszko, the editor of *Health and Strength* (September 17, 1910) observed, "I actually received letters from readers in India pointing out that if they [the Indian wrestlers] kept on winning, their victories would give a dangerous filip to the seditions amongst our dusky subjects that menace the integrity of our Indian Empire. But that is another story, upon which I do not propose to enter."

A more common view, though, appeared in a letter to the magazine by a John Moore. In praising the Indians, Moore wrote (*Health and Strength,* July 29, 1911: 112), "They will meet all comers, not waiting for a large sum of money; there is no hugging the mat, no resting, no fake. Let the best man win, whatever his colour or nationality!"

This was an age, of course, that thought in terms of race, and the question was always there. It usually expressed itself as a concern that the Indians' crushing victories over Western opponents might indicate that these "dusky subjects of the British Empire" were actually representatives of a physically superior race. When the editor of *Health and Strength* concluded his report on the match between Ahmed Bux and Armand Cherpillod, his last paragraph was a lament on the feebleness and lack of enterprise of British wrestlers:

It is certainly time some white man came forward to extend the Indians. Mr. Benjamin, after the match, advanced to the front and addressed the audience. "Ahmed Bux," said he, "is a British subject, born under the British flag....I do not grudge the Indians their victories; I only want to see our race victorious too." (*Health and Strength,* July 15, 1911: 60)

In any event, the Indian incursion was short-lived, and outside India, its details were soon forgotten. Nonetheless, to judge by the performances of Gama, Imam Bux, Ahmed Bux, and Gulam Mohiuddin, they were an exceptional group of wrestlers and a level above the professionals of the Western nations. A unique combination of circumstances—a group of talented and dedicated athletes, a culture which embraced wrestling, and a group of wrestling-mad maharajahs who financed the sport—produced a great era of Indian wrestling which can never be repeated.

THE LITTLE DRAGON:
BRUCE LEE (1940–1973)

James Halpin

Lee Yuen Kam was 18 years old in 1959 and washing dishes for his room and board in Ruby Chow's Seattle restaurant. They buried him 14 years later in Lake View Cemetery overlooking Lake Washington. In the interim, he had worked hard and succeeded—succeeded beyond anyone's imagining, possibly even his. And so there were 180 mourners at the gravesite, and among the pallbearers were James Coburn and Steve McQueen. It was really his second funeral. A crushing mob of 30,000 people attended the first one held a few days earlier in Hong Kong, where he had died under circumstances as lurid and perplexing as his own brief life.

Lee Yuen Kam was, of course, the given name of Bruce Lee, the Seattle scullion who became the hottest international superstar of his time, the dropout whose movies grossed up to $100 million apiece, the 132-lb. Eurasian who became the best-known martial artist of the century, the ex–juvenile delinquent who is among the biggest movie cult figures of all time. Indeed, decades after his death in July of 1973, Bruce Lee devotees continue to flock to his old reruns like pilgrims to a holy shrine. Many see each film dozens of times, watching his every move, listening to his every word.

An earlier version appeared in David Brewster and David M. Buerge (Eds.), (1989), *Washingtonians,* Seattle: Sasquatch Books. Copyright © 2002 by James Halpin. Adapted by permission.

Gravesite of Bruce and Brandon Lee, Seattle, Washington, 2002. Courtesy Joseph Svinth.

The theme of Lee's films is revenge. In them, Lee plays a humble *gongfu* (although a common name for Chinese martial arts, the word means "effort" rather than martial arts) practitioner who is essentially non-violent, but whom evildoers provoke until he turns on them in cold fury and destroys them. In *The Chinese Connection,* for example, Lee avenges himself for outrages committed against *gongfu,* himself, his *shifu* (master), and all Chinese everywhere. The film opens in Shanghai around 1908 when envoys from a Japanese martial arts dojo present Lee's school with a tablet engraved, "The Sick Man of Asia." When Lee, while imposing vengeance for this and other affronts, yells, "Chinese are not sick men," Chinese audiences frequently stand and howl in agreement and empathy.

It adds up to a message, particularly for Third World fans, although the last thing Bruce Lee's producers wanted in their films was social significance. "Bruce went beyond being a hero," Fred Weintraub, developer of television's *Kung Fu* series, once commented. "The blacks, Chicanos, and Chinese took Bruce as a hero because he made it. He was the first [non-white] hero they ever had. They felt as if he came from the same barrio that they lived in."[1]

No other action film star ever had this *authenticity.* When we watch Bruce Lee overcome impossible odds for a worthwhile cause, there is something there as brave as flags and as convincing as poetry. And so

James W. DeMile. Copyright © 1996 Olan Mills. Courtesy James W. DeMile.

young men still sit in dark theaters and pray, "Please, God, make me like him." They stare at those movies and those moves, hoping to figure out how Bruce Lee, scullion, transformed himself into Bruce Lee, superhero.

The metamorphosis took place in Seattle. How it occurred has remained a tantalizing mystery because the half-dozen or so Seattleites who witnessed this remarkable event have heretofore refused to talk with writers about it, tired of the way the movies and exploitative books and magazines had turned a man they loved into a one-dimensional cartoon character. Many of these witnesses were part of Seattle's now-vanished street-fighting scene, which consisted of a couple hundred kids who fought for turf and status with fists, knives, razors, and an occasional gun. Because they fought mostly themselves, Seattle and its police dealt with the problem mostly by leaving them alone, hoping they would go away. They did: By the early 1960s most were gone, some to prison, some to the hippie movement, and some into the drug scene. While the street fighters lasted, they served Lee well. It was by matching himself against these dangerous young men that he developed his extraordinary techniques.

One of these former miscreants remembers Lee with great clarity. He is James W. DeMile, today an entrepreneur, psychologist, lecturer, author, and world-class martial artist. "Bruce Lee was the most interesting and complex human being I've ever met," DeMile said in 1986. "Knowing him not only changed my life but determined its course forever."

The story of how Lee met DeMile sounds like something out of a movie script. It probably was, according to DeMile, who suspects that Lee lifted his recruiting technique whole cloth from Kurosawa's film classic, *The Seven Samurai.* "If you've seen the movie, you know the scenes in question," says DeMile, "the ones where the hero provokes passing masterless samurai he encounters into dueling with him so he can judge whether they have the mettle to fight against overwhelming adversity for a worthwhile purpose."

Aside from the fact that the worthwhile purpose Bruce Lee had in mind was Bruce Lee, his first encounter with DeMile does have the hallmarks of a classic movie confrontation. However, it took place in 1959 at Edison Technical School (now Seattle Central Community College) instead of the OK Corral.

"It was something called Asian Day," DeMile remembers. "There were maybe 40 students, including me, who showed up in a classroom to do a kind of show and tell on *gongfu,* which the notice on the bulletin board said was a Chinese martial art."

Lee, DeMile recalls, was "all dressed up in a dark suit and a tie and so neatly turned out that all he needed was a black book under his arm to make him look like a Mormon missionary. The suit, of course, hid his physique so that what you saw was this frail-looking, 18-year-old kid wearing thick, round spectacles—the stereotype of the filial and studious Chinese teenager. On top of that, he had this weird Hong Kong accent and what seemed to be a speech impediment that made his r's sound like w's, as in 'I wecently wealized I'm weally not weady to whessle.' If somebody had told me I'd spend the good part of the next two years watching him transform himself, I'd have thought he was hallucinating."

DeMile recalls that Lee began by telling his audience that they had never heard of *gongfu* because it had never been taught to Westerners. The Chinese kept it secret, he said, so that it could never be used against them, as had other Chinese discoveries such as gunpowder. *Gongfu,* Lee went on, was a bare-handed fighting system that priests and peasants developed thousands of years ago because Chinese warlords promoted domestic tranquillity by slaying any civilians they happened to catch carrying weapons. The Buddhist and Taoist priests therefore learned how to turn the human body into a weapon by studying the ways in which animals and insects fought.

Through the millennia, priests perfected *gongfu* and gradually realized that patience, exercise, and meditation could prepare a man to face any adversary or adversity. The *gongfu* masters eventually transformed their fighting system into a full-fledged philosophy that taught its practitioners not only how to survive but how to prevail.

"Bruce saw no reason to disenchant his audience by telling them that many of the fellow *gongfu* fighters he'd left behind in Hong Kong were punks and thugs who used it as a philosophical excuse for robbing and chastising those who didn't know how to fight as they did," DeMile recalls.

At first, Lee did not exactly electrify his audience. Nonetheless, he began to demonstrate the fighting styles named and patterned after animals. As DeMile reconstructs it, Lee first assumed the eagle stance with his hand extended in a claw. Then he transformed himself into a praying mantis with his forearms making piano-hammer strikes. Then he was a white crane with its wings spread and its leg raised in the defense position. Finally, he was the monkey stealing the peach, a euphemism for ripping the opponent's groin. "It was a beautiful performance," DeMile continues, "sort of a cross between ballet and mime. But it sure as hell didn't look like fighting and the audience began to titter."

Lee suddenly became stock still, "Like a cat that's just seen a robin," DeMile says. "The audience got very quiet very quickly, too, and I got my first intimation that this guy might really not be all talk. He got some sucker to come up front, and suddenly he's all over this guy like flies on manure. He starts explaining how he would tear this guy apart like an overcooked chicken while he's miming out how he'd cave in his temples with a praying mantis strike, then rip his muscles apart, whip his windpipe out, and tear his rib cage asunder. It was vivid and nobody was laughing any more. Next thing I know, Bruce is looking right at me and saying, 'You look like you can fight, how about coming up here for a minute?' "

DeMile was then 20 years old and 220 pounds of gristle. He could indeed fight. He was a former undefeated heavyweight champion of the Air Force as well as the unscarred veteran of street fights. It took a very self-confident man to invite DeMile to fight. DeMile joined Lee on the platform.

Lee said he would now demonstrate his own system, named wing chun (Pinyin: *yongchun*) after the Buddhist nun who had originated it. Wing chun, Lee told the audience, had gotten her inspiration while watching a fight between a broken-winged eagle and a fox. The eagle's tactic was to keep the talons of one foot always pointed directly at the fox's face. The fox tried a dozen feints but the eagle just kept turning to face him and clawing his muzzle whenever the opportunity presented itself, until the fox slunk off with nothing to digest but the day's lesson. Now DeMile was about to learn the same lesson.

Lee continued that in wing chun, you fought in close and controlled your opponent by redirecting his strikes or entrapping his arms with "sticky hand," a technique where you keep pressure on so that the friction makes him feel like he is punching under water. He now turned to DeMile and matter-of-factly invited him to hit as hard as he could, with either hand, whenever he was ready.

"I couldn't believe this guy," DeMile recalls. "It's easy to block a fast punch if you know which hand is coming first, but if you don't, it's quite another matter. Anyway, I fired a straight right hoping it wouldn't take his head off in front of 40 witnesses. I needn't have worried. He blocked me as easily as you'd brush away the hand of a baby, and gave me a left that stopped just short of my nose. From then on, no matter what I did, he tied me up with sticky hands and punched back at will, always stopping the blow in the last possible millimeter. I can't tell you how devastating this was. Here I was all tied up and as helpless as if I was in some giant roll of flypaper. It was Br'er Fox punching out the tar baby and I felt like I was in a slow-motion nightmare. And it didn't help things when Bruce ended it all by knocking on my forehead and asking if anyone was home. I knew that I had to either find out what this guy knew or go into intensive therapy, so after the demonstration I swallowed what little was left of my pride and asked him if he'd teach me some of his techniques."

Thus, DeMile and another Edison student named LeRoy Garcia, who had also watched the demonstration, enrolled in an informal *gongfu* class that Lee held in the parking lot of the Blue Cross clinic at Broadway and James. This place chosen because it was secluded, partially covered, and next to Ruby Chow's restaurant.

With the addition of DeMile and Garcia there were now eight students, a pan-racial microcosm of Lee's future worldwide audience of blacks, whites, yellows, and browns. Like many of Lee's fans, they were poor and mad at a world that seemed to have no place for them.

They included a very smart, very angry, black kid named Jesse Glover who became Lee's first disciple after seeing his *gongfu* demonstration in Chinatown during the 1960 Seafair. Glover had been studying Japanese martial arts for several years, obsessed with plans to revenge himself against an alcoholic Seattle cop who in a drunken fury had beaten him savagely when he was 12 years old.

Another student was Glover's roommate, Ed Hart, a white who had boxed professionally and was the inventor of the Hart Attack. This was a ploy that Hart resorted to in barroom brawls. Hart would sink to the floor grasping his chest and apparently gasping out his last breath. Then, when his foe bent over him, Hart would corkscrew off the floor and knock the sucker out of his socks.

There was DeWelle "Skip" Ellsworth, a handsome University of Washington student who was the Gentleman Jim of the group. Ellsworth was courteous and soft-spoken, but beneath the veneer was a boy who had grown up poor in a wealthy Midwest town and had achieved status there by pounding the pie out of any rich kids who even looked like they thought they were better than he.

There was Charlie Woo, who had grown up in an era when school bullies felt perfectly safe about beating up Chinese kids. Charlie's feelings of inferiority about size had driven him to earn a second-degree black belt in judo. He was the gentlest and best-liked guy in the gang. He had trained diligently to defend himself against the huge people he saw all around him, but he was kicked to death by a skittish horse a few years after he joined the group.

There were others who had studied martial arts, such as Howard Hall, LeRoy Porter, and Pat C. Hooks, a black belt in judo whose arms were crisscrossed with scars earned for wrong moves during knife practice with naked blades in Manila.

"None of us then had the least inkling that anything big was happening to us," DeMile says. "Being all of us about 20 years old, it seemed perfectly natural that an 18-year-old Chinese kid should be unveiling to us the forbidden secrets of a secret martial art in a Blue Cross parking lot. At that age, you think that is the way life is."

Why was Bruce Lee in Seattle teaching an arcane craft in a parking lot? We have to go back to San Francisco. On November 27, 1940, Lee was born to Mr. and Mrs. Lee Hoi Cheun in the year and the hour of the dragon. He would have dual American and Chinese citizenship, and the time would come when Bruce would need America badly.

His father was a famous comic star with the Cantonese Opera Company, which was performing in San Francisco's Chinatown at the time of Lee's birth. Bruce's half-European mother, Grace, christened him Li Jun-fan, which means, "Return to San Francisco." The Lees returned to Hong Kong shortly after his birth, where he grew up in relative affluence.

Throughout his life, Lee acquired new names with the frequency of a check forger. First, his parents changed his name to Lee Yuen Kam because the characters were similar to his dead grandfather's. A nurse at the hospital at San Francisco had given him the American name of Bruce. In the family he was called "Small Phoenix," a girl's name that was pinned on him to confuse demons looking for little boys' souls. Later, a movie director named him Lee Sui Loong, meaning "Little Dragon," because of his birthday. With all these names and all these identities, with a Buddhist father and a Catholic mother, with mixed blood and dual citizenship, it is small wonder that Bruce Lee spent much of his 32 years trying to find out who he was and what he was here for.

No man ever tried harder, but Bruce Lee was never able to measure up to his own expectations. Some of his dissatisfaction came from his inability to become a scholar, as his father wished. His grades were terrible because he simply could not sit still long enough to study. With his metabolism, to expect him to pore over books was like expecting a hummingbird to turn into an owl. These feelings of inferiority were exacerbated by Lee's jealousy of his brother, Peter, a wonderful student who became a noted scientist and the fencing champion of the British Commonwealth. Peter was the eldest son, studious, filial, never in trouble; he earned most of his father's praise. Bruce was none of these things; he earned most of his father's disapproval. To vent his frustration, Lee took to the streets. His father, who was a registered opium smoker, hardly noticed that his younger son was seldom home.

The Lee family wanted for nothing, since Mr. Lee had made profitable investments in Hong Kong real estate immediately following World War II. Bruce was sent to private schools, where he fought because his British classmates harassed him for being Chinese. He also had to fight Chinese peers who taunted him for being one-quarter Caucasian. Thus, Lee was able to convince his mother that he was going to end maimed if she didn't enroll him in wing chun lessons. Both of them kept this arrangement secret from the father, who still entertained fantasies about having two scholars in the family. Bruce enrolled in the school of the master, Yip Man, an ancient and frail-looking man of less than 100 pounds.

Lee began spending all his spare time working out at the wing chun gym. When he was not there, then he was doing secret isometrics at his school desk, sit-ups while he was reading his homework, or exercising one hand at mealtime while he ate with the other. He was soon one of the half-dozen top wing chun fighters in Hong Kong.

The admiration denied him at home was richly accorded in Yip Man's school and in the streets, where he became, at least in his own mind, the fearless righter of wrongs who makes everything come out all right in the end. In reality, he was a street punk who went around looking for trouble. Sometimes, he would represent the wing chun clan in illegal matches against the champions of other *gongfu* styles, of which there were hundreds. These clandestine matches were held on rooftops, because the crown punished severely any participants it caught.

In one such combat, Lee made the mistake of littering a rooftop with the permanent teeth of a *choi lai fat* (Pinyin: *cailifo*) representative. *Cho lai fat* pugilists harden their arms by pounding them on things until they are hard as crowbars. In battle, they swing these lethal arms in a furious figure-eight pattern. The parents of this detoothed human windmill unsportingly lodged a complaint against Lee with the crown police. His mother offered to save the Queen boarding expenses by shipping Bruce forthwith to his other homeland.

Lee landed in San Francisco in 1959 with $400 in his pocket and a maternal order not to return home until he had made something of himself. He migrated to Seattle, where he expected to be received as an honored guest by Ping and Ruby Chow. Ruby was the most flamboyant Chinese in Seattle. She had a remarkable talent for getting free publicity for herself and her restaurant, the Hong Kong. She later became a King County councilwoman and a powerful spokesperson on minority issues. Her husband Ping was a former Chinese opera singer who had worked with Lee's father and probably would have allowed the son of an old friend to sponge off him. But Ruby believed in the work ethic and immediately put Bruce to work washing, waiting, and busing at her restaurant. This was a precipitous drop for the playboy of the Eastern world, so there was bad blood between Bruce and Ruby right from the start. Lee claimed he was being exploited under the guise of a family friendship.

Lee also missed Hong Kong. The move interrupted his career as a rising wing chun champion; it also terminated his career as a movie actor. By the time Lee was 18, he had made 20 films for the Southeast Asian market, sometimes in starring roles. Usually he played the tough, wily street urchin with the heart of gold, a kind of Chinese Artful Dodger. Without a doubt, he preferred who he was in the movies to who he was in real life.

The kitchen help at Ruby Chow's restaurant tried to give the fresh-off-the-boat kid a hard time, mimicking his accent and mocking his claims to being a movie star and a wing chun expert. One day, Lee invited one of his persecutors, who was armed with a meat cleaver, to take a swing at him. The cook wisely backed down, and there was a hasty rearrangement of the pecking order. Bruce reinforced his social position by setting up a wooden dummy in the corner of the kitchen and pounding it to splinters when business was slow. In Seattle, at least, Lee was soon what he had never been in Hong Kong—the toughest kid in town.

"He was always the center of attention," DeMile recalls, "and he worked hard to stay that way. He'd gotten all that early recognition as a child movie star and had gotten hooked on it and needed it like an alco-

Guay Lee, Warren Chan, Wing Luke, Liem Tuai, Ping Chow, Mabel Yuen, Ruby Chow, and George Yee, at the Chow's restaurant, ca. 1960. Courtesy Guay Lee/Wing Luke Asian Museum Exhibition.

holic constantly needs a drink." A voracious eater and a nonstop talker, Bruce Lee's subject was always the same—Bruce Lee and *gongfu*.

Skip Ellsworth would introduce Lee around at fraternity and sorority parties. He would invite people he hadn't met to try and punch him in the face, or he'd suddenly start doing thumb push-ups in the middle of a dance floor. Sometimes the things he would do were dangerous—for example, blowing a police whistle at crowded downtown intersections just to see people's reactions or potting birds from his bedroom window with a pistol.

Despite Lee's self-centeredness and occasionally odd behavior, his tough young friends loved him and, as much as it was possible for him, he returned their affection. "I don't think Bruce ever again had friends with whom he was so open," Ellsworth says, "or who cared for him as much."

Although an essentially lonely man, Lee hid it by putting on a nonstop, one-man show. He would grab a dime out of your hand before you could close it and leave a penny in its place. He could catch two flies in the air at the same time or kick a 7-foot ceiling. "He had a 10-year-old's love of disguises," DeMile remembers. "He used to get all dressed up and swagger into a restaurant surrounded by us guys as a kind of guard of honor and let it be known that he was the son of the Chinese ambassador and that we were his bodyguards."

Lee remained as serious about wing chun as a fundamentalist about salvation. He worked out with his students for hours every day, and he exercised relentlessly. He continued to develop the beautiful physique that millions of men would envy and millions of women would fantasize about.

Lee's relationship with his students was generous but exploitative. He did not charge them anything, but he made no attempt to teach them the fundamentals of wing chun, merely the techniques in which he wanted to improve his own skills. "Bruce didn't give anything," DeMile comments. "You had to take it, and this he didn't mind, even respected, in fact. He had premonitions of an early death and so he was a man in a hurry. He'd tell you what he knew, but you had to pick it up the first time. He felt he didn't have time for people who were too slow or too lazy to learn as fast as he did."

Eventually, Bruce got his general education degree from Edison and went on to the University of Washington, although he never graduated. There he fell in love with a Nisei, Amy Sanbo. Now a ballet dancer, choreographer, and actress in Southern California, Sanbo remembers her first meeting with Bruce as one of the least suave on record. He reached out as she was passing his table at the University of Washington student union building, squeezed her arm so forcefully that it was black-and-blue for days, and informed her that this proved how much power could be exerted with just two fingers. She saw something about the guy she liked—the chip on his shoulder. Sanbo had one, too; one of her earliest memories was of armed soldiers rummaging through her mother's underwear in the Tule Lake relocation camp where they had been interned with other Japanese Americans during World War II. She had come out of the experience with the determination that no one was ever going to put any fences, real or imaginary, around her again.

Sanbo shared with her new boyfriend a drive to break through barriers. She had been Garfield High School's first Nisei homecoming queen; besides studying ballet, she was working her way through the university by singing in a band, all rather risqué as far as the prim Japanese American community was concerned. "What I liked about him," Sanbo says, "was that in a time where so many Japanese Americans were trying to convince themselves they were white, Bruce was so proud to be Chinese that he was busting with it."

Another Japanese American who found this fierce pride irresistible was Taky Kimura, who owned a supermarket at Eighth and Madison. Kimura too had been psychologically devastated by his incarceration during World War II. "I thought I was white, until they sent me to the camps," Kimura recalled in the back-room office of his supermarket. "They wouldn't even delay shipping me off one day so I could graduate from high school. They took away my identity because if I wasn't white and I wasn't free and I wasn't American, then who was I? When I got out of the camps I was a derelict, except that I don't drink. I was walking around half-ashamed even to be alive. Then I hear about this Chinese kid giving *gongfu* lessons in a parking lot near my supermarket. And there he is, bubbling over with pride, knocking these big white guys all over the place easy as you please. And I got excited about something for the first time in 15 years. So I started training and bit by bit I began to get back the things I thought I'd lost forever."

Kimura was 36 years old, and would become a surrogate father and unpaid business manager for Lee, helping him to establish and manage martial arts studios in Seattle. Yet to this day, he regards Bruce Lee as the man who saved his life and gave it meaning; he still gives free martial arts lessons to a select group of students in memory of the man to whom he owes so much.

Amy Sanbo saw Lee in a less uncritical light. "He had a childlike naïveté that was touching," she says. "But he also had the emotional maturity of a 12-year-old, and he made me feel like his grandmother. For example, he insisted that I have a bodyguard of his friends when I went around China-town. Who in the hell were they supposed to be protecting me from? I mean, I grew up in Chinatown."

One day on the University of Washington campus, Lee pulled her into an open office on the pretext they could study there in privacy. "In walks [Professor] Theodore Roethke, who tells us his name and asks what the devil we're doing in his office," Sanbo remembers. "Bruce sticks out his hand, says he's glad to meet him and says that he is Bruce Lee, the *gongfu* master. He then goes to the blackboard and gives Roethke a 15-minute lecture on *gongfu,* complete with diagrams and an explanation of the principles of yin and yang. After it's all over, Roethke thanks him and invites him to come back whenever he wants to talk more about *gongfu.*" Sanbo was less impressed. Furious, she told him, "Maybe you can impress those thugs you run around with, with this yin and yang bullshit, but we both know you don't believe a damn word you're saying."

When he was not being impossible, Lee would be wonderful. He could do anything physical with the ease of an angel making his first flight. He was everything a girl could want—handsome beyond credulity, brave as a

Theodore Roethke, mid-1950s. *Seattle Post-Intelligencer* Collection, Museum of History & Industry.

matador. He danced like Fred Astaire, fought as elegantly as Muhammad Ali, and moreover, he was attentive. In love, as in combat, his technique was to overwhelm the target. He cooked Sanbo ginger beef every morning at Ruby Chow's and took it to her for breakfast at her nearby home where she lived with her mother.

Amy grew weary of ginger beef every morning for breakfast and of proposals pressed with ever-greater insistence. She felt crowded but her repeated demands to Bruce that he give her more room were about as effective as ordering an advancing glacier to back off. There was another problem, too: Lee's attention was focused like a laser beam on making himself better at martial arts, but he had not the faintest interest in making the world a better place, while Amy, an activist, had tried repeatedly to involve him in her causes.

For the first time in her life, Sanbo ran away from something. She fled to New York after instructing her mother not to tell Lee where she was.

She took a job there and did not return west until she heard that Lee had married Linda McCulloch, a pretty, blonde Seattle girl who had also been a Garfield High homecoming queen.

Meanwhile, Lee became as ubiquitous as the Northwest rains, giving *gongfu* demonstrations on television, at the Seattle World's Fair, at the university, at high schools. He also wrote a book grandly titled *Gung Fu: The Philosophical Art of Self-Defense*. The book was impressive only because it was written by a teenager, but it made him $5,000. Copies today are worth thousands of dollars each. Lee also went around lecturing to high schools on Chinese philosophy. Lee was riding high. He had been telling people how good he was for so long that he began to believe it himself. So he went back to Hong Kong in 1961 to visit his parents and show Yip Man how far he had progressed in wing chun.

"His progress was zip," says DeMile. "He came back from Hong Kong shattered. He could hit the good wing chun men maybe once out of every three times they could hit him. He thought seriously about giving up martial arts."

But Bruce Lee, though he lived in a world of dreams and fantasies, also could think as coldly as a computer, and he analyzed how he had been bested in Hong Kong. "He came to a conclusion that would revolutionize the martial arts," DeMile recalls. "He concluded that *gongfu,* like any system, is set up to ensure that the top people are not threatened by talented newcomers. *Gongfu* students, in other words, were trained so they would be sure to fail if they ever challenged their teachers, who had held back from them the techniques that really work."

"When you think about it," DeMile continues, "this is the system that people use everywhere to perpetuate their power, whether they're businessmen, professors, politicians, police, or Mafia. They all guard the secrets of what makes things really work as though their existences depended on it, because they do."

"Bruce Lee now came up with a remarkable solution to this problem. He decided that he would create a system that worked better for Bruce Lee than for anyone else in the world—a system designed for a man of his size, his speed, his brains, and his aggressiveness."

"There is no doubt that between 1960 and 1962, Bruce Lee entered the most creative years of his life," says DeMile. "He was driven by now, more than ever, to succeed by the bitter experience of having for the first time failed at something he set out to do. Even worse, he had failed at the two things he cared most about—winning Amy Sanbo, and proving to Hong Kong that he was, or at least would be, the best wing chun man of them all." He could not do anything about Amy, but he could do something about traditional *gongfu*. So he now set out to purify it, strip it of everything that was superfluous. (After he left Seattle, Lee later named the martial arts system he was developing Jeet Kune Do.)

"He studied all the sports," DeMile says, "looking for principles and techniques he could incorporate into wing chun—football, baseball, basketball, the martial arts, and track, where he learned a lot about leverage by watching javelin throwers." One way he increased his speed, which was phenomenal already, was by working against timing devices. He developed what he called "the startle response" by "fighting" his television set: He would make his move only when there was a cut in the picture.

Lee also explored the arts and sciences, studying anatomy assiduously and making accurate sketches of muscles and bone structures. To study how people tapped their emotional resources, he read copiously in psychology and watched acting classes at the University of Washington. This eventually would help him master the extraordinary power of summoning his *qi* (the body's intrinsic energy), apparently at will.

So far as anyone knows, Lee did not study wild animals, perhaps because that had already been done. But he did explore the Northwest wilderness with LeRoy Garcia, who lived in a log cabin in the foothills near Issaquah. "LeRoy hated the city," recalls DeMile. "He was kind of the last of the mountain men. He came into Seattle only because he had to earn a living when there were no more beaver pelts to trap and sell." Lee did not like to shoot and hunt, but he loved to practice the quick-draw against LeRoy, using blank cartridges. Because Lee always won, LeRoy after a while refused to play.

"The Northwest environment influenced Bruce a lot," says Amy Sanbo. "He loved the freedom and openness. Northwest people often accomplish tremendous things when they go elsewhere, because they haven't been taught that what they want to do is impossible, like they teach you early on in, say, New York or Los Angeles."

However he created it, the achievement was astonishing. To the extraordinary innate quickness of his reflexes, he brought relentless training, an incredible capacity for work and exercise, and a compulsion to be without rival. What he invented, ironically, could not be used in his movies, for the action was too fast to see. Nonetheless, he finally made it, finally laid the ghosts of inferiority to rest—or so it seemed.

By now, there was no way for Lee's Seattle friends to keep up, and one by one they began dropping out of the classes he had been holding in a storefront at Sixth and Weller. "We were growing up and getting jobs and wives and responsibilities and interests beyond fighting," says DeMile, "so we closed down the place on Weller and had a few farewell dinners at the Tai Tung, and broke up."

By 1964, Lee was in Hollywood working as a stuntman and giving *gongfu* lessons to celebrities such as Coburn, McQueen, Elke Sommer, and Kareem Abdul Jabbar. Though still an unknown, Lee dominated and enthralled celebrities as easily and completely as he had the Seattle gang. "In my whole life," declared Sterling Silliphant, the Academy Award-winning screenwriter, "no man, no woman, was ever as exciting as Bruce Lee." Silliphant, Coburn, McQueen, and others used their power and influence to get Lee a starring role, but to no avail. Although he finally got a part as a flunky chauffeur in the *Green Hornet* television series, Hollywood's moguls refused him any major roles, claiming Caucasian audiences would never identify with an Oriental hero.[2]

And so, an angry Lee returned to Hong Kong and made two *gongfu* movies that drove audiences so wild and made so much money that Hollywood was soon begging him to come back.

The attention that Lee craved insatiably was now given without stint and without letup. Hong Kong adored its gaudy boy. Crowds followed him everywhere, fools tried to goad him into fights, and once, when he lost his temper and checked some persistent provoker, the press portrayed him as a bully. Starlets vied to seduce him or at least be seen in his company.

Lee took to spending most of his off-the-job time in his Hong Kong apartment with his wife Linda and their children Brandon and Shannon. He lamented that the freedom and openness of the Northwest he loved was now gone and he was, as he frequently complained, a prisoner in his own house. On the few occasions when he did go out he put on a false mustache and glasses to hide his identity—an ironic switch from the days in Seattle when he disguised himself to attract attention.

Lee now worked on his films with even more demonic energy than he had on *gongfu*. He would do ten retakes on an exhausting fight scene without rest; he was badly cut in a fight scene against an opponent who was armed with a real broken bottle because the producers considered a prop an unnecessary expense.

By all accounts, he was growing physically and emotionally exhausted. When the breaking point came, it was fatal. On July 10, 1973, Lee and a producer were in the flat of a beautiful actress named Betty Ting-pei, purportedly going over the script of a film called, chillingly enough, *The Game of Death*. When Lee complained of a headache, Ting-pei gave him a tablet of Equagesic, a kind of super-aspirin prescribed for her by her physician. Lee went into the bedroom to lie down; the producer went out to eat. Two hours later, Bruce was unconscious and could not be revived. An ambulance took Lee to Queen Elizabeth Hospital where he was pronounced dead.

It turned out to be the most unexpected and suspicious death of a celebrity since Marilyn Monroe's. Both had the same melodramatic ingredients, drugs, sex, and dark tales of murder. According to the coroner's report, Lee had died of a swelling of the brain brought on by a hypersensitivity to Equagesic. Hardly anybody at first believed the coroner and many people never would. That one of the most perfectly fit men on earth could die from taking a big aspirin seemed almost beyond belief. The press began circulating rumors that Lee had been given some undetectable poison by a Hong Kong film king who believed Lee was trying to take over his turf, or by *gongfu* masters who hated Lee for teaching *gongfu* to non-Chinese. Many of Lee's intimates, who knew how he drove himself, wondered if had not simply worn himself out driving his flesh and spirit beyond all human endurance.

SURVIVING THE MIDDLE PASSAGE: TRADITIONAL AFRICAN MARTIAL ARTS IN THE AMERICAS

Thomas A. Green

INTRODUCTION

The Americas are home to various African-descended martial traditions. In the Caribbean, there are the unarmed arts of *maní* (Cuba), *chat'Ou* (Guadeloupe), *ladjiya* (Martinique), and *pingé* (Haiti). In Central America, there is *Congo*. In South America, there is capoeira (Brazil), *broma* (Venezuela), and *susa* (Surinam). Even in the United States, there are reports of knocking and kicking (a.k.a. pushing and dancing) and side hold wrestling, which may have been the system called "leg flip" wrestling in some areas. There are also armed African-descended fighting traditions. Most involve sticks, but some also use whips. Examples are found in Brazil, the Caribbean, and the southern United States. Common names for these arts include *kalenda, kalinda,* and *calinda*.

With the exception of capoeira, which has become popular throughout the world since the 1970s, these arts are generally unknown to members of the European, Hispanic, and Asian American communities.

WHY TRADITIONAL ARTS ARE OBSCURE

Throughout the twentieth century, journalistic and academic descriptions often depicted African American males as oppressed into passivity (e.g., Elkins, 1959/1976). This is inaccurate. Although it is beyond the scope of this article to explain the political, social, cultural, and psychological reasons for this caricatured image, some suggestions are in order.

"Negroes fighting, Brazils." Watercolor by Augustus Earle, 1793–1838 [picture ca. 1822]. Rex Nan Kivell Collection NK12/103. National Library of Australia. PIC T141la.pic-an2822650. By permission of the National Library of Australia.

Misunderstanding of African culture is part of the explanation. African (and their African American descendant) combat systems are commonly carried on to the accompaniment of percussive rhythms. Therefore, even sympathetic outsiders often described African martial play and practice as mere tribal dance (e.g., Gorer, 1935/1949).

Furthermore, the venues in which African martial arts take place often conceal their true natures from outsiders. For example, overseers and slave owners staged "human cockfights" (Bibb, 1850/1969: 68; Danmyé, 2002). These were usually private affairs. Consequently, African combative arts (especially those involving stick fighting and wrestling) receive their greatest public exposure during festivals such as pre-Lenten Carnival. Carnival is a festival in which disorderly and bizarre conduct is expected, tolerated, and often officially ignored. Thus, in the upside-down world of Carnival, fighting is not really fighting (Lewis, 1999). Moreover, these occasions usually show martial arts in conjunction with music and dance. This further obscures the combative nature of the performance.

Boys wrestling by the side of the road: Person County, North Carolina, July 1939. Photo by Dorothea Lange. Library of Congress, LC-USF34-020254-E.

Finally, sport itself was not developed in the modern sense until the mid–nineteenth century; neither was it studied seriously by academics until the mid–twentieth century (Baker, 1983).[1] Consequently, even African Americans have downplayed sport as distracting people from "important" issues.[2]

CHARACTERISTICS OF TRADITIONAL AFRICAN MARTIAL ARTS

Introduction

Whether armed or unarmed, African martial arts generally share at least three of the following characteristics:

- Association with festival or celebration
- Use of supernatural assistance
- Accompaniment by percussive music, leading to a blurring with dance and performance art
- Boasting, bragging, and similar agonistic behavior

Traditional African martial arts in the Americas exhibit the same characteristics. Therefore, the following describes these traits in some detail.

Association with Festival or Celebration

In traditional African society, martial games such as boxing, wrestling, and stick fighting were played at highly developed levels. Moreover, they served social, political, and religious needs far beyond their capacity for developing military capabilities. Throughout Africa, martial exercises accompanied important points of the agricultural year. They marked rites of passage (coming of age, marriage, death, etc.), established status and hierarchies within political units, and sublimated competitions between political units such as villages and states.

For example, among the Nuba of the Sudan, the season when wrestling matches took place was tied to the agricultural cycle of planting, cultivation, and harvesting. Wrestling season extended from the first harvest in late fall to spring. Because the number of wrestling matches increases in direct proportion to the yield during a growing season, "wrestling may be regarded as a ceremony to celebrate a good harvest" ("Wrestling in the Nuba Mountains," 2002).

As a life cycle rite, the Ibo of southern Nigeria associated wrestling with the rites of male maturity. Thus, Ibo wrestled at male initiations. Similarly, the baNngala of Angola held boxing tournaments at male and female initiation and as part of wedding celebrations (Desch-Obi, 2000: 46).

Competition between villages (and larger political organizations, up to state level) was common. For example, the Bachma of Nigeria invited their neighbors (the Bata, Bwaza, Jen, and Mbula) to attend and compete in wrestling tournaments associated with Bachma agricultural festivals (Godia, 1989: 68). Likewise, Edward Powe has described the young men who travel about Nigeria competing in the Hausa boxing art of *dambe*. For these athletes, says Powe, the "sport is a vehicle to overtly demonstrate one's strength and courage and in so doing bring honor to one's village, family, and self" (1994: 20). He adds that *dambe* is associated with butchers, and that a butcher who does not box is unlikely to find a wife (p. 21).

Similar examples can be found on African-populated islands in the Indian Ocean (Powe, 2001)[3] and in South Africa (Coetzee, 2002).

Use of Supernatural Assistance

In premodern Africa, as in premodern Europe and Asia, magical or divine protection was as important for combative preparations as were quality arms and good training. Therefore, warriors of Nigeria's Bini culture defended against iron weapons using shields and armor that offered magical as well as physical protection (Spring, 1993: 49–55). Five hundred years later, Nigerian *dambe* boxers still put faith in various "medicines." These concoctions reportedly have magical powers useful for increasing strength and reducing risk of injury (Powe, 1994). This use of medicines, amulets, prayers, and similar supernatural aids is virtually universal in the African martial practices.

Similar practices are also seen in African American settings, as the following two examples illustrate. In eighteenth–century Saint-Domingue (Haiti), a mulatto called Jerome (a.k.a. Stake) sold *mayombo* (fighting sticks) that supposedly gave their users the power to defeat opposing stick fighters "at no risk to themselves" (Debien, 1972).

Additional details about Jerome's practices show that he was a practitioner of the religion called *vodun* (voodoo). This religion derived from the same West African sources (Kongo, Angola, Dahomey) as did Cuban *santería* and Brazilian *candomblé*. Although contemporary Europeans labeled Jerome a witch and accused him of mesmerism (Debien, 1972), the ties to African martial traditions of supernaturally strengthening weapons are clear.

Similarly, J. Lowell Lewis has suggested that some capoeira practitioners use *candomblé* to protect against "swift, stinging kick[s]" whose impact is compared to "the strike of a snake" (1992: 179). In this case, they use amulets containing knots. Lewis finds allusions to this in capoeira lyrics such as: "In the knot I hide the end...no one knows how to untie" (1992: 179).

Accompaniment by Percussive Music, Leading to a Blurring with Dance and Performance Art

Percussion music often accompanies African combatives. The movements of the fight, both choreographed and ad-libbed, are coordinated with the tempo of the music. The tradition is venerable; according to Dutch geographer Olifert Dapper, around 1648, the armies of the Angolan queen Nzinga Mbande trained in combat techniques using dance accompanied by traditional percussion instruments (Thornton, 1988).

In the military arts of Angola and the Kongo peoples, skills are encoded in dance. At least in the case of Queen Nzinga's troops, not all soldiers learned the same techniques. Specialists, called *imbare* (singular *kimbare* or *quimbare*) and often drawn from slave populations, were recruited to learn the art. John Thornton suggests that this specialized form of dance (called *sanga* in the Kikongo language, and *sanguar* in Ndongo) taught

Festival drummer, New York City, August 1973. Photo by Tom Hubbard. National Archives and Records Administration, ARC identifier 553234.

hand-to-hand combat skills, the use of sticks and other weapons, and "the ability to twist, leap, and dodge to avoid arrows or the blows of opponents" (quoted in Rath, 2000: 110).

The pattern of fighting, singing, and challenging used among the baNgala (Angola) for *kadenka* (boxing) (Desch-Obi 2000: 54) is shared by players of *dambe* (boxing) in Nigeria and *moringue* in Madagascar (Powe, 1994, 2001). Powe provides a detailed description of the ensembles that accompany traditional Hausa combat games *dambe*, *kwambe* (kickboxing), and *kokawa* (wrestling). Each has distinctive percussion ensembles and traditional songs that accompany the action.

In Dakar, among the Wolof, Kirsten M. Jensen (2001) notes that competition among the drum ensembles that accompany the traditional *laamb*
wrestling matches assumes almost as much importance as the matches
themselves. As in the previous cases, percussive music and martial dance
are intertwined arts.

Boasting, Bragging, and Similar Agonistic Behavior

In South Africa, Coetzee (2002) describes solo dancing accompanied by
boastful song as the prelude to Zulu stick fighting. In addition, the *ukugiza*
is a stamping dance performed by female spectators as an accompaniment
for the fight. The integration of percussive music and verbally abusive
song is a widespread phenomenon.

Powe, in fact, describes songs containing challenge, boasting, and derision as pervasive aspects of African combat sports. As an example, at
Hausa *dambe* matches the fights are preceded by drummers playing the
boxers' *take-take* (signature drum call) and praise singers extolling the
virtues of the combatants. The boxers shout boasts, insults, and taunts, and
on occasion the musicians will enter in as well (Powe, 1994: 19).

Similarly, some of the traditional songs accompanying capoeira contain
derisive, boasting, or taunting comments directed toward one of the two
players in the circle. The following is representative: "cry little boy/ nyeh,
nyeh, nyeh/ big cry baby/ nyeh, nyeh, nyeh/ he wants his mother" (Lewis,
1992: 165).[4]

Finally, throughout the West Indies, traveling bands of performers and
stick fighters on encountering one another escalate from song duels, to
verbal invective, to physical combats (Fayer and McMurray, 1999).

THE SURVIVAL OF AFRICAN TRADITIONS IN THE NEW WORLD

Introduction

The sixteenth century was the period of greatest transportation of slaves
from Africa to the Americas. (Portugal, the major European slave traffick-
ing nation, moved more than 1,000 slaves a month throughout the century.)

Besides their labor, these captives also brought their indigenous traditions. Among these were martial traditions. Included in the latter were the
times, places, and attendant features of practice, plus the techniques of
their various combat forms.

During the first half of the twentieth century, academic debate developed surrounding the survival of elements of African culture in the Western Hemisphere. On one side, E. Franklin Frazier contended that African heritage had been destroyed by the oppressive system. In opposition, Melville Herskovits pointed to literally hundreds of Africanisms in the Americas (Rath, 2000: 122).

After considerable initial resistance, the survivalists prevailed, after a fashion. As Richard Cullen Rath argues (2000: 122), African American culture is neither so simple as a reaction to bondage, nor a straightforward transplantation of unaltered Africanisms to the New World. Instead, the products of the African diaspora in the Americas bear the marks of both their origins and the forces encountered in the Western Hemisphere.

Political, Religious, and Military Survivals

Although there were individual variations, the policies of the various slave systems were a combination of coercion and conversion. The slave population was (as far as possible) coerced into abandoning elements of culture that slave owners considered disruptive in the plantation context. Typical subversive behaviors included conduct that represented breaches of the public order or challenged owners' domination, or that provided rallying points for bonding and the preservation of an African identity.

Targets included cultural markers such as language, political systems, and religion. Outward trappings of such institutions were often the easiest points of attack. For example, governments regarded drumming as sufficiently pernicious to require banning in Jamaica (1688), Barbados (1689), St. Kitts (1711), and elsewhere in the Caribbean. The fact that Jamaica was required to pass further legislation in 1717, as was St. Kitts in 1722, demonstrates that laws that required fines and the burning of drums were not particularly successful (Rath, 2002: 107). Even with the legislation, in 1804 the wife of the Jamaican governor reported hearing "bongoes, drums, and tomtoms" during the Christmas celebration (Liverpool, 2001: 104–105).

Among other things, these drums perpetuated Yoruba, Kongo, Arada, and other West African religious practice. Therefore, it appears that the colonial policy of converting the slaves from traditional to Christian belief and practice was not especially successful. In fact, a *vodun houngan* (priest), Boukman, triggered the Haitian Revolution by means of a *vodun* service held in August 1791.

Colonial repression was not always successful. In Stono, South Carolina, in 1739, a "conjure man" named Gullah Jack (Pinckney, 2000: 49) led a group of "twenty slaves, all sharing a common central African [Angolan] background" in an attack on a warehouse. During the raid, they killed two white guards and seized arms and ammunition (Rath, 2000: 111). Eventually, a group of between 60 and 100 escaped slaves assembled near Charleston. The force used drums for both signaling and dancing, Rath contends, in patterns that were distinctively Central African (2000: 111–112). Likewise, in El Salvador, in February 1720, a man saw about a hundred slaves gathered.

> I calmly approached them, inquiring whether they knew the gravity of their action and the penalty for such a display. They simply replied that they were through paying the [tax]. I said that the *alcalde* would probably give them the *garrote* [cudgel] that very night, to which they answered, without even removing their hats from their heads, that they were aware that a *visitador* was in town from the archbishopric in Guatemala, and they were going to ask him to take their part against the *alcalde*. Fearing violence from them, I retired to inform the *alcalde,* and along the way found more *mulatos* running about the streets. (Fiehrer, 1979: 51–52)

Ludic Survivals

The playful elements of African culture were not fully suppressed, either. Indeed, when they took the forms of art, entertainment, or sport, they were sometimes encouraged. For example, Rath observes that in the Carolinas, slave musicians (fiddlers) provided entertainment for the masters' revels. Moreover, he notes that the violin was used subversively, as a percussive instrument, thereby providing a "reinvention of the drum music so feared by planters" (2000: 115).

In the West Indies, whites joined in Carnival festivities; some even dressed like slaves and attended the dances of their servants. Indeed, in Trinidad, members of the white population actively participated in the *kalenda* (a festive dance connected to stick fighting) (Liverpool, 2001: 151–152).

Throughout the Americas, festivals provided an important public arena for the preservation and display of African identity. Over time, tolerance became the general rule for activities attached to Christian religious holidays. For example, the Black Codes in force throughout the Caribbean enfranchised holidays for enslaved Africans. Hollis Liverpool notes that Christmas and Easter, in particular, were seasons when Africans in Trinidad were permitted license to celebrate, and even received extra portions of food and drink with which to enhance celebration (2001: 104, 147–148).

Convicts at Angola Prison, July 1934. The man with the guitar is probably Huddie Ledbetter, a folk and blues singer better known as Leadbelly. Ledbetter served three terms in prison for assault and died poor, but the recording industry subsequently sold millions of copies of records featuring his music. The Lomax Collection, Library of Congress, LC-USZ62-121169.

Sinister Survivals

Sinister survivals included the human cockfights conducted for the amusement of bettors. For example, in Martinique it was reported that

> the owner...used his [slave, referred to as a] black stallion...as a fighting cock that he could exhibit during celebrations. Yet, the [fear of the] loss of his best slave or his being temporarily disabled led the *béké* [master] to put an end to this kind of events [*sic*]. (Danmyé, 2002)

Similar practices occurred in the United States. Henry Bibb, who ran away from slavery in nineteenth-century Kentucky, reported that on Sundays and holidays when slaves were freed from their work duties, men were sometimes forced by their masters to fight. During these contests, "The blows are made by kicking, knocking, and butting with their heads; they grab each other by their ears, and jam their heads together like sheep" (Bibb, 1850/1969: 68; see also Wiggins, 1977). This is a reference to the African American martial art of "knocking and kicking," known also as "pushing and dancing" (Rath, 2000: 109–111), which persisted well into the twentieth century (Gwaltney, 1981).

Cubans called a similar game *maní* (peanut dance). The former slave Esteban Montejo recalls that owners bet on the outcome, but forbade slaves to hit each other so hard that they would be "too bruised to work" (Montejo, 1968: 30–31). The reason was that healthy slaves were worth hundreds, if not, thousands, of dollars, whereas severely injured ones had little value, yet still consumed food.

There may be connections to British-style prizefighting under Broughton's Rules.[5] According to D. Wiggins (1977: 273), "Informal boxing matches between slaves was a common occurrence on the individual plantations. Also planters would frequently organize formal boxing contests and pit their slave champion against other slave champions from different plantations of the community. Many times more money was won on wagers during these fights than on the horses." Thomas Desch-Obi adds that bondsmen often fought using a style that he labels "cutting." Cutting combined elements of British-style boxing, the handwork of *kadenka* (slap-boxing), head-butts and kicks, and the throws of African wrestling (2000: 163, 1995).

The success of black pugilists during the slave period is documented in the careers of fighters such as Bill Richmond. The son of a Georgia slave, Richmond started his boxing career while a servant to the British General Hugh, Earl Percy (Mee, 2001: 60). He went to London with Percy and there became a bodyguard/boxing instructor to the eccentric Lord Camelford (Mee, 2001: 46). From there, he became "The Black Terror" of the British prize ring (Mee, 2001: 60), and later a respected publican.

Allegations of a connection between boxing and African American street styles emerge from time to time. Recent speculations include a link between "prison systems" such as Jailhouse Rock and the ring strategies of former heavyweight champions Floyd Patterson and Mike Tyson. Although this denies the influence of Cus D'Amato, who trained both Patterson and Tyson, Jailhouse Rockers such as Dennis Newsome strongly assert the relationship (personal communication with Dennis Newsome, September 2002).

THE ROLE OF FESTIVAL

Introduction

In the New World, African martial arts were preserved in the context of festival and holiday. Common contexts included religious holidays such as Christmas and the Carnival period preceding Lent. Other occasions included points of transition in the work calendar such as "Cropover" (a harvest festival that is reminiscent of the Nuba practice of wrestling at harvest), Saturday paydays, and other occasions featuring dancing, masking, and music.

Thus, in the New World, African-based martial arts remained largely within the settings established in the Old World. That is, they were not primarily defensive systems. Instead, they incorporated elements of festival, celebration, and equivalent public displays. In these contexts, they openly developed a sense of community (which can relate to locale or ethnicity) within the African American population. At the same time, they introduced (or juxtaposed) players to other segments of society, particularly "sensible," refined segments of the community (see Abrahams, 1983). Finally, they attracted sexual partners and established prestige within a young man's social group.

Free Space

Within the expressive limits defined by society, law, and one's group, festivals such as the pre-Lenten Carnival are psychologically "free space." This term describes situations where potential untapped in mundane life can be realized. Because so much of this involves individual fantasies, excess is common. This is allowed because, as folklorist Roger D. Abrahams observes, festival and ritual

> are both unusual but recurrent ceremonies or celebrations. Both involve a spatial-temporal sense of "removal"...and a psychological sense of separation [from the everyday] usually referred to as the experience of liminality. (1983: 98)

For both slaves and freemen, Carnival served as a psychological free zone. There was the illusion of freedom, equality, and upward mobility, of a world in which the ordinary order was upturned. The King of Fools was crowned, public figures were derided, and the white gentry of the French Caribbean played at being *Negres de Jardin* (field laborers) (Liverpool, 2001: 128).

At one level, festival is subversive because it questions established authority, rules of polite behavior, and even gender and species distinction. At another level, however, it may support authority, by serving as an alternative channel for confrontations. Additionally, participation in festival rebellion may reveal to the authorities the most angry or outspoken members of the community. This second factor suggests a pragmatic reason for the persistence of masking traditions (Saltzman, 1994, 1995).

At any rate, festival provides opportunities for the practice and preservation of martial techniques such as whipping, stick fighting, wrestling, and fisticuffs under a façade of play.

Leadership Opportunities

The coordination of performance groups of any kind calls for organizational skills. In the African American community, the organization of performance groups was often based on church affiliation, and some individual groups have histories as long as three centuries in the Western Hemisphere (Abrahams, 1983: 49).

African military societies may have formed another basis for organizing groups. For example, Desch-Obi argues that in America, members of African warrior societies preserved martial techniques under various guises, among them the band of fighters that commonly accompanied the musical bands of Carnival (2000: 152–157). Of course, other opportunities for creating organizations existed in festival contexts, but these are less directly related to his arguments.

Whatever their origins, leadership within performance groups created status in local society. While discussing the social power roles of Carnival in the West Indies, Abrahams offers this description of the performer who gains reputation through martial ability:

> In those troupes that involve dancing, acrobatics, or fighting [the troupe leader is]...the man of action, the physically adept one who brings focus to the proceedings by his leadership and performance abilities. (1983: xvi)

This "man of action" role is typically titled "King," "Pierrot," or "Paywo" (French, *pierrot,* meaning harlequin; Creole, *paywo*). The position is desirable because, while on the throne, kings accrue money and status for themselves, their groups, and their communities. Consequently, the same person often fills these roles year after year, until defeated by a challenger who then assumes the leadership position.

Given the opportunity, troupe leaders sometimes tried to transform festival power into real world action. An example is the thwarted rebellion in Antigua, South Carolina in 1736, during which

> a "Coromantee" (Western Kwa) slave leader "announced his intention to stage an uprising 'in open Day-light, by a Military Dance and Show, of

which the Whites and even the Slaves (who were not Coromantees nor let
into the Secret) might be Spectators, and yet ignorant of the Meaning.' "
(Rath, 2000: 108)

Recreation

During festival, African combat tradition survived as sport-game-dance.
(All these labels have been applied at various times.) As festival events,
they were portrayed (and perceived) as not entirely serious. Accordingly,
they were permissible under universal festival rules. Moreover, the action
was directed (ostensibly) toward other members of the African American
community. Thus, the only danger apparent to the slave owners was the
potential destruction of property. All these conventions serve to wrap the
martial elements in layers of art and play.

THE MARTIAL ARTS OF THE FESTIVAL

Although festival provided a context for the preservation of African
martial traditions, all combat systems were not equally preserved. For
example, pugilism is not widely distributed, and wrestling is not as developed as one might expect. On the other hand, arts involving the use of
sticks and whips are nearly universal.

On Martinique, the martial art is *ladjia* (or *danmyé*). Its matches combine wrestling and striking to musical accompaniment. It apparently has
roots in Benin, and like most Caribbean arts, it features prominently at
Carnival and is an element of the festival event known as *swaré bèlè*, or
"dance evening" (Danmyé, 2002: Michalon, 1987; C. Smith, 2001).

In Cuba, Esteban Montejo recalled from his days as a slave in the nineteenth century that *maní* was a pugilistic contest during which men fought
in the middle of a circle of rhythmically clapping spectators (1968: 30).
According to Montejo, the pugilism took place mostly on Sundays, the
day of the "biggest fiestas" (1968: 29). He further labeled the sport
extremely brutal. Even in the Protestant southern United States, Henry
Bibb reports (1850/1969) that the knocking and kicking battles between
slaves took place on Sundays and other holidays.

Throughout the Caribbean, the best known tradition is the stick-fighting
game known as *calinda, kalenda, bois,* and sticklickin', among other terms.
Other Caribbean stick fight/dances associated with festival are *masondi* and
battonie (Haiti), and outside the Caribbean, "battle dance" (Surinam), and
maculelé (Brazil) (Courlander, 1960: 131–133). *Kalinda* and stick fighting
extended into the southern United States as well.

Kalenda. Courtesy Dennis Newsome.

In these stick-fighting games, music is a prelude to the activities and a means of pacing action. Instruments included, to cite various examples, a single drum, a fife and drum ensemble, a battery of three drums called "Big Drum," and hand clapping.

The sticks serve various functions. For example, in Trinidad, the *paywo* (king of fools) carries a whip (often a wire wrapped in tape or, occasionally, a bull pizzle). He brandishes the whip as a symbol of authority, cracks it to punctuate his speeches, and uses it to strike his opponents (Hill, 1998).

In Curaçao, elegant fashion accessories among slaves and free blacks included the *garoti* or *koko makaku*. A thin walking stick, it was the subject of official sanctions from the eighteenth to twentieth centuries because of its role in the stick-fighting games (Rosalia, 1996: 234). Father Paul Brenneker described the Curaçao dance/fight:

> Each of two men held his stick at the ends, approached the other and danced and jumped around to the rhythm of the singing and clapping of hands of the spectators. A drummer would beat time. The men were supposed to defend their own head with their stick and simultaneously make efforts to strike the opponent with it on his head. They manipulated the sticks master-fully. If one of them saw an opportunity to deal a blow to the other on his head, he would be the winner. If the loser bled from his head wound, the bystanders would shout: "sanger pa tambú" (blood for the drum). The loser had to let some blood flow on the skin of the drum. (quoted in "Our Cultural Heritage," 2001)

In Haiti, the Rara festival follows Mardi Gras. In it, bands led by baton-juggling kings play songs of praise and ridicule. Each king has a unique dancing style that is competitive in nature and accompanied by drums. Here, the stick is a means of demonstrating physical dexterity. This use of the stick is a kind of baton twirling.[6]

The sticks of Rara are also used during wrestling matches (pingé) that accompany the festival. The competitors meet in a circle of spectators and grapple to the rhythm of musicians playing drums, flutes, and lengths of bamboo beaten by sticks (Courlander, 1960: 105–108).

Given its omnipresence and ability to pass as a tool necessary to the musical ensemble, the stick was an especially apt weapon in the festival context. Moreover, a stick could produce the blood that was an element of African traditional combat (compare to "blood for the drum"), but represented less danger to combatants than bladed weapons.

In the last analysis, however, these African American martial arts, whether played unarmed or armed, fill the same temporal slots as their African precursors. That is, they are part of festival entertainment.

CAPOEIRA

The origins of capoeira are documented only in the traditions of the art. There is some argument about whether capoeira developed in Africa or Brazil. In discussing the controversy, Lowell Lewis portrays this argument as arising, in part, as an element in an internal debate in the Americas over whether a person is African, African Brazilian, or Brazilian (1992: 18–21; see also Lingo, 1996: 13–18). In this interpretation, historical questions take on social and political freight, with participation in capoeira becom-

Capoeira. Courtesy Dennis Newsome.

ing a way of playing out ethnic identity. In terms of anthropological arguments, however, Daniel Dawson (1993), Thomas Desch-Obi (2000), and
Robert Farris Thompson(1992) have presented compelling evidence that
the art is African in both esthetic and origin.

During the seventeenth century, legend locates capoeira among fugitive
slave communities in the Brazilian bush. In these communities, the surviving accounts of festival entertainment are tantalizing. For example,
there are descriptions of dancing to percussive music. The dancing is
described as including competitive kicking and tripping, and names
included *batuque* (which also involved verbal dueling), *samba duro* (hard
samba), and *roda de pernada* (circle of leg blows).

Capoeira unmistakably entered the written record during the nineteenth
century, at which time government officials suppressed its practice in urban
centers. However, even in this context, capoeira remained attached to festival. For example, during Carnival, the various *maltas* (gangs) and their
attendant *samba* bands sometimes met in violent clashes in the streets. During these fights, knives and razors commonly complemented kicks, grap-

ples, and head-butts. Consequently, capoeira earned a reputation as the weapon of *malandros* (tough guys) (Holloway, 1993; Lewis, 1992: 49; Powe, 2002a: 94). Nonetheless, there was still culture in capoeira, especially in its music. The most important of capoeira's accompanying musical instruments is the *berimbau,* which is a musical bow using a gourd resonator that one plays by striking its metal bowstring with a stick. Thus, the capoeira *maltas* were analogous to the Caribbean stick fighting groups.

During the late 1920s, capoeira began acquiring another face. In 1927, Manoel dos Reis Machado (1899–1979), or *Mestre* (Master) Bimba, began teaching private lessons in Bahia. Five years later, he established an academy that catered to a more middle-class (and European Brazilian) clientele. Toward satisfying this population's expectations, Mestre Bimba developed a more structured curriculum and a more gymlike atmosphere (Powe, 2002a: 97).

Mestre Bimba's training hall, called *Centro de Cultura Física e Capoeira Regional* (Center of [for] Physical Culture and Regional Capoeira), lent its name to his newly structured system—*capoeira Regional.* Older styles of play that survived on the streets or under the instruction of conservative teachers such as *Mestre* Pastinha (Vicente Ferreira Pastinha, 1889–1981) were labeled *capoeira Angola* (Powe, 2002a: 179).[7]

Livio Sansone (1999) contends that this mid–twentieth century development helped form distinctions between Brazilian and African Brazilian identities. After capoeira Regional disavowed its heritage as a pastime for "rough youth" (p. 22), it became (along with Umbanda, "a whitened form of black religion" [p. 19]) associated with Brazilian identity. In contrast, capoeira Angola and *candomblé* (a religion closely tied to Yoruba religious practice) remained associated with African identity, that is, "blackness" (p. 23).

Capoeira Angola (and to a lesser extent, capoeira Regional) contains links to West African spirituality. For example, the songs that accompany a capoeira *jôgo* (Portuguese for "game") contain references to *candomblé orixás* (supernatural entities whose spirits possess devotees during religious events). Similarly, there are gestures associated with Kongo religious practice such as making a cross on the ground before entering the *roda* (literally "wheel," but describing the human circle in which capoeira is played). Finally, some players use *patuá* (fetishes) to provide supernatural protection.[8] Of course, whether these practices are matters of sincere conviction or mere habit varies from person to person.

Abroad, Sansone notes the irony of the ethnic exclusiveness of some U.S. capoeira Angola schools. Despite European Americans having enthusiastically supported the revival of capoeira Angola, some schools cater exclusively to African Americans, and therefore establish policies against admitting white members (1999: 41).

CONCLUSION

The foregoing glimpses of African martial arts in the Western Hemisphere tantalize us with visions of rich variety. Nonetheless, much additional research is required to flesh out the record.

At the outset, investigators must bear in mind that African martial arts did not really survive in the New World. Despite strong family resemblances, anything that survived the Middle Passage was forced to accommodate. As with other cultural forms brought from Africa, what endured eventually emerged as a creole.

Some of the contexts in which these arts were preserved were essentially the same as contexts in the African homeland. Examples include harvest festivals analogous to Cropover. Other contexts were modifications of general types, but not duplicates. For instance, Carnival, although festive, is not precisely like anything in traditional Africa. Therefore, the African-descended martial arts in the Americas were elements of a creole complex.

One important distinction is that the African martial arts in the Americas were not part of the dominant culture. Therefore, unlike their parent forms, New World hybrids had to deal with culturally and racially plural systems from a position of political weakness. Thus, much of their ethos involved confrontation with politically and socially powerful "others." Methods of accomplishing this confrontation included the assertion of African identity. The preservation of martial traditions operating as licensed play represents one aspect of this assertion.

During the twentieth century, some traditions lapsed. *Maní* is an example. Others, such as capoeira Angola, adapted and flourished. Still other traditions were revivals, usually via reconstruction. In most cases, this reconstruction was organized by government agencies operating relatively independently of the tradition bearers. A project on *ladjia,* for example, was the object of a cultural study program at Lorrain High School in Martinique (Danmyé, 2002). Commercial interests were also involved in reconstruction. For example, in Martinique, Haiti, and Brazil, tourist agencies advertise various stick arts as cultural performances.

In this regard, capoeira Regional is noteworthy because it made the transition from folk art to popular culture. Its teachers achieved this by changing it into a martial sport and system of self-defense. Subsequently, capoeira Regional became popular internationally, and it even formed the basis for Hollywood movie fight choreography.[9] This represents the extreme (and to date, the most commercially successful) adaptation of African martial tradition.

KENDO IN NORTH AMERICA, 1885–1955

Joseph R. Svinth

INTRODUCTION

Before World War II, people of Japanese ancestry living in North America did not practice kendo (Japanese swordsmanship) for military prepared-ness, or even sport. Instead, they used it as a cultural artifact that con-nected students, expatriate businessmen, immigrants, and their families to traditional Japanese culture and values. As George Izui put it, "Many of us started out to train in kendo as a sport, but later became more involved in the more difficult combination of mental and physical disciplining. There was no room for any conceited superstars" (personal communication, July 4, 1998).

KENDO COMES TO NORTH AMERICA

A kendo dojo, or "place for studying the Way," was established in Hono-lulu in the late 1890s. Other early kendo clubs include ones in San Fran-cisco (before 1907), Seattle (before 1909), Denver (1912), Steveston, British Columbia (1913), and Los Angeles (1914).

As a rule, these early clubs catered to comparatively educated men, men who might be termed exchange students or expatriate businessmen rather than immigrants. Various reasons prevented immigrants from practicing fencing, or teaching it to their children. One reason was time. Japanese immigrant men typically worked for wages 10 hours a day, six days a week. Afterward, they went home and cleared land during the winter and

Men demonstrating kendo in Tacoma, Washington, during the mid-1930s. Courtesy Tacoma Public Library.

picked fruit or went fishing during the summer. Obviously, this did not leave them much time for recreational activities.

A second factor was money. As few immigrants were wealthy, even dedicated kendo practitioners had trouble arranging for the second set of armor and *shinai* (a pliant bamboo practice sword) that a partner required.

A third factor was prejudice. Visions of Japanese agricultural workers attacking their overseers with sticks set off waves of Yellow Peril paranoia, and consequently early community leaders often downplayed Japanese martial traditions.

Finally, it was hard to find someone both qualified and willing to teach. For example, in 1921, the Japanese Association of San Pedro, California hired Noriyoshi Toyama to teach kendo to members' children. Unfortunately, Toyama died soon after, and consequently, when the current teacher (Sasamori Junzo) returned to Japan in 1923, the Los Angeles kendo community was shattered.

During the late 1920s, community leaders decided to bring professional kendo instructors to the United States. This represents a fundamental change, and is largely responsible for the rapid spread of kendo during the 1930s. The organization most responsible for the necessary exchange program was the Hokubei Butokukai, or North American Martial Virtue Association. In 1932, it established a kendo federation in California, and in 1935, it received official recognition from Japan.

The Hokubei Butokukai had its headquarters at Alvarado, California, which was a Bay Area community incorporated into Union City in 1959. Its early professional instructors included Nakamura Tokichi, who started teaching at San Pedro in October 1929, Mori Torao, who taught in Los Angeles from 1936 to 1940, and Fukagawa Susumu and Iwasa Yuji, who started teaching in San Francisco in January 1930. By the mid-1930s, reasonable numbers of American-born teachers were available, and by 1940, most Hokubei Butokukai teachers were American born. In September 1936, the Hokubei Butokukai began spreading kendo instruction into Washington and Oregon. Financial patrons included a Seattle Japanese-language newspaper *(North American Times),* the Fukuoka Prefectural Association (Nakamura Tokichi was from Fukuoka), and the Seattle business community (notably Heiji "Henry" Okuda, who was also from Fukuoka).

Members of Seattle's existing kendo club (the Seattle Kendo Kai) were not happy to see the Californians. Indeed, as far as they were concerned, Nakamura Tokichi was a dojo-robber who bought members by promising higher ranks and lower standards. They were not shy about saying so, either (Jim Akutsu, personal correspondence, January 13, 1998; FBI 100–5006: 10; George Izui, personal communication, October 19, 1998; Paul Kurose, personal communication, January 27, 1998).

The animosity ran deep. Consequently, in June 1938, the two clubs could not come together long enough to organize a joint tournament with which to welcome a visiting Waseda University kendo team. This embarrassed the Japanese consul and led a local paper to complain, "There are two self-centered kendo groups—the Hokubei Butokukai and the Dai Nippon Butokukai[1]—in this city, each of which seemingly has no use for the other, and are obviously unwilling to cooperate with each other" (*North American Times,* June 28, 1938: 8).

The opprobrium stung. Consequently, "after we [the Hokubei Butokukai] built our new hall [in Seattle in 1940]," said Heiji Okuda's son Kenji, "the Kendo Kai's teachers [Junichi] Yoshitomi and [Umajiro] Imanishi used to come over all the time and teach classes" (personal communication, May 9, 1998). Nevertheless, the Hokubei Butokukai and Seattle Kendo Kai never

Left to right: Yeikichi Matsumura, Yuichi Akune, and Moriharu Tanigami of
Steveston, British Columbia, following the Hokubei Butokukai's 1937 Seattle
tournament. Courtesy Joseph Svinth.

organized any joint tournaments. Moreover, as late as 1941 the Japanese consul was still grumbling that the two groups wasted his time calling him to complain about the actions of the other (FBI 100–5006: 2–5).

The Hokubei Butokukai did not just establish clubs in downtown cores. For example, in southern California, it had clubs in Brawley, Chula Vista, El Centro, Huntington Park, Redondo Beach, and Riverside, while in Oregon, metropolitan Portland had two clubs (Columbia Boulevard and Gresham-Troutdale) that were located miles from downtown.

Although not affiliated with the Hokubei Butokukai, British Columbia kendo clubs often participated in tournaments with its Seattle branch. In 1940, British Columbia had six kendo clubs, located at Vancouver, Steveston, New Westminster, Sunbury, Whonnock, and Woodfibre. The instructor at Vancouver and Woodfibre was a Canadian-born but Japanese-educated man *(kibei)* named Motoo Matsushita, while the Steveston instructor was an immigrant *(issei)* named Yuichi Akune.

NUMBERS OF PRACTITIONERS

Researcher Ito Kazuo once asked how many people did judo in the Pacific Northwest before World War II. The response was that there were probably 400 *yudansha* (literally, "grade holders," but figuratively, black belts), plus another 1,000 of lesser grade (Ito, 1973: 241).

So, if perhaps 1,400 boys and men did judo, how many practiced kendo? In addition to the two big kendo clubs in downtown Seattle, there were six smaller clubs in the Puget Sound region, three in Portland Metro, and scattered enthusiasts. Between them, the two downtown clubs reported several hundred students, which was probably more than everyone else combined. (To give an idea of the size of outlying clubs, in 1941, Tacoma reported 30 members, while in 1938, Bellevue advanced its nine current members and welcomed five new members.) Numbers in British Columbia are unknown, but there were still just six clubs, with the largest being in Steveston and Vancouver. Therefore, all told, there were probably 150–200 kendo practitioners in Canada and another 300–400 in Washington and Oregon.

However, this is not what one usually hears. Instead, one reads that before World War II, 10,000 Japanese Americans practiced kendo, 2,500 in Los Angeles alone (Azuma, 2000: 85). Admittedly, California had more practitioners than Washington and Oregon. Nonetheless, I have seen nothing to convince me that the dozen or so Los Angeles clubs averaged several hundred members each. Neither has anything caused me to believe that nearly 8 percent of the approximately 126,000 Japanese Americans

Kendo tournament at Gresham, Oregon, February 1940. Courtesy Joseph Svinth.

living on the U.S. mainland in 1940 practiced kendo. So, if we assume this statistic is exaggerated, then the question is to identify who started this story, and why.

One possibility is jingoistic newspapers. For example, on February 4, 1907, the *New York World* reported on page 1 that hundreds of Russo-Japanese War veterans living in Hawaii drilled with broomsticks in anticipation of the arrival of the Japanese fleet. True, many Japanese immigrants *(issei)* referred to the Japanese Navy as "our Navy." However, it is also true that in 1907, there was only one kendo club in Hawaii, and its members could have been counted on fingers and toes. Therefore, if this is the source, then it is a brilliant example of what Kaiser Wilhelm II called "the Yellow Peril."

A second possibility is that Hokubei Butokukai leader Nakamura Tokichi was a man who liked to blow his own horn. For example, on July 21, 1940, *Japan Times* (p. 3) quoted Nakamura as saying that his classes had aroused interest "in over 10,000 Nisei[2] living in America." Because

Japanese culture does not encourage juniors to question seniors, it is doubtful that any kendo enthusiasts would have questioned Nakamura's statement. Nor would the U.S., Canadian, or Japanese governments have bothered to doubt him, either. After all, he said what they wanted to hear.

A third possibility is mistranslation. In 1942, federal agents asked Heiji Okuda, the head of the Hokubei Butokukai in Seattle, how many people practiced kendo in the United States. Okuda replied, "Ten thousand" ("Henry H. Okuda," n.d.). Although Okuda's statement is documented, he may have meant the number figuratively rather than literally. After all, in Japanese, one can say *"ichi-man"* (10,000) in contexts where in English one would say, "Uncountable." Perhaps Okuda meant to say "an indeterminate number, but many," but the interpreter, who probably was not a native speaker, misunderstood him to mean an exact number?

No matter. Although regional kendo associations clearly had hundreds of active members and thousands of supporters, treat the estimate of 10,000 kendo practitioners in North America before World War II with caution.

HOW TRAINING WAS CONDUCTED

Before World War II, North American kendo training usually took place at a Japanese-language school, church gym, or other shared community space. Before classes began, older youths swept and mopped the floors, while younger children, in the words of Kenji Okuda (personal communication, May 1998), "horsed around until the teachers showed up."[3] Once the teachers arrived, then everyone lined up in rows, with the instructors facing the students, the senior-most person kneeling to the right, and his juniors arrayed by seniority to his left. Positioning in these rows was exact and changed only following formal promotion.

Classes started with formal bows to tradition and instructors, followed by a brief lecture. Next, students practiced basics—about 30–45 minutes of every hour were devoted to practicing proper strikes and parries. After that, students put on their armor and fenced. During the fencing, fundamentals were everything, with enormous stress on how the hands were placed, how the *shinai* was gripped, how the feet moved (Ken Hibi, personal communication, August 1, 1999). At the end of training, everyone knelt in a formal position while the teacher spoke about morals and ethics. Finally, everyone bowed to thank each other for participating in training, and then headed home (FBI 100–5006, 10; Ryo Munekata, personal communication, August 3, 1998).

Japanese and Japanese American teachers of the Hokubei Butokukai, in Japan, ca. 1934. Back row, left to right: Yamamoto, 1-*dan*; Nakamura Sensei; Hirano, 5-*dan* (from Japan). Front row, left to right: Hara, 2-*dan*; Maruyama, 4-*dan* (from Japan); Fujii Sensei; Nakano, 2-*dan*; Imada, 2-*dan*. Courtesy Joseph Svinth.

The formal position in which practitioners knelt was called *seiza*. "Sometimes you'd sit so long, your legs became numbed," recalled Kenji Okuda. "When they had you stand up, people would topple over. It was painful!" (personal communication, May 9, 1998). Such hardship was intentional, as it was supposed to forge the spirit. As Ruth Nishino Penfold put it, "We also practiced *seishin shuyo* (meditation of the inner spirit). We sat in Japanese style on the bare floor. This was difficult for me because I was very young and inexperienced in life. It was hard keeping unnecessary thoughts from crowding in" (personal communication, April 2, 2001).

Originally, parents ordered kendo armor from Japan, but by the late 1930s, local merchants began stocking armor. Thus, most students had their own set (Kazuo Kinoshita, personal communication, April 1, 2001). Yeikichi Matsumura recalled that armor cost about $100, which was a lot of money in those days (Janet Matsumura Zilberman, personal communication, September 12, 1999). Once suitably attired, proud parents rushed their children to a photographer for a formal portrait and then sent the resulting prints to relatives in Japan. Unfortunately, Japanese Americans usually destroyed such photos after Pearl Harbor, while their Japanese relatives often lost their photo albums during the fire bombings of 1945. Consequently, such pictures are somewhat rare today.

Intermediate students—say 3-*kyu* or higher—sometimes learned special breathing and meditation techniques. These methods helped calm the practitioners, and teachers said that they might help students understand their opponents' motivations. With complete understanding, Jim Akutsu (personal correspondence, January 13, 1998) recalled, "You were supposed to know what your opponent was going to do before he did."

Kangeiko, or winter training, was an ascetic discipline *(shugyo)* commonly associated with prewar kendo classes. Although *kangeiko* was meant to build practitioners' character through overcoming shared hardships, as far as most young Japanese Americans were concerned, it mostly involved training during the middle of winter with the heat turned off and the windows opened wide.

Obviously, the discipline was not always so Spartan. Otherwise, no one except a handful of masochists would have stayed with kendo training, especially not once they discovered cars and the opposite sex. To demonstrate through actions rather than words that they truly had the best interests of the younger generation in mind, club supervisors routinely included social activities in their training schedules. For example, when the Tacoma Kendo Kai held its first meeting of the season in October 1940,[4] its first order of business was planning a party (*Great Northern Daily News,* October 16, 1940: 8). Likewise, on March 2, 1941, the Seattle Hokubei Butokukai hosted a bazaar featuring dancing and "good things to eat served by beautiful girls" (*Great Northern Daily News,* February 28, 1941: 8).

FEMALE PARTICIPATION

Circa 1940, about 10 percent of the kendo students in Tacoma and Seattle were teenaged females. These girls trained together with the boys. "I was most nervous about practicing fencing with Mr. [Tamotsu] Takizaki's daughter, Teresa, when she showed up," Henry Itoi recalled. "The fellows were reluctant at first to hit her. But we found out in a hurry that she could dish it out vigorously, and take it too" (personal communication, August 24, 1999).

Girls also trained in California, and during tournaments, the California girls sometimes competed with boys (*Japanese-American Courier,* December 18, 1937: 3). However, in the Northwest, boys and girls competed separately. As this made winning trophies much easier, the girls never complained. (Although winning trophies is not the goal of kendo competition, it is always hard to convince young people of that) (Taeko Hoshiwara Taniguchi, personal communication, March 30, 1998).

In Seattle and Los Angeles, girls also practiced with *naginata,* which are six-foot polearms fitted with a single wooden blade. In Japan, schoolgirls started wielding *naginata* during physical education classes in 1924, and on December 15, 1929, Seattle's Miyo Inouye gave a demonstration at Seattle's Nippon Kan Theater (*Japanese-American Courier,* December 14, 1929: 2). Inouye evidently taught the Seattle class, as in February 1940, she and Teresa Takizaki, who had recently returned from a year in Japan, gave a *naginata* demonstration in Vancouver, British Columbia (*Japanese-American Courier,* February 3, 1940: 4).

Outside these communities, Japanese American girls could not develop fearless posture and alert eyes using *naginata* because there were no available instructors. Therefore they did kendo instead (Taniguchi, personal communication, March 30, 1998). Tacoma girls who did kendo included Sachiko Yamamoto, Taeko Hoshiwara, and Kai Nakagawa. On August 1, 1937, Yamamoto earned special distinction for winning her division against Californian opponents. "Although us girls were few in number," recalled Sachiko Yamamoto Oyanagi, "we strived to do our utmost" (personal communication, March 30, 1998).

In Oregon, there were just three female kendo practitioners. These were Gresham's Arie Shiiki and Portland's Ruth Nishino and Chiye Tomihiro (Ray Shiiki, personal communication, February 20, 2001). Nishino's parents encouraged her to study kendo because "it seemed to produce slim, taller bodies. This results because the participants do not have to concentrate on keeping upright and on their feet [as in judo]. The emphasis is on speed and accuracy in hitting the vital spots: *o-men* (head), *o-kote* (wrist), *o-do* (waist), and *o-tsuki* (throat)" (Penfold, personal communication, April 2, 2001).

Finally, in British Columbia, the only known female practitioner was Eiko Matsushita, sister of Vancouver kendo teacher Motoo Matsushita (*Japan Times,* March 13, 1941: 3).

PROMOTION

Taeko Hoshiwara Taniguchi doesn't remember exactly how rank was judged or awarded. "I know *dan* rank came from Japan," she said. "The instructors looked at you and wrote to Japan and you got a certificate. But for *ikkyu, nikyu,* etcetera, you didn't get any certificates. I guess they just looked at us during competition and said okay, you're this rank" (personal communication, March 30, 1998).

To this, George Izui added, "A nominee's personal character was considered as well as the proficiency with a *shinai.* To emphasize its significance, I recall going to my *sensei* [teacher] with my father and making the sad request to strike my name off the list of *shodan* nominations. The reason was my unpredictable temper" (personal communication, July 4, 1998).

Fees for these promotions were nominal, and were paid by clubs through dues rather than charged to individuals (FBI 100–5006: 9).

The practice form *(kata)* taught in North America was generally the *Dai Nippon teikoku kendo kata.* This curriculum descended from police kendo forms developed around 1885–1886 and was periodically updated. Until *dan*-graded, few students learned *kata.* Explained Taeko Hoshiwara Taniguchi, "None of us kids was good enough to do *kata.* The instructor, the *renshi,* he did *kata.* It was dangerous because you used a real sword. We hardly saw those *kata,* except during an exhibition or something. All we did was practice *men, do, kote*" (personal communication, March 30, 1998).

Equally, few second-generation Japanese Americans *(nisei)* ever handled a real sword. For example, George Izui only began practicing with real swords during the 1970s, and then mostly because he had grown bored with the game of tag played in local kendo tournaments (personal communication, July 4, 1998). Reasons included the secrecy that surrounded the transmission of traditional Japanese sword arts. Nakamura Taizaburo taught swordsmanship to Japanese army officer candidates from 1935 to 1945. "Until the end of the [Second World] War," says Nakamura, "sword techniques and forms were prohibited from being shown even to the parents and brothers of a practitioner." The reason, he said, was that "this way the styles could be transmitted only to the direct students of certain styles" (Nakamura, 1998).

Therefore, if students wanted to learn *kata* and *iaido* (quick draw using real swords, also called *batto-do*), they had to go to Japan. Travel was expensive and because of political disagreements between governments, it was hard to organize and arrange. One youth who overcame these difficulties was Dick Yamamoto, who went to Japan in the mid-1930s to train with the Hokubei Butokukai. As Yamamoto recalled:

> I received my 5-*dan* and took my *renshi* exam at the Dai Nippon Butokukai in Japan in 1939. I came back to the States soon after. I instructed kendo at

Seattle, South Park, Tacoma, Sumner, Puyallup, and Portland. I was what you call a *junkai kyoshi,* or roving teacher.

I don't think you know about the kendo ranking of *renshi, kyoshi,* and *hanshi.* A *renshi* [someone who has mastered himself] is ranked 4-*dan* or 5-*dan.* A *kyoshi* [instructor] is someone ranked 6-*dan* or 7-*dan.* A *hanshi* [master instructor] is someone ranked 7-*dan* to 10-*dan.* To get *renshi,* a degree exam was held at the Dai Nippon Butokukai in Kyoto. The test included a written exam in kendo knowledge, *kata,* and *shiai* [competition]. It took three days to test. (Personal communication, April 16, 1998)

Yamamoto's experience was of course exceptional. Furthermore, his description of grading and testing refers solely to the prewar Hokubei Butokukai.[5] Nonetheless, his description still gives an idea of how prewar kendo teachers were trained and selected.

REGIONAL TOURNAMENTS

Although there were local kendo tournaments on Oahu as early as the 1890s, regional tournaments *(taikai)* appear to date to the 1920s. For example, during the early 1920s, Sasamori Junzo organized regional tournaments in Los Angeles. Steveston hosted British Columbia's first known regional tournament on April 18, 1931. The Seattle Kendo Kai organized Washington's first major regional tournament on July 4, 1933. Finally, Gresham-Troutdale held Oregon's first major regional tournament on February 11, 1940.

By this time, many people attended these tournaments. For example, in February 1941, 140 practitioners gathered for a tournament in Vancouver, British Columbia. Clubs competed as teams, and a typical team had about 10 members. "The competition make-up was to align all contestants of a division by instructor-graded ability," said Frank Muramatsu. "The two lowest ranked players began the competition with the winner matched against the next in line. The division winner was the player with the most wins. My personal best was thirteen consecutive wins" (personal communication, March 5, 2001).

Upon starting a bout, contestants were expected to give a spirited shout, or *kiai.* "I had a fearsome, loud *kiai,*" recalled Ruth Nishino Penfold, "I stood at the start and bellowed in a loud voice, '*Saa-kita,*' 'Beware, here I come!' The first time the Portland kendo team went to Seattle, my *kiai* really frightened my opponents and startled them, but as there was more skill in kendo, I lost my rounds" (personal communication, April 2, 2001).

Katashi "Ken" Hibi of Steveston, British Columbia, following the Hokubei Butokukai's 1938 Seattle tournament. Courtesy Joseph Svinth.

According to George Izui:

> Rules regarding contests yesterday did not seem as complicated as they are today. A contest was refereed by one person. His calls were never questioned. If a contestant had a doubt about the official's call, he tried to do better next time, so there would be no doubt. There may have been penalty rulings, but I cannot recall anyone having been charged with one. Teammates did not applaud or shout any encouragement, advice, or joyous approval. The spectators may have applauded a good contest, but I do not remember. (Personal communication, July 4, 1998)

For prizes, divisional champions received new *shinai* while overall champions received cups. Once the tournament was over and the trophies handed out, then everyone attended a banquet at a local (usually Chinese) restaurant.

WORLD WAR II AND BEYOND

North American and Hawaiian kendo clubs closed following the Japanese attack on Pearl Harbor, and many club leaders were arrested as potentially dangerous enemy aliens. The U.S. government simultaneously passed legislation prohibiting people of Japanese descent from possessing swords or firearms. Consequently, *shinai,* armor, and trophies were hidden away or destroyed. "My father felt that all things Japanese should be destroyed so the kendo equipment was burned and buried," said Frank Muramatsu. "It would now be in the ground about where the terminal building of the Portland Airport is now located" (personal communication, March 5, 2001).

Similarly, ancestral swords were buried or broken. As Frank Chuman told Bill Hosokawa, "Disposal of these beautiful pieces of Japanese workmanship seemed to be a symbolic rite. It was as though a tangible cultural tie with Japan were being severed" (Hosokawa, 1982: 135).

The ties stayed broken inside the "relocation centers" into which the U.S. government moved about 120,000 Japanese Americans. True, a few young men practiced kendo, in part as a way of protesting their incarceration. Thus, there is a photo of California's Hiroji Miyohara in kendo armor at Heart Mountain (Ozawa, 1965). However, upon release from the camps, few Japanese Americans continued with kendo. Some were too busy resuming their lives. Others viewed kendo as too closely linked to Japanese militarism. Finally, everyone was intimidated by ongoing FBI surveillance. Therefore, in 1951, Heiji Okuda sold his vacant Seattle kendo hall to the Nisei Veterans Committee for $1,000 and lawful considerations (*Northwest Times,* October 31, 1951: 1; *Northwest Times,* December 19, 1951: 1; "Henry H. Okuda," n.d.).

The upshot was that in the mainland United States, kendo had to be reintroduced from scratch.[6] Southern California pioneers included Mori Torao. Mori had helped introduce kendo into California before the war. He had returned to Japan in 1940, but in 1951, his work brought him back to Los Angeles. He soon contacted his old kendo friends (notably Yutaka Kubota and Hiroji Miyahara) and subsequently organized a dojo at a local Buddhist church. In 1956, Mori took 17 Californians to participate in tournaments in Japan, and by 1965, there were at least 250 people practicing kendo in the greater Los Angeles area (Hazard, 2001: 4; Ozawa, 1965).

There was a kendo club at a Buddhist church in San Francisco during autumn 1952, but it did not last long and there is no record of its members. Therefore, the pioneers of the reintroduction of kendo in northern California were the returned servicemen Benjamin Hazard and Gordon Warner. Hazard had learned kendo while serving in Japan between 1948 and 1952, while Warner had done kendo in Japan before World War II and resumed it afterward as a form of physical therapy. (He lost a leg at Bougainville.) In the spring of 1953, Hazard and Warner were graduate students at the University of California at Berkeley, and with the support of fencing coach Arthur Lane and physical education dean Henry Stone, they established a kendo club.[7] A few months later, a separate kendo club was established at Dom and Helen Carollo's Danzan Ryu jujutsu school in Oakland. This club's founders included Hiroshi Uemoto, Yoshinori Miyata, Soichi Fujishima, and Seiichi Uemoto. In 1955, a northern California kendo federation was organized, and in 1956, annual tournaments with southern California began (Asawa, 1962; Hazard, 1973; Benjamin Hazard, personal communication, June 7, 2002).

Sargeant Martin Di Francisco started Washington's first postwar kendo club at Spokane's Fairchild Air Force Base in 1956. This club lasted until at least 1960 (*Fairchild Times,* June 29, 1956: 1; *Fairchild Times,* May 20, 1960: 5). In Seattle, kendo resumed sometime after September 1956. The pioneers were Umajiro Imanishi, Kazuo Shoji, and Kiyoshi Yasui. All three men had taught kendo in Seattle before the war, and their inspiration included seeing Japanese sailors practicing kendo aboard their ships. However, kendo did not return to Tacoma until the winter of 1966–1967 (the pioneer was Rod Omoto) or Portland until 1975 (the pioneers were Stephen Strauch and Tomotsu Osada) (Stroud, 2002; Tacoma Kendo Club, 2002).

By contrast, in Canada, kendo continued unabated throughout the war, then played an active role in building the modern Japanese Canadian identity. As in the United States, in December 1941, the Canadian government started arresting suspected Japanese sympathizers, and by September 1942, it had relocated most Japanese Canadians to internment camps. Although the United States guarded its "relocation centers" with soldiers and barbed wire, the Canadians guarded their equivalent "inland housing centres" with open space. However, while the U.S. camps had fences, they also had schools, electricity, and running water, amenities that most Canadian camps lacked until the summer of 1943. Furthermore, Japanese Canadians were told that they must either relocate away from the Pacific Coast or repatriate to Japan. The result was severe disagreement within the Japanese Canadian

Members of the kendo club at POW Camp 101, 1944–1945. Courtesy Joseph Svinth.

community—those who chose to relocate were called dogs and those who chose to repatriate were called fools (Takashima, 1971).

So far, there is little difference between the U.S. and Canadian experiences. However, here is a significant one. In early 1943, the U.S. Army began accepting Japanese American recruits. While some Japanese Americans opposed service on principle, no one said that volunteers were wrong for choosing to serve their country, or wished them bad luck. Therefore, by the end of the war, Japanese Americans viewed anything too closely tied to Japanese militarism, to include kendo, as somewhat unpatriotic. (Judo escaped this opprobrium because during the middle of 1943, it was made part of U.S. military training programs.) On the other hand, Canadian Forces refused to enlist Japanese Canadians until January 1945. Consequently, Japanese Canadians came to view kendo as a form of passive (and almost patriotic) resistance to racial prejudice and wartime hysteria.

One center of Canadian wartime kendo was Prisoner-of-War Camp 101, located near a railway stop in Ontario called Angler, inside what is today Neys Provincial Park. Hundreds of Japanese Canadian men were sent here in 1942 for protesting relocation, and in 1943, Motoo Matsushita, the former Vancouver kendo teacher, established "Mr. Matsushita's Lakeside Kendo Club." (The name was an ironic allusion to Angler's proximity to Lake Superior.) The Angler kendo club had maybe 50–60 members. Most had never done kendo before the war, but by the time they left, several were ranked first *dan*. Instructor Matsushita gave his own certificates to these people, as there was no access to the Japanese associations at the time.

Following his release in April 1946, Matsushita went to Moose Jaw, Saskatchewan, but after a couple years, he accepted relocation to Japan. Nonetheless, several of his students became leaders of postwar Canadian kendo. Of these, the most prominent is probably Kiyoshi Ono of Montreal.

Canada's inland housing centres also produced their share of postwar kendo practitioners. For example, from 1943 to 1945, kendo was openly taught in the towns of Kaslo, British Columbia, (J. V. Humphries School, 2002) and Raymond, Alberta. The Raymond instructor was Moriharu Tanigami. Tanigami returned to Steveston as soon as it was legal to do so (1950) and almost immediately joined with Rintaro Hayashi to reorganize the Steveston Kendo Club. Throughout the 1950s, Steveston kendo practitioners worked with members of the Steveston Judo Club to organize permanent training areas. In 1972, the City of Richmond, the Steveston Community Society, and the Japanese Canadian Community Association rewarded their efforts by building the Steveston Martial Arts Centre. The first structure of its kind outside Japan, and featuring judo, karate, aikido, kendo, and a public library, the Centre played an important role in preserving Japanese Canadian culture into the twenty-first century (City of Richmond Archives, 2002; Moriharu Tanigami, personal communication, June 19, 1999).

OLYMPIC GAMES AND JAPAN

Kano Jigoro

EDITOR'S INTRODUCTION

Kano Jigoro was both the founder of judo and a member of the International Olympics Committee, and from 1932 until his death in 1938, he was a leader of Japan's bid for the 1940 Olympics (Bernett, 1980).

Judo became an Olympic exhibition sport in 1964, and today one often hears that one of Kano's ambitions was to see judo in the Olympics. However, that is not quite true. Instead, as Kano told Britain's Gunji Koizumi, "My view on the matter, at present, is rather passive. If it be the desire of other member countries I have no objection. But I do not feel inclined to take any initiative" (Koizumi, 1947: 7). Nonetheless, Kano was a pioneer of sport in Japan (Guttmann and Thompson, 2001), and as such, he (perhaps unhappily) contributed toward judo becoming a sport rather than remaining a martial art.

It is more than 40 years ago that Baron Pierre de Coubertin together with a few people who had a similar idea, started the modern Olympic Games (Young, 1984). At the time of the Greeks it was an affair between Greek states, but the aim of the modern Olympic Games was to be an affair of the world.

First published in *Dai Nippon* (1936) (pp. 197–199). Copyright expired; in the public domain.

Japan's member of the International Olympic Committee, Kano Jigoro (left) with Canadian judo pioneer Shigetaka Sasaki at Lake Louise, Banff, Alberta, during July 1936. Courtesy Joseph Svinth.

In 1909 [French ambassador to Japan] H.E. Monsieur Gérard communicated to me one day the contents of a letter from Baron Pierre de Coubertin, who was at that time President of the International Olympic Committee:

> Since the time the Games were started the number of countries participating has gradually increased, but there is no country in the Far East which has yet joined. And he thinks that Japan is a country worthy of being represented, so he asked me to represent to Japan.

International committee members are chosen by vote, so I replied that if I were elected, I would represent Japan, being desirous of a revival of the Games from the view of both physical and spiritual culture. Then the report came that I was elected, and I consented to become a member. At that time I had a fair idea of what Olympic Games were, but I had no accurate knowledge of what had been done since its inauguration and what measures to take to fulfill a member's duties. While I was pondering over those things I got letters and a number of pamphlets from the Swedish

Olympic Committee inviting Japan to the 5th Olympiad to be held in Stockholm.

After reading those pamphlets I got a fairly good idea of what the Olympic Games were, and I was able to take a step towards fulfilling my duty as a member. First of all, I thought it necessary to organize an association which represents Japan in the Olympic Games. Even before this time athletic sports were being practiced here and there, but there was no organized body for the whole country. As I was the president of the Higher Normal School in Tokyo, I wrote to presidents and directors of several of the important educational institutes in Tokyo requesting them to send some competent persons to my college.

After consulting with such representatives I organized the Japan Amateur Athletic Association, and in 1912, after eliminating competitors from the different schools in Tokyo that desired to compete, I picked two entrants, Yahiko Mishima[1] from the Tokyo Imperial University and Shizo Kankuri from the Higher Normal College, one a sprinter and one from the Marathon. I sent these two competitors with a person who could take care of them, Mr. Omori who had lately come back from America, having studied physical education there, and I also followed them a few days later. These two young men, although they were our best runners at the time, had no success. After the Games these two young men travelled through the different countries of Europe, and I myself also went from one country to another to study physical education in Europe and America, and after coming back to Japan I reorganized the Japan Amateur Athletic Association and added all available competent people I could find to the staff. The next Olympiad, which was to be held in Berlin in 1916, was suspended on account of the Great War, so that the next Olympiad, the 7th, took place in Antwerp. This time we could send 14 competitors, including Kumagai and Kashio, both of whom were sufficiently recognized in lawn tennis [that is, they won medals].

In the 8th and 9th Olympiads Japan was represented by a larger number and more worthy participants, and at the time of the 10th Olympiad in Los Angeles we sent 131 competitors and 69 other people including officers, managers, coaches, etc.

In swimming we were ahead of all the competitors from all the different countries; and besides, in horsemanship and jumping and some other events we also showed remarkable success; and it was from that time that Japan became to be counted among the important countries in the field of athletics, and considering the number of years from our first entry, nobody can deny that Japan may rightly be considered a country of great future.

Kano Jigoro (left) and Shigetaka Sasaki at the Nitobe Memorial in Vancouver, British Columbia, shortly before Kano's death in May 1938. Courtesy Joseph Svinth.

It was in this same year [1932], at the time of the committee meeting in Los Angeles, that I was asked by the mayor of the city of Tokyo to read his letter of invitation to hold the 12th Olympiad in Tokyo. After reading the letter of the mayor I spoke of manifold reasons for holding the Games in Tokyo.

During the Games I spoke on different occasions why Tokyo should be the site of the 12th Olympiad, and for two consecutive years after the Los Angeles meeting I myself was present at the meetings and spoke to my colleagues of the manifold reasons for holding the 12th Olympiad in Japan. Out of these the most important one is, that, since its inauguration the Olympiads have been held either in Europe or in the United States of America, and never in other countries.

The modern Olympic Games has become an affair of the world and not of Europe and the United States, why shall we not hold the 12th Olympiad in Tokyo? The aim of the modern Olympic Games is to promote the physical condition of the whole world, certainly not only that of Europe and America, and also to spread the Olympic idea to countries outside of Europe and America. It is only by holding such Games in countries outside of countries already having had them, that the Olympic ideal can be fostered in those parts of the world. Since the time of its first entry, Japan has been true to the ideal of Olympicism, every time we are sending a larger number of competitors and we have encouraged the games, and every time we are sending better and better competitors.

We hope to hold the 12th Olympiad in Tokyo because we are very enthusiastic in the promotion of the Olympic ideal for holding the Games. One must be prepared to spend a large amount of money as well as people's energy, and that is no easy task—but we are prepared to do so because the 12th Olympiad falls in the year of the 2,600th anniversary of the founding of our Empire, and such an undertaking can most completely be carried out at such a time. We are going to hold an International Exposition on that occasion, but there has been talk among our colleagues that to hold the Olympic Games together with the International Exposition may prevent peoples' attention from concentrating on the Olympic Games. Attaching great importance to such a remark, we have decided to end the Exposition before the opening of the Games.

People may say that Japan is a country far from Europe, where the largest number of participating countries are situated, and many countries may find it inconvenient because of the expense of travel and the greater number of days that must be spent, and as the meeting is held generally in summer, Japanese summer being warmer than that of most other countries of Europe, most of the competitors of Europe may think the Japanese climate may not be favourable to them in doing their best. I think such an objection is not strong enough, because Japan is sending a larger and larger number of competitors to places very inconvenient from the point of expense and time. Can there be any reason why Japan should always bear the inconvenience, and European countries should go where it is convenient for them? If European countries urge faraway countries from Europe always to stand in an inconvenient position, does not that reason make faraway countries be severed from the world Olympic Games, and organize such Olympic Games or athletic meetings where countries nearer to one another form an independent group, and make the ideal of the modern Olympic Games become faded?[2] Hearing that notwithstanding the setbacks Japan has always been true to the ideal of Olympicism and has been participating with greater and greater enthusiasm in the world's Olympic Games, hearing that there are people who object to coming to Japan because Tokyo is far away, requiring larger expense and time, and consequently objecting to participating, there are already voices heard that these far away countries ought better to be severed from future Olympics and hold their own independent organizations.

Those who are true to the ideal of Olympicism should endeavour by all means to prevent faraway countries from running in such a direction. For many reasons, and even for this single reason, the 12th Olympiad should be held in Japan.

One great object the Olympic Games should try to attain by this kind of gathering of people of all nationalities, is that mutual understanding shall be promoted which conduces to the harmony and peace of the world. Difference in manner and custom has due reasons for its formation, and if one understands such reasons, what was once a cause of antipathy or dislike may become a reason for sympathy and love.

People are prone to think what they are accustomed to do is good and right, and whatever is foreign to them is mistaken or harmful. Therefore, a gathering of people for a common cause, which all of them participate in with interest, is likely to see the difference in other people with friendly feeling. It is always from noticing the difference in other people that we come to get hints for progress.

I deem therefore, very important that the differences among different people are recognized, and a hint for progress or bettering be detained from such a recognition. For this point of view of appreciating the differences in a friendly spirit, I firmly believe that the great gathering should be held in a country out of Europe and America where common civilization, manners and customs are so close together.

ORIGINS OF THE BRITISH JUDO ASSOCIATION, THE EUROPEAN JUDO UNION, AND THE INTERNATIONAL JUDO FEDERATION

Richard Bowen

INTRODUCTION

The years slip by and much that should be remembered is forgotten. This is a brief account of the creation of three judo organizations (one British, one European, and one global) over 50 years ago.

The story starts with Gunji Koizumi, who during the early 1930s suggested to a group of judo friends on the European continent that a union should be formed to facilitate international judo matters. Probably the concept originated earlier during discussions between Koizumi and Kano Jigoro, who made five visits to Koizumi's London judo club, the Budokwai, between 1920 and 1933.

Much is known about judo's founder Kano Jigoro, but what about Gunji Koizumi? Koizumi arrived in London in 1906 and some nine months later went to the USA. By 1910, he was back in London, where he set up an antique business. Although he never became a British citizen, he wished to contribute something to his adopted country, and so he organized at his own expense a martial arts society in London, the Budokwai, which opened its doors on January 26, 1918. This was, and is, a strictly amateur and democratic body, one run and owned by the members.

An earlier version appeared in *Journal of Asian Martial Arts* (1999) 8: 3 (pp. 42–53).

Gunji Koizumi, ca. 1948. Courtesy Richard Bowen.

In 1929, Western Europe's first international judo contests took place in Germany between the Budokwai and the Frankfurt-am-Main and Wiesbaden clubs. The initiative for this competition came from the Frankfurt Jiu-Jitsu Club. Although these started as inter-club matches, by 1931, they had assumed the character of full international contests. Within a year or two, Judo Instructional Summer Schools were taking place in Frankfurt, and it would have been at these that plans were made for some form of European union. A skeleton organization was indeed formed, but came to naught with the rise of the Nazis and the threat of war. In later years Koizumi was prone to say, "The European Judo Union was formed but never matured" (personal communication). At times, he would refer to this early organization as the First European Judo Union.

In passing, the instructors at the three or four prewar summer schools were G. Koizumi, Y. Tani, and M. Otani, all from the Budokwai; M. Kawaishi from Paris; Dr. Rhi from Switzerland; and Dr. Kitabatake from Berlin. All, with the possible exception of Dr. Rhi, were members of the Kodokan.

BRITISH JUDO ASSOCIATION

After World War II ended, Koizumi discussed with the Budokwai Committee the possibility of forming a British national judo body and of reviving a possible European organization. Early in 1948, he decided to act, and John Barnes, then chairman of the Budokwai, sent out invitations to a conference of all known British clubs. A further invitation went to all known judo and jujutsu clubs in Europe. These two conferences were timed to coincide with a Judo Summer School run by the Budokwai in London in July 1948, a suitable time for matters international as the first postwar Olympic Games were being held in the city.

The British conference took place in Committee Room A, at London University's Imperial College Union, Prince Consort Road, on Saturday, July 24, 1948. The meeting convened at 2:30 p.m.

The meeting examined a proposed constitution put forward by Koizumi which, after some amendments and additions, was unanimously adopted. This is not the place to set out the agreed constitution, but it could hardly be called lengthy, running to twenty-nine lines. How nice! With the British Judo Association (BJA) now formed, the meeting went on to elect committee members, chairman, secretary, and treasurer. But the treasurer had nothing to treasure, so Koizumi lent a few pounds to allow the baby Association to stagger forward.

EUROPEAN JUDO UNION

The Association then got down to discussing ideas for the forthcoming international conference on the proposed European Judo Union (EJU). A draft constitution was formulated for consideration at the international conference. And that was that, with the meeting closing at 5:30 p.m.— three hours to form the first amateur national judo association in the world.

The number of clubs attending gives an indication of the size of judo in Britain at that time. There were about 18 clubs affiliated to the Budokwai. Doubling that number gives the likely number of clubs in the country in 1948. A few years later, there were 110 clubs affiliated to the Budokwai and about 40 in the BJA. Subsequently, however, the number of clubs in Association gradually overtook the Budokwai affiliates.

On Monday, July 26, 1948, the International Conference was convened in the same Committee Room A at the Imperial College Union, commencing at 2:45 p.m. Only four votes were allowed, equaling the number of countries represented (Britain, Austria, Holland, and Italy, France being an

Second general meeting of the International Judo Federation in Zurich, August 30, 1952. Courtesy Richard Bowen.

observer). Leggett of the Budokwai was elected Chairman for the Conference, and Imperial College's Hylton Green was appointed scribe. The Budokwai's draft constitution, which was actually based on a proposed constitution from the thirties, was tabled. Leggett then explained that the object of the proposed Union was the standardization of judo rules and procedures and the establishment of an international body for arbitration.

It being generally agreed that the members did want to form a Judo Union, they went on to examine the draft constitution. A detailed examination followed, with each section being scrutinized, hacked about, taken out, put back in, altered, and put to the vote, all no doubt with varied expletives in various languages. At one point, France's de Jarmy tried to vote, until he was reminded that he was there as an observer and not as a member of the conference. By 5:25 p.m., everyone had enough, so the meeting was adjourned until the following Wednesday, giving the delegates time to recover and to examine further details at leisure.

The meeting resumed in the same Committee Room on Wednesday, July 28, at 2:30 p.m. Chew of the South London Judo Society joined the conference as a new delegate and Italy's Castella was unable to attend, but otherwise the delegates remained unaltered. Leggett continued to chair the conference and France's de Jarmy, who was allowed to express opinions but not to vote, continued to raise objections about certain points, although the delegates had approved of these. Finally, Britain put forward the motion: "That the European Judo Union be now formed on the basis of the Constitution as approved, and that all other European countries be circulated with a copy of it and be invited to join." This was seconded by Holland and approved unanimously.

THE FIRST GENERAL MEETING OF THE EJU

The members then opened the First General Meeting of the EJU and proceeded to the election of officers. This resulted in Leggett being appointed Chairman and Thieme of Holland Vice-Chairman. The next move was to form a Judo Council (a technical body as opposed to the General Committee). Those elected were Koizumi, Feldenkrais, Bonet-Maury, Mossom, and Leggett.

The French representative intervened with the suggestion that each of the important judo countries should be represented on the Council. As Chairman, Leggett replied that the purpose of the Council was not to represent national interests but to be composed of real judo experts. Just before the meeting closed, Holland issued a formal invitation to the EJU for the next General Meeting to be held in Holland. The meeting concluded at 4:30 p.m. with a vote of thanks to Britain for taking the initiative in organizing the Union. Shortly after the close of the meeting, Leggett relinquished the position of Chairman of the General Committee (but retained his position on the technical body), because mat judo was more important to him than was *kuchi waza* (mouth technique).

Because the position of Chairman was now vacant, it was suggested that Barnes should act as pro tempore Chairman until the Holland gathering. This was agreed. The first Constitution of the EJU was naturally more comprehensive than the 29 lines of the BJA's Constitution, so, including titles and subtitles, it ran to 68 lines. Once again, it was a triumph of judo over bureaucracy.

No doubt the creators of the first continental judo union then retired to the Union bar to celebrate, in the time-honored manner of judo folk everywhere.

THE SECOND GENERAL MEETING OF THE EJU

This took place in Bloemendaal, Holland, on October 29, 1949. Members from Britain, Holland, and Italy were present, and observers represented France. Denmark, which earlier had applied for membership to the Union, was unanimously elected.

Most of the discussions centered on the contest rules; it was decided that in international contests between Union members, the Kodokan contest rules should be used. The Italian was elected Chairman for the coming year with the Dane as the Vice-Chairman. Kawaishi of France and Rhi of Switzerland were elected to the Judo Council, the other members being Koizumi, Leggett, Bonet-Maury, Mossom, and Feldenkrais.

Subsequently, an account appeared in an official Union publication that claimed not only that this was the First Annual General Meeting, but that it was at this meeting where the Union was formed. The English version, which was accompanied by French and German versions, reads, "On 29.10.1949 in Bloemendaal (HOL) the EJU was founded and the following countries were present: Denmark, France, Great Britain, Holland and Italy. Mr Torti (ITA) was elected President" (Secretariat, 1976).

That the EJU was founded on that date and place is false.

An earlier paragraph in the same document says that a meeting took place in London on July 26, 1948, to prepare the basis for the foundation of the EJU. It is correct to write that a meeting took place, but the rest of the EJU report is also false; I have the minutes of the 1948 meeting. There was also a report ("Club News") in the October 1948 issue of the *Budok-wai Quarterly Bulletin* on the founding of the Union, and there is other documentary evidence. John Barnes, a vice-president, eventually took up the matter with the Union, and it is hoped that these errors, which surely are the result of inadequate research, have now been remedied in the official records.

THE THIRD GENERAL MEETING OF THE EJU

This took place in Venice on Sunday, October 29, 1950, with delegates from Italy, Britain, Holland, Belgium, Austria, and Switzerland, under the chairmanship of the Italians. It was thought that the term of chairmanship was too short so it was extended to four years. The General Committee was enlarged to include three vice-presidents and two advisors. A Briton and an Austrian were elected vice-presidents, with Dutch and Swiss as advisors. The third vice-presidency was left vacant pending the Chairman's invitation to France to join the Union.

I do not possess the minutes of this meeting, and although I do have a long report in three languages by Dr. Torti, this does not give the names of the delegates. It is certain that John Barnes represented Britain and Dr.

Uchimata. By Janet Bradley.

Torti, Italy. The identity of the others is yet to be resolved. France sent an observer in the person of Mr. Marcelin. Switzerland, Belgium, and Germany, were elected to membership of the Union, and a fourth language, German, was added to the official languages (French, Italian, and English) of the Union.

The French observer explained the failure of France to join the Union. France had four separate judo organizations: two amateur and two professional. As a consequence, there were difficulties in forming a single national body to represent France, and of course the Union would only accept a single national body. Similar trouble arose with Holland, where two organizations were competing for national supremacy. The Union solved this by rejecting the claims of one body for nonpayment of the Union fees, and accepting the other body as the new representative for Holland. This General Committee meeting was relatively short, but not so the meeting of the Judo Council, which ended five hours after the other group's discussion had finished. The Council went through the contest rules with the diligence of an elephant searching for fleas. It ended with the adoption of the Budokwai's contest rules, which were based on those of the Kodokan, with some minor alterations of wording to avoid ambiguity.

Things change little. After offering some praise for the British attitude to judo, the report of the Chairman, Dr. Torti, continued with, "though I deplore their lack of a federal outlook." As one of the bloody-minded islanders, who am I to contradict his judgment?

A few weeks after the Venice conference, the French managed to reconcile their internal differences and applied to join the Union. At about the same time, Argentina also applied, with others outside Europe having similar thoughts. The Statutes of the Union had already been widened to allow for this. Europe was very stretchable in those days.

THE FOURTH GENERAL MEETING OF THE EJU AND THE FIRST GENERAL MEETING OF THE INTERNATIONAL JUDO FEDERATION

This important meeting was held in a private room at Choy's Chinese Restaurant, Frith Street, Soho, London, on Thursday, July 12, 1951, no doubt to the comforting rattle of chopsticks. Eight countries were represented: Italy, Britain, Belgium, France, Holland, Germany, Austria, and Switzerland.

The desire of Argentina to join (and with others outside the European ambit just as keen) required serious thought. A proposal, which had been circulated earlier with a suggested constitution, was tabled. After discussion and agreement on the proposed constitution for a new organization, the EJU was formally dissolved and replaced by an International Judo Federation. Instead of holding individual elections for officials to serve on the new Federation, it was agreed that the officials of the now extinct EJU.

take up similar positions on the new body. How sane, how peaceful, how logical!

The other main subject was the position of the judo colossus in the Far East—Japan. Koizumi, who had been corresponding with Kano Risei (the president of the Kodokan and son of the founder) read a letter from him, in which Kano explained that he regretted being unable to attend the meeting or send a delegate. The letter contained the suggestion that the headquarters of a world federation should be in Tokyo. The meeting declined this on the grounds that Japan was too distant. Furthermore, Japan was not a member of the Federation.

THE SECOND GENERAL MEETING OF THE INTERNATIONAL JUDO FEDERATION AND THE RESURRECTION OF THE EJU

This meeting, a real humdinger, was held in Zurich, Switzerland, on Saturday, August 30, 1952. It started at 10:00 a.m. and continued, apart from breaks for food, to midnight; "discussion raged!" (Barnes, 1952) The outstanding problem was how to find a way for Japan to enter the Federation. The problem was the same as France had earlier faced—there was not a single national body. It was finally decided to offer Kano Risei the presidency of the International Judo Federation (IJF). A diplomat acting on behalf of the Japanese Ambassador, whom Kano had asked to represent him at the conference, thanked the meeting.

With the presidency of the Federation now in the hands of Japan, the conference dealing with the Federation came to an end and discussions switched to Europe. But without a Union nothing could be done, so the EJU was reestablished. Bonet-Maury expressed the wish that a Frenchman should be elected its president. His reasoning was that France's importance in Europe was parallel with that of Japan in Asia, that it was essential for the progress of the judo movement in Europe that France assume this important role, and failing this, France might not take a very active part in the Union. This subtle, diplomatic, and canny statement resulted in an Italian being elected to the presidency. Members from France and Britain were elected vice-presidents with a Belgian as treasurer.

Among other problems was the application of East Germany to join the EJU. This was temporarily solved by admitting East Germany as an Observer for one year, without voting rights but with the right to participate in competitions. Further discussions ranged about the question of weight categories, which Britain, France, Belgium, and Holland opposed. A French

Trevor Leggett, 1950s. Courtesy Richard Bowen.

proposal was eventually adopted, this being that those nations who wished to have weight category competitions do so in their own countries, and in the European Championships special weight category events should be held for them which do not interfere with the customary non-weight category competitions of Britain, France, Belgium, and Holland.

"On more than one occasion, differences of opinion in four or five quarters occasioned a full scale battle of words, the contestants excitedly flinging their arms in the air. Suddenly, a split-second silence. Somebody smiled and the whole room dissolved into laughter!" (Barnes, 1952).

Strictly speaking, some were not delegates but instead were present as advisers or in some other capacity. Koizumi was one example of this, being present as a Technical Adviser, Barnes being the official BJA delegate.

The young lions of the time took little interest in the first tottering steps of the three new organizations. Apart from lacking the experience and seniority necessary, they were far more interested in forwarding their personal prowess on the mat. This was certainly the case in Britain, and it is unlikely that their counterparts on the European continent differed. It was during the 1950s that Leggett encouraged and helped many on the trek to Japan, some 16 from the Budokwai including myself. France provided the next largest number of "Exiles," with other countries supplying smaller numbers. But to return to the Zurich meeting of 1952. Koizumi, who had been at a separate technical meeting, was invited to address the delegates, and among other things, he warned, "All these [organizational] problems arose from the basis of competition—championships and international contests. For a cure, I should like to advise you to extract this tooth—that is, to do away altogether with championships and international competition." A few words of explanation are required here. Koizumi was not against contests per se. Like Kano Jigoro, he was against championships because they tend to deceive people into believing that contests of this nature are the ends rather than the means of training (Koizumi, 1947). Contests are a form of training and nothing more. A failure to understand this is really a failure to fully understand judo. For those who never had the privilege of knowing Koizumi; he was teaching until the day before he died in April 1965. Altogether he spent over 64 years in judo and, apart from nine months in 1906 and 1907, he was a strict amateur throughout his life. At his death he held the Kodokan grade of eighth *dan.*

Much more could be written about the early years, but this short article will suffice to acquaint readers of the origins of the three organizations. Before closing, here is an opinion from Mr. Somsak of Bangkok, a Kodokan third *dan,* written in 1948:

Emphatically Judo should not be a mass movement. Its confinement to a select membership will curtail abuse which will result if it is an open affair to all and sundry. To cover up their inferiority complex or to feed their egotistical sense of importance those with a rudimentary grasp of it are liable to make a detrimental use of this art, thus violating the Kano principles. It should not be taken up lightly and treated as any other game or sport. Just look what has been done to wrestling. (Letter to E. J. Harrison, in author's collection)

Was he right? Many years later, I wrote to the General Committee of one of the three bodies about its abuse of Kano's principles, and particularly its efforts in spreading the falsehood that Kano wanted judo in the Olympic games. I concluded, "The Committee is striving to attain mediocrity—without much success." The remark could apply to all three.

Who started the canard that Kano wanted judo in the Olympic Games is unknown. But I suspect the matter can be laid at the doors of the organizations noted in my article. And so-called authority after authority has contributed blindly to this without troubling to research the matter.

THE EVOLUTION OF
TAEKWONDO FROM
JAPANESE KARATE

Eric Madis

Taekwondo (*t'aegwondo,* kicking and punching way/art) is a Korean martial art and combative sport distinguished by kicks, hand strikes, and arm
blocks. Its sanctioned history claims that taekwondo is 2,000 years old,
that it is descended from ancient *hwarang* warriors, and that it has been
significantly influenced by a traditional Korean kicking game called
taekyon. However, the documented history of taekwondo is quite different. By focusing solely on what can be documented, the following essay
links the origins of taekwondo to twentieth-century Shotokan, Shudokan,
and Shito-ryu karate and shows how the revised history was developed to
support South Korean nationalism.

Imperial Japan began its domination of Korea and Manchuria in the
1890s. Both Russia and China unsuccessfully attempted to control Japan's
expansion into the region. The Japanese victory in the Russo-Japanese
War (1904–1905) resulted in the Treaty of Portsmouth, which placed
Korea under the "guidance, protection and control" of Japan (Harrison,
1910: 499). Finally, on August 29, 1910, King Sunjong (ruled 1907–1910)
of the Yi Dynasty (1389–1910) was forced to abdicate his throne, thereby
completing Japan's annexation of Korea (Lee and Wagner, 1984: 313).

Japan's colonization of Korea lasted from 1910 to 1945. Japanese policy toward the Korean populace was guided by factors such as Japan's
economy, Japan's international situation, and the policies of individual
governors-general (Lee and Wagner, 1984: 346). Therefore, treatment of

A scene of breaking eight pieces of tile with the fist, circa 1958. Courtesy Joseph Svinth.

Koreans varied from paternalism to severe repression (Breen, 1998: 103–115; Korean Embassy, 2000). At all times, however, Koreans were treated as second-class citizens.

Under Japanese rule, the Koreans were compelled to participate in Japanese imperialism (Breen, 1998: 105). Nearly one million Koreans emigrated to Manchuria (Schumpeter, 1940: 70). Some worked in agriculture while others worked in mining, petroleum, and heavy industry. Furthermore, low-status security forces in Manchuria largely comprised Koreans (Jones, 1949: 33). The primary employer was the South Manchurian Railway, a huge, multifaceted Japanese company, similar to the British East

India Company, which spearheaded Japanese expansion into Manchuria and northern China (Harries and Harries, 1991).

By 1940, another million Koreans resided (sometimes involuntarily) in Japan (Schumpeter, 1940: 70), and during World War II, this number grew to as many as 2.4 million (Chin, 2001: 59). The majority of them worked in factories or coal mines. Many Koreans served in the Japanese military, while others involuntarily served Japanese war efforts as laborers or "comfort women" (Breen, 1998: 113)

Conversely, some affluent Koreans chose to send their children to preparatory high schools and universities in Japan, both for education and to establish the peer relationships necessary for success in Japanese-dominated society (Lee Jeong-kyu, 2002).

OKINAWAN KARATE COMES TO JAPAN

After participating in an exhibition of Japanese martial arts in April 1922, Okinawan educator and karate adept Funakoshi Gichin (1868–1957) remained in Tokyo. Later that year, Funakoshi began teaching karate at the Okinawan student dormitory *(meisi juku)* at Japan University in Tokyo (Funakoshi, 1975: 69–71). Interest in karate grew steadily, allowing Funakoshi to establish a training hall (Japanese, *dojo;* Korean, *dojang*) at Keio University in 1924 and another at Tokyo University in 1926. Between 1928 and 1935, Funakoshi established more than 30 *dojo,* most of which were at educational institutions (Cook, 2001: 76; Funakoshi, 1975: 75).

Growing interest in karate encouraged other Okinawan instructors to move to Japan. Examples include Uechi Kanbun (1877–1948) in 1924, Mabuni Kenwa (1889–1952) in 1928, Miyagi Chojun (1888–1953) in 1928, and Toyama Kanken (1888–1966) in 1930 (McCarthy and McCarthy, 1999: 18, 126). Mabuni established *dojo* in Osaka, including several at universities. Toyama established the Tokyo Shudokan in 1930 and taught at Nihon University. It was in these Japanese university clubs that some Korean students studied the arts that would become the foundation of future Korean karate styles.

The introduction of karate to Okinawan public schools began in 1901 (Bishop, 1989: 102). The pioneer was Itosu Ankoh (1832–1915). A leader and innovator from the Shorin-ryu (Shaolin school) karate lineage, Itosu not only modernized but created many of the forms (Japanese, *kata;* Korean, *hyung*) that are practiced in karate today. Examples include the *pinan* (peaceful mind; Japanese, *heian;* Korean, *pyongahn*) *kata,* which were a series of five forms designed to advance students from beginning to intermediate level

Funakoshi Gichin, 1922. Courtesy Patrick McCarthy.

in a class setting (Cook, 2001: 52). Itosu also taught and mentored many of the major figures of modern karate, including Funakoshi, Mabuni, and Toyama. In addition, Itosu embraced the promotion of karate as a means of developing Japanese spirit *(yamato damashi),* which contributed to karate's acceptance and popularity in Japan (Bishop, 1989: 103; Cook, 2001: 25)

Yabu Kentsu (1866–1937), who was a student of Matsumura Sokon (1809–1901) and Itosu, also had a profound influence on modern karate training. A former officer in the Japanese army, Yabu introduced many procedures still practiced in karate schools worldwide, including the Korean styles. These innovations included the following:

- Bowing upon entering the training hall
- Lining up students in order of rank

Yabu Kentsu, about 1927. Courtesy the Yabe/Yasui Family collection.

- Seated meditation (a Buddhist practice further developed in Japan as a result of kendo influence)[1]
- Sequenced training (warm-up exercises, basics, forms, sparring)
- Answering the instructor with loud acknowledgment
- Closing class with formalities similar to opening class (Cook, 2001: 26–28, 52–53; Donahue, 1993)

Most of these procedures already had been implemented in judo and kendo training and reflect a blending of European militarism and physical culture with Japanese neo-Confucianism, militarism, and physical culture (Abe, Kiyohara, and Nakajima, 1990/2000; Friday, 1994; Guttmann and Thompson, 2001). However, these procedures did not exist in China, or in Okinawan karate before Yabu; neither were they part of *taekyon* practice in Korea (Pederson, 2001: 604).

Pioneers and promoters of karate in Japan, several of whom were also influential in the development of karate in Korea, ca. 1934. Left to right: Toyama Kanken, Ohtsukua Hironori, Mr. Sato, Funakoshi Gichin, Motobu Choki, Mabuni Kenwa, Nakasone Genwa, and Taira Shinken. Courtesy Patrick McCarthy.

Yabu was a primary assistant of Itosu in Okinawa. Thus, his methods were widely adopted by other Okinawan instructors in Japan, including Mabuni, Funakoshi, and Toyama. These training procedures, which were not found in karate books, set the standard for modern Korean karate training and clearly indicate Japanese influence.

The use of belted white cotton martial arts uniforms (Japanese, *dogi;* Korean, *dobak*) is relatively recent, having been introduced in Japan during the late nineteenth century by judo founder Kano Jigoro (Cunningham, 2002; Harrison, 1955/1982: 43–44). Funakoshi modeled the designs of his karate uniforms after Kano's judo uniforms and introduced them into his classes around 1924 (Cook, 2001: 62; Guttmann and Thompson, 2001, 147; McCarthy and McCarthy, 2001: 130). Before these uniforms, students practiced in loose-fitting everyday clothes or, in subtropical Okinawa, as little clothing as possible. Anyway, modern taekwondo uniforms are essentially identical to the ones used in karate, providing further evidence of Japanese influence.

THE ESTABLISHMENT OF THE MAJOR KOREAN SCHOOLS

Before the Korean War (1950–1953), the Republic of Korea's (ROK) six major karate *(kongsoodo)* organizations were the Chungdohwe, Songmookwan, Yunmookwan, YMCA Kwonbup Bu, Jidokwan, and Moodukwan. The organizational leaders made many attempts to develop standards and unity, and generally, good relations existed between *kwan* (organizations, institutes). Most of the leaders of these organizations had studied karate in Japan, and all taught curriculums that were karate based. At that time, Japanese training was respected within the Korean martial arts community; consequently, there was no need or desire to conceal it (Capener and Perez, 1998).

During the Korean War, many Koreans fled from Seoul to Pusan. During this period, *kwan* leaders maintained communications by establishing the Korean Kongsoodo Association. Indeed, the Korean Kongsoodo Association's first president, Jo Young-joo (Kang and Yi, 1999: Chapter 2, Section 2), had been president of the *mindan* (literally, "public group," but meaning a Korean residents' association) in Japan (Jinsoku, 1956) and was himself a practitioner of judo (Burdick, 1997/1999).

Immediately following the Korean War, there was a period of disunity among the *kwan.* This started with the withdrawal of Hwang Kee and the new Chungdokwan director, Son Duk-sung, from the Korean Kongsoodo Association. Hwang, for example, attempted to form the Korean Tangsoodo Association (*tangsoodo* is an alternative name for karate) and join the Korean Amateur Athletic Association.

The following provides some background regarding each of these major organizations.

Chungdokwan

Lee Won-kuk (born 1907) was possibly the first Korean student to study karate. Lee moved to Tokyo in 1926 to attend high school. (Korean children started school at about age 11. Consequently, they also went to high school later.) He subsequently majored in law at Chuo University. At Chuo, he studied Shotokan karate under Funakoshi Gichin and his son Yoshitaka (Gigo). Since the Chuo University *dojo* was founded after 1928 but before 1935 (Cook, 2001: 76), this suggests that Lee began studying karate during the early 1930s.

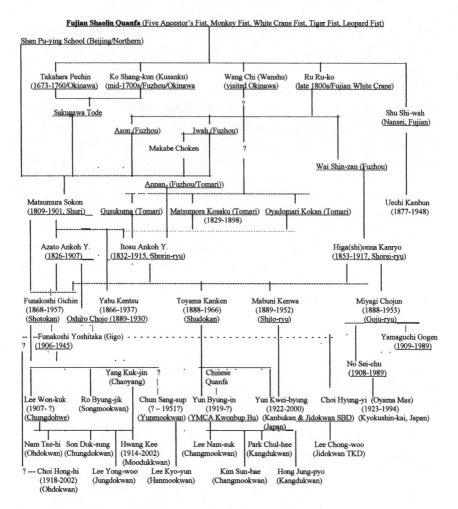

Korean Karate Lineage Chart for The Evolution of Taekwondo from Japanese Karate. Copyright © Eric Madis 2002. Courtesy of Eric Madis.

Although Lee has not specified his Shotokan rank, several clues allow an estimation of second or third *dan* (degree of black belt). Noted Shotokan instructor and historian Kase Taiji states that, in 1944, only three students (Hayashi, Hironishi, and Uemura) held fourth *dan* rank. Kase remembers only one Korean with second *dan* rank, who later returned to Korea (Graham Noble, personal communication, July 2000). Subsequently, Lee was the acknowledged senior student of Shotokan in Korea.

After returning to Korea in 1944, Lee received permission to teach karate, first to Japanese nationals and later to a select group of Koreans at the Yungshin School gymnasium in Seoul (Kang and Yi, 1999: Chapter 1, Section 1–1). Lee named his organization the *Chungdohwe* (Blue Wave Association), which became known as the *Chungdokwan* in 1951. Lee called his art *tangsoodo* (China hand way) (Hwang, 1995: 26; Massar and St. Cyrien, 1999). The name was the Korean pronunciation of Funakoshi's mid-1920s spelling of "karate-do" using the Tang/China character.

As Korea's leading Shotokan-trained instructor, Lee played an important part in Korean karate development from 1944–1947.

In those days, training at the Chungdohwe generally reflected the training Lee received with Funakoshi Gigo. For example, it emphasized strong basics and forms, used the striking post (Japanese: *makiwara;* Korean: *tal yul bong*), and included one- and three-step sparring drills (Cook, 2001: 76–96; Lee, 1997; Massar and St. Cyrien, 1999). As Lee has said:

> The lessons were popular and many people wanted the training. We had to be careful to recruit and keep only the best, most highly motivated students. The students we kept included some of the prominent figures in modern taekwondo. We worked hard to keep up the quality of instruction and our students, and to promote tangsoodo as a positive influence in Korean society. Our main objective was to instill discipline and honor in young people left without strong moral guidance in those troubled times. (Lee, 1997, 47–48)

In 1947, the head of Korea's national police, Yun Cae, approached Lee with an offer from the ROK President Rhee Syngman (Yi Sung-man). If Lee could convince his entire 5,000-member institute *(kwan)* to join Rhee's political party, he would be appointed Minister of Internal Affairs. Lee refused. According to Lee, "I was concerned that the government's motive for enrolling 5000 martial artists in the president's party was not to promote justice, so I politely declined the offer" (Lee, 1997, 48).

Immediately, Lee was accused of being pro-Japanese and the leader of an assassin group. This is ironic because, according to the noted Korean scholar Lee Jeong-kyu, "during the 12 years of Syngman Rhee's administration (1948–1960), 83% of 115 cabinet ministers were Japanese agents or collaborators under Japanese colonial rule" (Lee Jeong-kyu, 2002). Soon after, Lee, his wife, and several of his top students were arrested.

After his release in 1950, Lee continued to feel threatened by the political climate, so he relocated to Japan (Lee, 1999; Massar and St. Cyrien,

Koreans breaking three pieces of 1-inch board, late 1950s. Courtesy Joseph Svinth.

1999). His absence, combined with Korean War disruption, led to some of his senior students establishing their own institutes. These included Hwang Kee, *Moodukkwan;* Son Duk-sung, *Chungdokwan;* Kang Suh-chang; *Kukmookwan;* Choi Hong-hi, *Ohdokwan;* Lee Yong-woo, *Jung-dokwan;* and Ko Jae-chun, *Chungryongkwan* (Kang and Yi, 1999: Chapter 1, Section 1; Lee, 1997; Massar and St. Cyrien, 1999).

Songmookwan

During the late 1930s, while attending a Tokyo university, Ro Byung-jik (dates unknown) received first *dan* ranking in Shotokan karate from Funakoshi. Ro subsequently returned to Korea. Exactly when is not known, but Lee Won-kuk has stated that he met Ro in 1940 in Tokyo and that Ro worked as a policeman in Seoul during World War II. In any event, on March 11, 1944, Ro opened a *dojang* in Kaesong (now North Korea), calling it the *Songmookwan* (Martial Life Institute) (Losik, 1999). *Song* also means "pine" and alludes to Ro's prior Shotokan (Pine Wave Institute) training (Funakoshi, 1975: 84–85; Kang and Yi, 1999: Chapter 1, Section 5).

Despite his close association with his senior, Lee Won-kuk, Ro called his art *kongsoodo,* meaning, "empty hand way," rather than *tangsoodo,* meaning "China hand way" (Hwang, 1995: 26; Kang and Yi, 1999: Chapter 1, Section 5). The name preferences are significant, as they reflect changes that occurred in Japan during the years that Lee and Ro studied Shotokan karate.[2]

Owing to Kaesong's underdevelopment and remoteness, the Songmookwan soon closed. It reopened in 1946 at the Kwandukjung archery school in Kaesong. It is unclear if this newer *dojang* closed before or after the establishment of the People's Democratic Republic of Korea on September 9, 1948. However, Ro relocated to Pusan in 1950, where he served as executive director of the Korean Kongsoodo Association. In 1953, Ro reestablished the Songmookwan again in Seoul. True to its Shotokan karate roots, training in Songmookwan emphasized basics, forms, *makiwara* training, and traditional sparring (Kang and Yi, 1999: Chapter 1, Section 5).

Yunmookwan

During Japanese occupation, the Japanese government allowed Koreans to practice judo and kendo. Consequently, in 1931, Lee Kyung-suk (dates unknown) founded a judo school called the Chosun Yunmookwan (Losik, 2001). During the 1940s, Lee hired Chun Sang-sup (dates unknown) to teach judo and *kongsoodo.* Chun had gone to school in Japan, and there he studied judo during high school and karate during college. Although virtually nothing has been published about Chun's Japanese karate experience, recent evidence reveals that he attended either Toyo University or Takushoku University.[3] This would indicate that he studied either Shitoryu or Shotokan karate. Indeed, a noticeable Shotokan influence has remained from the Yunmookwan to its predecessor (the Jidokwan), suggesting that Chun studied at Takushoku University with Funakoshi.

After Korean independence, Chun assumed leadership of the *kwan,* reopening it March 3, 1946. He named it the *Yunmookwan Kongsoodo Bu* (Kang and Yi, 1999: Chapter 1, Section 2).

From 1946 to 1949, the Yunmookwan and the Chungdohwe were the predominant Korean karate schools (Hwang, 1995: 26). As Yunmookwan membership grew, Chun hired Yun Byung-in and eventually Yun Kweibyung as senior instructors (Lee Se-ree, 2002; Losik, 2001). Both of these individuals had studied under Toyama and had distinguished themselves in Japan. Chun disappeared during the Korean War. Reports vary from his abduction to his volunteering for a mission into North Korea (Kang and Yi, 1999: Chapter 1, Section 2; Park, 1989: 4).

In 1950, Yun Kwei-byung assumed leadership of the *kwan* and renamed it the *Jidokwan*.[4] After returning to Seoul in 1953, another Yunmookwan student, Lee Kyo-yun, taught *tangsoodo* in several locations, eventually establishing the *Hanmookwan* in 1956 (Kang and Yi, 1999: Chapter 1, Section 8).

YMCA Kwonbup Bu

Yun Byung-in (1919–?) was raised for eight years in Manchuria (Kimm, 2000), where he studied *quanfa* (Chinese, fist art; Korean, *kwonbup;* Japanese, *kenpo*). He also reportedly studied *quanfa* in Shanghai (Kimm, 2000), which had a large martial arts community during the 1920s and 1930s.

Neither Yun nor his students have specified his Chinese instructor(s) or style(s). However, based on Yun's legacy, his training appears to have included *changquan* (long fist) and Yang *taijiquan,* two styles that were taught liberally to non-Chinese during the early twentieth century (Hsu, 1986; Harvey Kurland, personal communication, March 21, 2000).

In 1937, Yun enrolled at Nihon University in Tokyo, where Toyama reportedly taught karate to Yun in exchange for *quanfa* lessons. Toyama later included *taijiquan* in his curriculum for advanced students (International Shudokan Karate Association, 2002). Yun became captain of Nihon University's karate team and was awarded fourth or fifth *dan* (depending on the source) and a master's certificate by Toyama (International Shudokan Karate Association, 2001; Kang and Yi, 1999: Chapter 1, Section 4). According to Choi Hong-hi, Yun also taught karate and *quanfa* on a Tokyo YMCA rooftop (Kimm, 2000).

Yun returned to Korea in 1945. On September 1, 1946, Yun began teaching *kongsoodo* and *kwonbup* at Kungsung Agricultural High School (Burdick, 1997/1999). Shortly thereafter, he also began teaching at the Yunmookwan and, in addition, established his own school, the *Kwonbup Bu,* at the Jong Ro YMCA in Seoul (Kang and Yi, 1999: Chapter 1, Section 4).

Evidence exists that Yun taught some Chinese forms (Yates, 1991) and that he varied students' training according to body size (Kang and Yi, 1999: Chapter 1, Section 4). Otherwise, no evidence exists of a curriculum that included Chinese training methods, such as *qigong* (energy mastering), push hands, sticky hands, and specific conditioning, all of which make the

Koreans breaking 10 roofing tiles, late 1950s. Courtesy Joseph Svinth.

forms applicable. Instead, Yun's legacy indicates a karate-based curriculum. In addition, Yun's assistant was Lee Nam-suk (1925–2000), whose primary martial arts experience reportedly consisted of self-study of karate from a Funakoshi text (Dussault and Dussault, 1993).

Like his friend Chun Sang-sup, Yun disappeared during the Korean War. His students Lee Nam-suk and Kim Sun-bae reopened his school after the war in 1953, renaming it the *Changmookwan*. In 1956, Yun's students Park Chul-hee and Hong Jung-pyo separated from the Changmookwan and established the *Kangdukkwan* (Kang and Yi, 1999: Chapter 1, Section 4).

Jidokwan

Yun Kwei-byung (1922–2000) began his karate study while attending high school in Osaka, Japan. His teacher was Shito-ryu founder Mabuni Kenwa. Yun continued karate study under Toyama Kanken while doing undergraduate and graduate studies in veterinary medicine at Nihon University in Tokyo (Takaku Kozi, personal communication, October 12, 2000).

Because of his education, refinement, and karate skill, Yun distinguished himself in Japan. Therefore, although many Koreans studied with Toyama, he is one of just two to have received a master certificate (Takaku Kozi, personal communication, October 12, 2000; International Shudokan Karate Association, 2001). In addition, he was reportedly awarded seventh *dan* by Toyama (Losik, 2001). Considered an innovator in both sparring skills and sparring with protective armor (Nakamura, 2000), Yun soon attracted a sizable following (Nagashima Toshi-ichi, personal communication, November 19, 1999).

In 1940, Yun established the *Kanbukan* (Korean Martial Arts Institute) in Tokyo. This school, now known as the Renbukai, offered classes in karate and open exchange between different martial arts styles (Marchini and Hansen, 1998). Today, Yun is one of very few Koreans found on Japanese karate lineages, although his name is usually transliterated as "In Gihei" or "Yun Gekka."[5]

Yun was an active member of the Korean residents' association in Japan *(mindan)*. Even during World War II, he had a large banner on the Kanbukan that read, "Alliance for the Promotion of Establishing the Republic of Korea" (Jinsoku, 1956).

In 1948, Yun returned to Korea (Nakamura, 2000) to teach animal husbandry at Konkuk University (World Karate Championships, 1970). He later became the Yunmookwan's chief instructor, as well as founder and coach of the karate teams at both Konkuk and Korea Universities.

Following Chun Sang-sup's disappearance in 1950, Yun became director of the Yunmookwan, which he renamed the *Jidokwan* (Wisdom Way Institute) (Losik, 2001). Because of the chaos caused by the Korean War, regular training at all schools was disrupted. Therefore, most *kwan,* including the Jidokwan, are considered to have been reestablished in 1953.

In 1961, the Jidokwan joined Hwang Kee's Korean Subakdo Association, and, with the Moodukkwan, it brought Korean karate teams to Japan in 1961, 1964, and 1970 for goodwill competitions (Hwang, 1995: 39, 70; World Karate Championships, 1970). However, a split in the Jidokwan occurred in 1967, when senior instructor Lee Chong-woo (born 1928) led a group of Jidokwan members to join the Korean Taekwondo Association (Kang and Yi, 1999: Chapter 1, Section 2).

Moodukkwan

Hwang Kee (1914–2002), founder of the *Moodukkwan* (Martial Virtue Institute), originally called his art *hwasoodo* (flower hand art). By his own account, he built this art from three sources: 15 months study of *quanfa,* self-study of *taekyon* as a youth, and self-study of books on Okinawan karate (Hwang, 1995: 9–18).

In *The History of Moodukkwan* (Hwang, 1995: 12–14), Hwang stated that he studied *quanfa* with a Chinese instructor named Yang Kuk-jin from May 1936 until August 1937. This training took place in Chaoyang[6] while Hwang was an employee of the South Manchurian Railway (Hwang, 1995: 12). He stated specifically that his training consisted of the northern Shaolin *tam tui* (springing legs) exercise, the Yang *taijiquan* form, and exercises for conditioning and mastering basics (Hwang, 1995: 14).

In a 1990 interview, Hwang stated that he studied "the northern Yang style of kung fu" with Yang (Liedke, 1990). As Hwang described Yang as being around 50 years of age in 1936 (Hwang, 1995: 12), his birth date would have been in the 1880s. Therefore, he should be (but is not) a recognizable name in Yang lineage (Draeger and Smith, 1969: 35–39; Robert Smith, personal communication, December 31, 1999). Unfortunately, Hwang did not provide his instructor's name in Chinese characters, which would facilitate the verification of his existence and his place in the Yang lineage (Robert Smith, personal communication, December 31, 1999). Consequently, many in Korea's martial arts community doubted Hwang's claims of *quanfa* training, based on lack of evidence (Kang and Yi, 1999: Chapter 1, Section 3). Traditional Moodukkwan curriculum is devoid of Chinese training, with the exception of a *changquan* ("long fist") form and a Yang *taijiquan* form, which are taught only to high-ranking masters (Boliard, 1989).

Hwang further stated that from 1939 to 1945 he studied Okinawan karate books (Hwang, 1995: 16, 18). However, he has not stated specifically that he learned forms from books or which books he studied. Many Moodukkwan forms are nearly identical to, but contain movements that clearly predate, early Shotokan versions (Thomas, 1988). This is true whether comparing the forms shown in Funakoshi's 1922 and 1935 texts, or watching documentary film of circa 1930 showing Funakoshi at Keio University (Warrener, 2001).[7] Although various early karate books were available to Hwang at this time (Noble, 1996b), few offered adequate descriptions and illustrations, and none displayed what would later become Moodukkwan advanced forms. That the Moodukkwan used Shotokan-based class structure, forms, and training methods reinforces Lee Won-kuk's claims that Hwang studied at the Chungdohwe (Lee, 1997; Massar and St. Cyrien, 1999). Finally, Hwang was friendly with both Chungdohwe and Yunmookwan instructors (Hwang, 1995: 28), and he may have studied with them.

200   MARTIAL ARTS IN THE MODERN WORLD

Some sources (Loke, 2002) have suggested that Hwang studied with the future Renbukai and All-Japan Karate-do Federation president Kondo Koichi (1929–1967). These rumors apparently started because of Hwang's association with Kondo (Graham Noble, personal communication, September 15, 1998) and his mention of Kondo in his books (Hwang, 1995: 40; Hwang, 1978). However, Kondo's lifelong associate and Renbukai successor Nagashima Toshi-ichi states that Kondo, who began karate study in 1947, was Yun's student at the Kanbukan (personal communication, November 19, 1999). Furthermore, Renbukai spokesperson Takaku Koji states that Kondo first met Hwang in 1961 (personal communication, October 12, 2000).

Hwang made two attempts to establish *hwasoodo* classes at the Ministry of Transportation (his employer), but in both instances his small group of students soon resigned. According to Hwang, this was because Korean students lacked appreciation for Chinese-based arts (Hwang, 1995: 24–26).

If these classes are considered the Moodukkwan's inception, then it was founded on November 9, 1945. If not, then its inception dates to 1947, when Hwang reformed the Moodukkwan. It was at this time that he also changed the name of his art from *hwasoodo* to *tangsoodo* (Hwang, 1995: 26).

Taking advantage of space made available to him at little or no cost by his employer, Hwang established many schools along railroad lines. From the standpoint of expansion, this gave the Moodukkwan an advantage over other *kwan* (Kang and Yi, 1999: Chapter 1, Section 3). Other *kwan* accused the Moodukkwan of fostering its growth through overly generous standards of admission, discipline, and promotion (Kang and Yi, 1999: Chapter 2, Section 5). Therefore, despite considerable leadership, a legacy of many notable students, and a reputation for upholding tradition (Kang and Yi, 1999: Chapter 1, Section 3), Hwang often found himself in conflict with the Korean martial arts establishment. Numerous attempts in the 1950s and 1960s to include the Moodukkwan in the taekwondo community were unsuccessful.

In 1960, Hwang formed the Korean Subakdo Association (KSA), which would soon include Yun's Jidokwan. Because of Yun's friendship with officials in the All Japan Karate-do Federation (some of whom were his former students), the KSA participated in several tournaments in Japan between 1961 and 1970. By 1965, 70 percent of Korea's martial art practitioners were KSA members, the largest portion being the Moodukkwan (Hwang, 1995: 44). However, in March 1965, a majority of Moodukkwan students, led by Kim Young-taek and Hong Chong-soo, seceded from Hwang's organization to join the newly formed Korean Taekwondo Association.

Miss Kim kicking against an opponent, late 1950s. Courtesy Joseph Svinth.

GENERAL CHOI, THE OHDOKWAN, AND THE INCEPTION OF TAEKWONDO

In 1950, before leaving for Japan, Lee Won-kuk appointed a military officer named Choi Hong-hi (1918–2002) as honorary leader of the Chung-dokwan; Choi in turn appointed Son Duk-sung as acting leader of the Chungdokwan (Kimm, 2000). Although Choi's claims have been contradicted by several Chungdokwan leaders (Cook, 2001; 293; Kang and Yi, 1999: Chapter 2, Section 3), General Choi asserted that he received first *dan* in karate while attending high school in Kyoto, and second *dan* in Shotokan while attending Chuo University, from which he graduated in law in 1943 (Cook, 2001; Capener, 1995). Whatever his karate experience may have been, Choi's role in taekwondo's development was considerable.

In 1953, Choi founded the ROK Army's 29th Division, and assigned Nam Tae-hi and Han Cha-kyo (students of Lee Won-kuk) as senior *tang-soodo* instructors. Nam had taught *tangsoodo* at the ROK Army Signal School since 1947.

In September 1954, the 29th Division performed a demonstration of *tang-soodo* for ROK president Rhee Syngman. After watching with great interest,

Rhee expressed his desire for all ROK Army troops to be trained in what he preferred to call *taekyon* (Kimm, 2000). Consequently, in late 1954, a new gymnasium was built for the 29th Division. Choi named this gym the Ohdokwan, and he staffed it with instructors from the Chungdokwan.

In 1955, Choi assembled a committee to decide upon a new name for Korean karate. Through a process of compromise between those preferring *taekyon-do* (referring to the traditional Korean game) and those preferring *tangsoodo* or *kongsoodo,* the term taekwondo *(t'aegwondo)* was chosen. Choi especially liked the term because it referred to both kicking *(tae)* and hand *(kwon)* techniques. Rhee eventually accepted the taekwondo name, and it was first implemented at the Ohdokwan and Chungdokwan schools.

In 1959, Choi, the administrative leader of two *kwan,* invited representatives from four major *kwan* to his home. According to Choi, "My full purpose for this meeting was to get away from the Korean variations in pronunciation for Japanese karate, 'kongsoo' and 'tangsoo' " (Kimm, 2000, 51). Choi eventually persuaded the representatives to accept taekwondo as the name for their arts and to join the Korean Taekwondo Association.

Currently, in an effort to provide an indigenous Korean lineage for taekwondo, many taekwondo histories omit the karate and instead emphasize the influence of the traditional foot-fighting game of *taekyon* (Twenty Centuries, 1981: 25–29; World Taekwondo Federation, 2002a). However, investigation of *taekyon* shows this connection to have been fabricated (Capener, 1995; Pederson, 2001: 606).

The Yi Dynasty's (1389–1910) Confucian emphasis on intellectual pursuits brought about the neglect of military arts, including *subak* (hand strike), *kwonbup,* and *t'ang-su,* all of which were arts closely modeled on Chinese methods (Della Pia, 1994; Henning, 2000).

By the late 1700s, preference for the kicking art *taekyon* was replacing *subak's yaet bop* (literally, "old skills," referring to hand techniques) (Capener, 1995; Pederson, 2001: 603). Consequently, despite lack of formalized training, *taekyon* survived into the twentieth century primarily as a kicking contest. According to Song Tok-ki, practitioners included common people and gangsters (Capener, 1995; Pederson, 2001: 604).

After the Korean War, the ROK government under Rhee Syngman sought to associate Korean karate with *taekyon,* with its sweeps and kicks. This influenced the choice of taekwondo as a name for the new Korean art. However, serious interest in *taekyon* during taekwondo's formative years was almost nonexistent (Capener, 1995), and its influence on taekwondo's foundation was negligible (Pederson, 2001: 606).

POLITICS, NATIONALISM, AND THE OLYMPICS

The anti-Japanese sentiment that is so prevalent in modern Korean society is based on the Korean memories of Japanese occupation. Like their counterparts in Formosa and the Ryukyu Islands (other colonies seized by Japan between 1878 and 1895), many Koreans during occupation grew up believing that their destiny was to be second-class Japanese citizens (Ishida, 2000). As Lee Won-kuk said, "I never thought that Korea would win its independence from Japan" (Lee, 1997: 46). Nonetheless, after World War II, Korea was free of Japan, and ROK politicians used anti-Japanese sentiment to foster Korean nationalism. Therefore, in the case of taekwondo, this meant consciously separating taekwondo from its origins in karate (Capener, 1995).

In 1960, a student uprising ignited a political process that resulted in the overthrow of President Rhee and eventually the installation of a military government under General Park Chung-hi on May 16, 1961.

In 1962, General Choi organized a meeting of *kwan* representatives and the Korean Sports Union. After Choi left the meeting early, the visitors agreed on the Korean Taesoodo Association and elected Choi president. Choi reportedly declined the presidency because he had labored to popularize the name taekwondo (Kimm, 2000). However, he accepted the position in 1965 and was then successful in changing the name to the Korean Taekwondo Association. By 1965, Choi (or people under his direction) finished designing all of the *Chang-hon* forms, which were modeled closely on sequences from Shotokan forms (Thomas, 1988). Although they retained traditional karate movements and techniques, these forms received names based on Korean historical and nationalistic themes (A-KATO, 2002; World Taekwondo Federation, 2002b).

On March 22, 1966, Choi established the International Taekwondo Federation (ITF) to administer to the growing international taekwondo community (Burdick, 1997/1999). However, others feel that Choi formed the ITF because he had been forced to resign the presidency of the KTA.

On March 20, 1971, President Park proclaimed taekwondo as Korea's national sport, designating its full name as *kukki* (national) taekwondo (Kang and Yi, 1999: Chapter 3, Section 3). About the same time (January 23, 1971), Park appointed Kim Un-yong (born 1931) as president of the Korean Taekwondo Association. Kim was at the time an assistant director of both the Korean CIA (KCIA) and the Presidential Protection Force (Jennings, 1996: Chapter 9; Kang and Yi, 1999: Chapter 3, Section 2).

Miss Kim demonstrating form, late 1950s. Courtesy Joseph Svinth.

According to Kim, "I accepted the position of KTA president because the Korean government told me to correct the way taekwondo was at that time" (Kang and Yi, 1999: Chapter 3, Section 2). According to Choi (1981), "Park wanted access to the ITF. He saw it could be a powerful muscle for his dictatorship." Either way, for refusing to hand over the leadership of the ITF to the KCIA, Choi was threatened with jail, which prompted him to relocate to Canada (Jennings, 1996: Chapter 9).

In February 1971, the Korean Ministry of Education issued a requirement that all taekwondo schools have private school permits, thereby subjecting them to government regulation (Kang and Yi, 1999: Chapter 3, Section 5). With this, recalcitrant *kwan* leaders could be punished for retaining Japanese karate-based art names and traditions, and for refusing to comply with government standards and policies. Standard punishments included media blacklists, suppression of *kwan* publications, the inability to renew teaching contracts at educational institutions (particularly military and police academies), problems obtaining passports, threats of imprisonment, and assassination attempts (Hwang, 1995: 45–50; Kimm, 2000). This treatment marginalized some of taekwondo's pioneers, including Choi Hong-hi (moved to Canada), Son Duk-sung (moved to the United States),

Hwang Kee (moved to the United States) and Yun Kwei-byung (whose death in 2000 went virtually unnoticed by the taekwondo community).

In November 1971, the Kukkiwon (the Korean Taekwondo Association's Central Gymnasium) was established, with Kim Un-yong as director. According to Kim, "The Kukkiwon would be the monumental symbol of a nation. The objective of the Kukkiwon is to promote taekwondo as a means of general exercise for the benefit of public health as well as to spread taekwondo as a symbol of Korea and its traditions" (Kang and Yi, 1999: 84).

The following month, on December 23, 1971, Kim announced that he would popularize taekwondo internationally. Toward this end, he would soon publish an English version of taekwondo materials, to include new history and training concepts suitable for distribution in foreign countries (Kang and Yi, 1999: 66). This history attributed the appearance of taekwondo to ancient tribal communities on the Korean peninsula and claimed that taekwondo was chronicled in the eighteenth-century *Muyedobo-tongji* (*Illustrated Manual of Martial Arts*) (World Taekwondo Federation, 2002a; Cho, 1981).[8]

In 1973, President Park designated the Kukkiwon as the World Taekwondo Headquarters and appointed Kim Un-yong as acting president of the newly organized World Taekwondo Federation (WTF). During the inaugural meeting of the WTF, Kim was empowered to select all of the organization's officials. He further announced, "We are going to promise that taekwondo must become our national sport, as well as an international sport which represents Korea" (Kang and Yi, 1999: 65).

In 1974, the Korean Taekwondo Association consolidated more than 40 existing *kwan* into just 10 *kwan*. Additionally, the new *kwan* were identified by numbers rather than their traditional names. On August 7, 1978, presidents of the 10 remaining *kwan* signed a proclamation stating, "Taekwondo will strive hard to unify and will eliminate the different *kwan* of the past thirty years" (Kang and Yi, 1999: 98). Although perhaps not the primary intention, this served to erase connections to the karate-influenced past.

Meanwhile, Kim Un-yong got taekwondo admitted as an official Olympic sport. This was crucial to the ROK's emergence as a modern international power and to Korea's desire to have a uniquely Korean martial art.

Although frequently controversial,[9] Kim at various times presided over the WTF, the Korean Taekwondo Association, the Korean Amateur Sports Association, the Korean Olympic Committee, and the Kukkiwon. In addition, he eventually became an executive board member of the International Olympic Committee (Jennings, 1996: Chapter 9; One-hundred-twelfth IOC Session, 2001).

Kim lobbied tirelessly to bring the Olympics to Seoul and to get taek-wondo included in the Olympics. Through his efforts, taekwondo was an exhibition event in the 1988 Olympics in Seoul, and a regular Olympic sport in the 2000 Sydney Olympics. The value of this to the ROK was that the Korean victories in the taekwondo competition catapulted the ROK into tenth place in overall medal counts, which is an impressive achieve-ment for a country with a population of just 47 million (" 'Best Olympic Games,' " 2000).

Getting taekwondo into the Olympics meant converting it into a specta-tor sport. For example, the Olympic scoring system, which awards one point for a kick or strike to the body and two points for a kick to the head, perpetuates a Korean kicking tradition, but more importantly, it makes for an exciting spectator sport. It also distinguishes taekwondo from kickbox-ing, as in the latter, the fighters often throw the mandated number of kicks in the first moments of the round, and then resort to boxing.

Emphasis on free sparring has led to the adaptation of techniques from boxing, a sport in which Koreans have competed admirably since the late 1920s (Svinth, 2001b). For example, the modern sparring and forms use more upright stances than were seen during taekwondo's early years. These higher stances allow the mobility needed for point-fighting compe-titions in which throws and grabs are not allowed. Meanwhile, the rules used during point fighting are similar to those used in amateur boxing. Finally, the interest in free sparring contributed to the development of the foam sparring equipment used today during taekwondo and some karate competition. The Korean American Jhoon Rhee was a pioneer in this area. A distinctive pullover uniform jacket was introduced in the early 1980s for sport taekwondo. One advantage of the pullover is that it does not gap open during competition, causing lulls while the uniform is fixed.

Such changes have taken Olympic taekwondo far from its roots as a martial art: today it is a combative sport. According to Kim Un-yong, "We must continue to develop taekwondo into a sport" (Dohrenwend, 2002). According to Choi Hong-hi, "The WTF . . . simplified the complicated (tra-ditional) moves into a full-contact sparring event convenient for Olympic bouts and television coverage" (Jennings, 1996: Chapter 9). Either way, despite the technical and philosophical changes that accompanied the emergence of taekwondo as an Olympic sport, the desire to maintain Asian tradition still anchors taekwondo to its foundation in karate. Many taek-wondo schools still teach traditional karate forms, and the modern ITF and WTF forms use techniques and sequences borrowed directly from Shotokan karate (Nixdorf, 1993; Thomas, 1988). Characteristics such as basic techniques, forms, uniforms, training methods, and protocol still connect taekwondo to its roots in karate.

CONCLUSION

Taekwondo's origins in Japanese university karate clubs during the first half of the twentieth century is well documented. During and after World War II, Korean students returned home with experience in Shotokan, Shudokan, and Shito-ryu karate. Those who chose to establish karate schools taught their arts as they had learned them in Japan, and they called their arts *tangsoodo* or *kongsoodo,* which are Korean pronunciations of karate.

Shortly after the Korean War, the ROK government under Rhee Syngman recognized the value of these arts in promoting physical fitness and encouraged their dissemination. However, ROK nationalism demanded a uniquely Korean name for the arts, resulting in the term taekwondo. The person most responsible for the adoption of this name was General Choi Hong-hi.

During the 1960s and 1970s, the ROK government was controlled by a series of military dictatorships that viewed taekwondo as a strong tool for Korean nationalism. Because of the administrative efforts of Kim Un-yong, the ROK government had the ability to compel the unification of many schools into one style. Thus, by marginalizing dissent, supporting unification with financial and political incentives, and inventing history and traditions, taekwondo evolved into the Korean national sport and eventually an international Olympic sport. This evolutionary process included creating a revised history of taekwondo that claimed a 2,000-year, indigenous Korean heritage while obscuring the art's true origins in Japanese karate.

WOMEN'S BOXING AND RELATED ACTIVITIES: INTRODUCING IMAGES AND MEANINGS

Jennifer Hargreaves

INTRODUCTION

Women's boxing, in common with women's participation in other traditionally male sports, has been largely hidden from history. Therefore, my early investigations have resulted in an overview of the history of the sport from savate, through competitive boxing, to boxerobics. In the process, I outline analytical possibilities, mostly by considering a range of possible meanings attaching to the variants of women's boxing. I refer to the ideas of Bourdieu and Foucault in order to suggest that their theories might be applied more systematically in ways I do not have space for here.

My focus is on women. References to male boxing are made only to indicate the symbolic significance of a specific form of sporting maleness that signifies difference from femaleness. The discourse of men's boxing overrides class and racial differences between male boxers and suggests a homogeneous masculinity that creates specifically gendered relations of power. One reason that I looked at women's boxing is because it appears to deconstruct the "normal" symbolic boundaries between male and female in sport—the opposition between masculine and feminine, based on the body, argued by Bourdieu (1995: 93) to constitute "the fundamen-

Earlier versions appeared in David Chandler, John Gill, Tania Guha, and Gilane Tawadros (Eds.) (1996), *Boxer: An Anthology of Writings on Boxing and Visual Culture* (pp. 121–131), London: Institute of International Visual Arts, and *Body and Society* 3: 4 (1997) (pp. 33–49). Copyright © 2002 Jennifer Hargreaves. Adapted by permission.

Kim Messer, women's world junior flyweight boxing champion, circa 2000.
Courtesy Kim Messer.

tal principle of division of the social and symbolic world." However, I was
to find that even in combative situations, different meanings and dis-
courses applied to women's boxing, and in all its guises a diverse shaping
of the female body occurs.

The concern here is to indicate ways in which actual bodily experiences
have direct relevance to meanings and identities and how meanings are,
literally, embodied, a process that integrates the physical, psychic, and cultural dimensions of human experience. Fuller treatment of women's boxing is needed to explore the relation between the diverse and complex
bodies of the boxers and structures of power: gender, class, race, commercialization, and politics.

A SYMBOL OF MASCULINITY

Proponents characterize boxing as "the noble art of self defense," "the
sweet science," a channel for courage, determination, and self-discipline,
and the sport that, above all others, combines fitness with skill, strength

with artistry. In the following quotation, poet and ex-professional fighter Vernon Scannell compares the roles of great artists with those of boxers:

> But what it (boxing) can do—and here it is like art—is give a man a chance to behave in a way that is beyond and above his normal capacity. The great artist may be, outside the confines of his art, cruel, weak, arrogant, and foolish, but within them he can transcend his own condition and become noble, passionate and truthful beyond the range of ordinary men. Something similar happens to the great fighter, too. He may be stupid, vain, ignorant and brutish—though he is not, in fact, these things nearly as often as popular belief imagines—but in the exercise of his art he becomes the embodiment of transcendental courage, strength and chivalry. I have seen it happen and I have experienced the Aristotelean catharsis as powerfully in the boxing stadium as in the theatre. (1971: 48–49)

In contrast, opponents claim boxing is brutalizing, savage, and destructive, resulting in acute and chronic injuries, mostly to the eyes and brain, and sometimes causing massive hemorrhaging and death (British Medical Association, 1993). The following excerpt from Irvin S. Cobb's graphic account in the *New York Times* (July 3, 1921) of the world heavyweight championship fight between Jack Dempsey and Georges Carpentier describes the sort of incident used to support the anti-boxing lobby:

> I see the Frenchman staggering, slipping, sliding forward to his fate. His face is toward me and I am aware at once his face has no vestige of conscious intent. Then the image of him is blotted out by the intervening bulk of the winner. Dempsey's right arm swings upward with the flailing emphasis of an oak cudgel and the muffled fist at the end of it lands again on its favorite target—the Frenchman's jaw.
>
> The thud of its landing can be heard above the hysterical shrieking of the host. The Frenchman seems to shrink in for a good six inches. It is as though that crushing impact had telescoped him. He folds up into a pitiable meagre compass and goes down heavily and again lies on the floor, upon his right side, his face half covered by his arms as though even in the stupor following that deadly collision between his face and Dempsey's fist, he would protect his vulnerable parts. From where I sit writing this I can see one of his eyes and his mouth. The eye is blinking weakly, the mouth is gaping, and the lips work as though he chewed a most bitter mouthful. His legs kick out like the legs of a cramped swimmer. Once he lifts himself half-way to his haunches. But the effort is his last. He has flattened down again and still the referee has only progressed in his fateful sum of addition as far as "six." (Cobb, 1976)

In both accounts, a conventional sporting ideology appears. Boxing is an essentially masculine activity associated with the male physique and psychology, with no organic connection with femaleness. The blood, bruises, cuts, and concussion that accompany boxing's intrinsic aggression, violence, and danger, are popularly considered to be legitimate and even "natural" for men (Messner, 1992: 67), but at odds with the essence of femininity. Boxing, as Wacquant (1995: 90) argues, is deeply engendered, embodying and exemplifying "a definite form of masculinity: plebeian, heterosexual and heroic."

In working-class communities, fighting prowess provokes powerful images of machismo and virility. Dominance in combat is simultaneously feared and admired. In boxing subcultures maiming or even killing an opponent are rationalized, and contempt for punishment and pain is a sign of being a "real" man and a good boxer. Because the boxer's body is both a weapon and a target, it is constantly under surveillance and must be disciplined to stay strong and tuned for the fight. If Foucault's analysis (1979: 26) is applied to the male boxer, his is a subjected body, heavily invested with power and, furthermore, in a manner which produces a distinctly gendered form of embodiment (Sawicki, 1991). The investment of power in the male boxer's body can also be understood as a form of cultural capital, or, more specifically, as Bourdieu (1984; 1986) conceptualizes, a symbol of physical capital highly valued for males in working-class communities.

It seems surprising, therefore, that recently there has been an increase in the numbers of women who box, and, in particular, of women with middle-class and professional backgrounds. Their participation is stamping a new character on a sport that has traditionally symbolized the "essence" of working-class maleness. At first glance, women's boxing appears to be a radical intervention that blurs traditional male and female images, identities, and class alliances.

FIGHTING WOMEN

Few people are aware that women's boxing (or more correctly, prizefighting) can be traced back to the eighteenth and nineteenth centuries. The early bare-knuckle contests were crude and bloody, fights to the finish in a harsh world in which the bodies of working women were imbued with strength and aggression, similar to the physical capital of working men. In London from the 1720s onward, bouts were staged between women from laboring trades who thirsted for money and status. Some of these women became well known and their feats are recorded. For example, we read about "The famous boxing woman of Billingsgate," "The fighting ass-driver from Stoke Newington," "A female boxing blacksmith," "The vendor of sprats," "The market woman," "The City Championess," "The Hiberian Heroine" and "Bruising Peg." The contests were vicious free-for-alls, either topless or in tight-fitting jackets, short petticoats, and Holland drawers. They involved punching, feet- and knee-kicking to all parts of the body, mauling, scratching, and throwing, and often resulted in serious injuries. Large crowds and large bets were commonplace, and members of the nobility often donated lucrative purses (Daly, n.d.; Guttmann, 1991: 74–77; Park, 1994: 31). A bout between two women in 1794 was described as follows:

> Great intensity between them was maintained for about two hours, where-upon the elder fell into great difficulty through the closure of her left eye from the extent of swelling above and below it which rendered her blind through having the sight of the other considerably obscured by a flux of blood which had then continued greatly for over forty minutes...not more than a place even as large as a penny-piece remained upon their bodies which was free of the most evident signs of the harshness of the struggle. Their bosoms were much enlarged but yet they each continued to rain blows upon this most feeling of tissue without regard to the pitiful cries issuing forth at each success which was evidently to the delight of the spectators since many a shout was raised causing each female to mightily increase her effort. (Daly, n.d.)

A century later, women's prizefighting was taking place on both sides of the Atlantic. Because relatively few women competed, exhibition matches were often against men, and sometimes women won. More usually, women were seriously injured; at least one may even have been killed. On-the-spot stitching of large cuts was sometimes carried out so that a bout could continue, and women fought on with broken noses and jaws, smashed teeth, and swollen eyes. Because of the betting economy and the lure of a fat purse, women's fights continued to be staged as brutal spectacles. Although in some contests, only punching or boxing with the hands was allowed, "savate" fights (strikes with the feet as well as the hands) were popular at the turn of the 20th century, and sometimes girls as young as 12 years old headed the bill. Here is an extract from an article in the *Police Gazette* (1924) describing a fight between a woman of 25 and a girl of 17:

> One snapshot showed the woman shooting a kick at the girl's head; the girl was warding it off with her left arm and sending in her right fist to the woman's stomach. This fight ended in a victory for the woman. Another

such fight was won by Mlle. Fari, who, soon after an hour of bloody and bruising battle, broke the other girl's jaw by a savage kick.... About 1902 Mlle. Augagnier beat Miss Pinkney of England in a savage fight. It was boxing and savate against straight boxing. Pinkney was better with her fists and looked like a winner after about one and a half hours of bloody fighting, but Mlle. A. cleverly managed to kick Pinkney in the face. This blow made a terrible scar and stunned the English girl, then the French girl shot a smashing kick to Pinkney's stomach and knocked her out. The French girl was carried by her admirers in triumph from the ring.

Starting in the last two decades of the nineteenth century, the status of local champion was gradually replaced by national and even international titles. In 1884, Nellie Stewart of Norfolk, Virginia, claimed to have won the first "Female Championship of the World" (Eskin, August 1974: 30). The following year the title was claimed by Ann Lewis of Cleveland, Ohio, following an advertisement in the *Police Gazette,* challenging any woman in the world to fight her for $1,000 (ibid.). The first properly advertised Championship probably took place two years later in 1886. According to the published information, neither of the contestants had ever been beaten in a fight, and between them, they had accumulated 76 knockouts. On this occasion, Hattie Leslie was battered around the ring, knocked down for a count of eight, had her nose broken and blood drawn and one eye practically closed. Then, miraculously, she turned things around and became the first officially recorded "Female World Champion."

FEMININE CAPITAL

The development of women's boxing was quite separate from that of other women's sports. In a different social sphere, middle-class women were struggling to get into the "respectable" world of organized sports, but found themselves seriously constrained by dominant medical ideologies about the innate physical limitations of females and their unsuitability to take part in vigorous exercise (Hargreaves, 1994). Whereas the development of mainstream sports for women was based upon notions of sexual difference (and male and female bodies in most sports are signifiers of those differences), the basic symbolism of women's boxing seemed to contradict this trend. In its purest form, it celebrated female muscularity, physical strength and aggression. Power was literally inscribed in the boxers' bodies—in their actual working muscles—an expression of physical capital usually ascribed to men. Nevertheless, gender and sexuality received heightened expression. Although the battered body of the male boxer symbolized the defeat of heroic masculinity, the battered body of the female boxer was the very denial of the supposed essence of femininity. Instead, it symbolized brutalization and dehumanization, simultaneously creating an image of exciting and animalistic sensuality. No matter how serious the women were about their sport, because of its low-class, disreputable image, it remained "underground," or at best marginalized. Working women who used their bodies freely and powerfully were characterized as uncivilized and vampish, in distinct contrast to the listless, weak, and sexually repressed image of the well-bred middle-class Victorian lady. For that reason, women's boxing attracted male voyeurs—not only working men, but also local dignitaries and businessmen. Its explicit sexuality (through bare breasts and the ripping of clothes, the scope for male fantasies, and potential as a surrogate for male brutality against the "weaker" sex) increased the entertainment value of women's boxing into the 20th century.

OPPOSITION AND ADVANCES

As part of the suffragette movement of the late nineteenth and early twentieth centuries, female office workers were encouraged to box for fitness and self-defense (*New York World,* November 27, 1904, Sunday Magazine: 11; *Seattle Times,* November 20, 1910, Sunday Magazine: 7). Working women also participated in vaudeville acts featuring boxing and speed-bag punching; examples include Polly Burns, Belle Gordon, and Harriet Seaback.

Following World War I, physicians and social workers complained that boxing (and football, water polo, and various other sports; see Hargreaves, 1994) were too strenuous for girls. Nevertheless, there were a few female boxers and promoters in Western Europe, North America, South America, the Antipodes, and the Indian subcontinent. These women often were motivated by money. As Annie Newton, a war-widow who boxed to support her daughter, told a London reporter, "And really! All this talk about boxing for women being 'degrading' and 'risky' and 'too hard work' strikes me as very comic. Is it any more degrading, or half as hard work, as scrubbing floors?" (*Japan Times,* October 3, 1926: 6).

At the same time, the new emphasis on fashionable slenderness was attracting women to the gym. According to an article published in the *Seattle Post-Intelligencer* (April 8, 1928, Sunday Magazine: 4),

The gym of "Philadelphia Jack" O'Brien, located in the heart of Broadway's white light section, is now more sonorously entitled "The Flesh

Fräulein Kussin and Mrs. Edwards boxing, 1912. Library of Congress, George Grantham Bain Collection, LC-USZ62-113556.

Reducing Institute," and Mr. O'Brien's clients, who, a few years ago were almost 100 per cent. men, are now almost exclusively women....

"In a class of 22 fat women," said the impresario of the Flesh Reducing Institute, "we succeed in getting off a total of over fifty pounds in one day. In a period of a month each woman in the class lost an average of 26½ pounds. One woman, who weighed 291½ pounds when she entered the class, registered 259½ pounds at the close of her first month's treatment, a loss of 32½ pounds."

During the 1930s and 1940s, there were occasionally public matches and competitions featuring women. (But not in Germany, where Hitler considered female athleticism disgusting.) In common with other sports that previously had been characterized as suited only to men, women's boxing faced harsh and widespread opposition. Opponents argued that the training made women muscular and therefore ugly. Furthermore, it was said that hard hitting could cause cancer or harm reproductive organs, and thereby affect women's abilities to bear and suckle children (Fleischer,

March 1933: 20; Laird, 1936: 142–143). In fact, the female reproductive organs are firmly positioned and thoroughly protected inside the body cavity and are probably less susceptible to injury than those of men. And, of course, women, like men, can wear protective apparatus to protect vulnerable parts (Dyer, 1982).

The ethics of arguments to ban boxing are as appropriate to men as they are to women. However, the differential treatment of the sexes in boxing exemplifies the systematic application of biological arguments to women's bodies in order to control cultural practices. The repression of women's bodies in boxing symbolized the repression of women in society. In contrast, the possession by men of physical capital in boxing was transformed and exploited as cultural capital. Ironically, part of this process was the exploitation of male boxers themselves.

Despite this opposition, the 1940s, 50s and 60s saw increasing numbers of female boxers. One of the most famous female fighters was Barbara Buttrick, "a little toughie" originally from Yorkshire, England, who was the undefeated Women's World Fly and Bantamweight Boxing Champion from 1950–1960 (Eskin, 1974, August). "Battlin Barbara," as she became known, learned her trade in the fairground boxing booths of England and France. It was claimed, "she not only pulverised every woman she met, but swapped punches with over 1,000 men in exhibition bouts" (Philip, 1983: 39). Buttrick has been eulogized in boxing circles for her understanding of the very essence of the noble art. She was neither uncontrolled slugger nor a vamp, but a civilized and disciplined "artiste of the physical." Admired for her "speed, finesse and knowledge of boxing" and the way she moved "with the rhythm of a ballet dancer" ("British Girl," 1955), she became known as the "female Jimmy Wilde" (Philip, 1983: 39). In 1960, Buttrick became the first woman boxer to be elected to the International Boxing and Wrestling Hall of Fame, and in 1995, she became the first President of the newly founded Women's International Boxing Federation (WIBF).

Buttrick and other female boxers were unlicensed fighters, and as recently as the 1970s, boxing was recognized as a professional sport for women in only a few places. Then, in 1974, the push for female boxing coincided with the International Women's Year and the strengthening of radical feminism, and women's boxing was recognized throughout much of the world. Nonetheless, it remains commonplace for women to struggle for recognition and resources at both amateur and professional levels, and to compete amid hostile controversy.

Professionally, 1994 marked another watershed when Don King, a powerful promoter, signed up his first female boxer, Christie Martin, and promoted a Women's Championship event. The following year, the first fully sanctioned Women's World Championships in professional boxing history took place. Since then, women's boxing has developed at a remarkable rate and in a remarkable way, and by 2001, even Egyptian women had boxing clubs.

NON-COMBAT BOXING

Although gym owners taught boxing for fitness since before World War I, during the 1980s there was a huge escalation of interest in, and demand for, female boxing and associated activities such as "boxerobics" and "karaterobics." At one level this can be understood as an aspect of the consumerism of exercise, feeding off the modern obsession with body maintenance and its surface representation or the "look" of the body (Featherstone, 1982/1991). The power of consumer culture derives from its ability to harness for profit people's desires about their bodies—a form of "control through stimulation." Body maintenance requires hard work and discipline, but the perceived product of a well-toned body induces women to participate in exercise programs.

An advertisement for "Pony's Exerbox" sportswear recommends Boxerobics as a preferred form of exercise, claiming it "really sorts out the women from the girls." "After the first few rounds of training," the advertisement promises, "you'll start to lose weight and gain strength. You'll develop long, lean muscles, not bulk. Your body will feel firm and look hard." We see an image of a strong, muscular young woman, sitting in a changing room in a manly pose with her legs apart. She is wearing Exerbox gear—boxer's shorts, t-shirt, and trainers. Her hands are strapped, her boxing gloves beside her on the bench. In the picture, she looks more like Mike Tyson than a Cindy doll. Certainly, this representation supports Susan Bordo's (1990) contention that in recent years the athletic and muscular image of femininity, although quite solid and bulky-looking, has become highly desirable. This, Bordo argues, is because tautness and containment have become more valued than thinness, and that any form of excess, sagginess, or wrinkling (even on the skinny body) is considered to spoil its appearance. Whereas in the past muscularity was associated with masculinity, the new androgynous look acquired through workouts has become a symbol of both control and desirability. Thus, in the same way that muscularity has always symbolized the empowerment of men, representations of the athletic female body can also be understood as symbols of empowerment and the reconstruction of traditional images of femininity. Women are empowering themselves by appropriating male symbols of physical capital and shifting gender relations of power.

The burgeoning popularity of boxing and karate aerobics has made these activities akin to cults. They attract women who explicitly reject the "ultra-feminine" image of aerobics and who want more exciting and demanding forms of exercise. Evolving from "Executive boxing," originally devised by actor Mickey Rourke (once an amateur boxer) to relieve stress, and coinciding with the muscular and aggressive female image popularized by Linda Hamilton's performance in the *Terminator* movies, boxerobics spread to gyms in Hollywood and New York, and then became an international phenomenon. Screen actresses such as Jodie Foster, Michelle Pfeiffer, Cindy Crawford, and Claudia Schiffer have become devotees, and after boxerobics was introduced into England, the former "Page 3 Girl," Samantha Fox, made a boxercise video. Modeled on a boxer's workout, exhausting routines of skipping, shadowboxing, and pummeling punch-bags are performed to funky tunes.

Unlike "real" boxing, this mode of exercise severs the female agent from the worrying relationships between combat, aggression, pain, and injury. It is boxing without an opponent—a non-contact form of exercise during which, the Exerbox advertisement assures us, "The only pain you inflict is on yourself." The implied message coheres with the politically induced and popularized idea that women should take responsibility for their own bodies. The philosophy is introspective, reflecting widespread insecurities about the body and self that are mediated and reproduced through dominant modes of consumption such as advertising (Tomlinson, 1990). The resultant female body is ascetic and disciplined, and the product of a self-imposed physical regimen.

The discourse of female boxing training is complex and contradictory. The body trained through boxing practices is strong and athletic, illustrating the way in which power and lifestyle intersect. Reportedly, it symbolizes independence and suggests a body produced "for oneself" rather than as "the object of male desire" (Cole and Hribar, 1995: 361). In the open embrace of rigorous physicality, muscularity, and firmness, there is a broadening of femininity and a radicalizing of the link between the public female body and hegemonic heterosexuality. At the same time, there is a rejection of "contrived" muscle bulk supposedly produced by exercise regimes such as weight lifting, which allegedly mask the breasts and masculinize the "real" body. Training in boxing, claim its disciples, is the "best all-round work-out," because it burns fat faster while producing a muscular, but also long, lithe, and "attractive" body shape. Their rejection of

Tamami "Sky" Hosoya. New York City Golden Glove boxing champion, mid-1990s. Courtesy Tamami Hosoya.

Kate Moss's waif-like, submissive, and passive portrayal of femininity embodies the belief that sexiness is not in contradiction with power. The new super-paid super-models are tall, muscular and sporty, and "Uber-woman" (from Nietzsche's *Übermensche*—"a 'higher body' from Man": see Lash, 1984/1991: 271–272) is the term used to describe this radical athletic aesthetic (see Hargreaves, 1994: Chapter 7).

The contradictions of boxing images are apparent in a recent advertisement for Haliborange, which offers a line of nutritional supplements. A slice of a young woman's head showing her eyes appears above a huge boxing glove that is forefront in the picture and takes up most of the space. The eyes bore purposefully into the viewer, signifying that Haliborange, in common with female boxing, is a form of self-defense. Here we have a strong woman taking up a male sport, connoting the power and "extra PUNCH" of Haliborange. However, an alternative reading of the advertisement is possible. The eyes of the woman, highlighted because they are the only visible part of the face and because they "speak" to the reader with intensity, could be saying, "I am sexy. Come and get me." In this case, the message is that behind the boxer is the "real" woman. Rather than a subject of pleasure, the body is an object of desire. In sport, as in advertisements, the body is fundamentally semiotic; a place where meaning is both created and enacted, and a place for the inscription of multiple signs (Brooks, 1993: 38).

"REAL" BOXING

The link between women and boxing embodies another contradiction. A small but growing group of women deride boxerobics as "cosmetic," or, disparagingly, as "aerobics with gloves on." They prefer sparring and organized fights because, they say, that the demands of combat provide (for them) a more basic physical and psychic pleasure. One fighter explains her feelings as follows, "Boxing requires intelligence, and a combination of skill and the aesthetic that is deeply satisfying.... It's like you get to know your body inside out." This description coheres with Wacquant's (1995: 73) account of the effects of bodywork undergone by male boxers. He claims that "it practically reorganizes the entire corporeal field of the fighter, bringing to prominence certain organs and abilities and making others recede, transforming not only the physique of the boxer but also his 'body-sense,' the consciousness he has of his organism and, through this changed body, of the world about him."

Whether male or female, people go into competitive boxing for different reasons. For example, they want to get rid of aggression, to learn techniques of self-defense, to get physically strong, or because they relish the sportive challenge. However, they also share the belief that boxing is intellectually challenging, and enhances self-confidence, strength of character, and courage. They claim that facing danger and overcoming fear gives them an unbelievable buzz—they enjoy the physicality of fighting, the excitement, the roughness, and the risk. For them, it is a uniquely sensuous bodily experience, which, when mixed with the mental challenge is addictive. "The most terrifying thing I can ever remember doing is preparing for a fight," one boxer explains. "And just before the fight, getting into the ring, I feel so ill, I feel terrible.... But regardless of the result, win or lose, when you come out of the ring, you feel on top of the world for months and months." The over-riding sensation is one of empowerment, perceived to be inscribed both in the individual physical body and in the inner self. "It takes intense concentration and precision, a combination of physical and psychic energy. When I leave [the gym after boxing] I am clear, self-confident and peaceful." (Wendy G. Finch quoted in Mende Conny, 1993: 53)

After conducting a study of exercise routines, Cole and Hribar (1995) discuss a shift in emphasis in 1990s feminism from attention to the external body or surface self, to the inner or deep self. They see this as a new "commodity feminism," which, through the "sale" of female fitness, has become reconciled with capitalism. Featherstone (1982/1991: 171) also discusses the relationship between the inner and the outer body. "Within consumer culture," he argues, "the inner and the outer body have become conjoined: the prime purpose of the maintenance of the inner body becomes the enhancement of the appearance of the outer body."

DISMISSING DANGER

Boxing is intrinsically vicious and potentially lethal; to disregard this characteristic is implicitly to support or idealize it. Ann Parisio, director of Raging Belles, puts it bluntly: "Boxing is much more brutal than wrestling. They [boxers] are pumping the grey matter into jelly, but a lot of people make a lot of money out of it; that's why it's respectable" (quoted in Downes, 1989: 15). Without doubt, the recent promotion of women's boxing is due to its profit-making potential, but at present, there is little money to be made by the boxers themselves. Thus, the profit motive explains neither the growing penchant for participation, nor female boxers' apparent lack of concern about the likelihood of injury. The death of male boxer Bradley Stone in 1994 reopened the debate about the safety of boxing, but, ironically, coincided with an accelerating interest in the sport among women.

Boxing's main purpose is to disable or render an opponent unconscious, an action resulting from injury to the brain caused by a punch (or series of punches) to the head. One extreme consequence is death, but a more common occupational hazard in the men's professional game is the "punch drunk syndrome," a debilitating neurological disease which has features in common with Alzheimer's dementia and Parkinson's disease (Kemp, Houston, Macleod, and Pethybridge, 1995). Fighters are also at great risk of serious eye injuries. Nonetheless, supporters of boxing for women are quick to point out that boxing is only 30th on the list of dangerous sports. Moreover, they say, because women's upper bodies are less strong than men's and there are various regulations about wearing protective apparatus, the risk of serious injury is minimal.

This is perhaps disingenuous, as results of examinations of male amateur boxers (ibid.) have disturbing implications for women boxers. For example, the exams show that there is an accumulative build up of brain damage over time that goes undetected without elaborate testing. Further research took place at the Royal London Hospital following the death in the ring of a 23-year-old man who had been boxing since the age of 11 but had previously shown no signs of brain dysfunction. He suffered a massive brain hemorrhage and was found to have "long-standing brain damage, and some of the structural abnormalities common in the brains of elderly Alzheimer's patients" (Hunt 1996: 2). This report confirms, "Young boxers can develop permanent brain damage early in their careers without any signs or symptoms of injury" (ibid.), and at a time in their lives when the power of their punches is less than that of adult female boxers.

Although no research has been carried out on female boxers, there is no reason to suppose that their brains are less prone to injury than those of men. In 1996, Missouri's Katherine Dallam collapsed in the dressing room after her first professional fight. She had to undergo neuro-surgery to repair a burst blood vessel causing bleeding between the cranium and the brain. She now suffers from short-term memory loss and is unable to feed or dress herself. There was a similar case in Australia in 2001.

Like men, women boxers refuse to engage in a rational debate about the long-term effects of brain injury and become vehement and irrational in defense of their own sport when faced with the evidence. An interesting feature of this phenomenon is that boxing attracts increasing numbers of educated women from affluent social backgrounds. An example is Deirdre Gogarty, who during the 1990s was a contender for a world title. She comes from a middle-class Irish family—her father is a mouth surgeon, her mother is a dentist, she has a sister who is a doctor and a brother who directs an orchestra. Rene Denfeld, author of *The New Victorians,* is an aspiring world champion and Delia Gonsalez is a biochemist. Both of the latter are from the United States. There are accountants, attorneys, nurses and doctors, teachers and businesswomen, as well as women from working-class backgrounds, who box competitively and choose to ignore the dangers.

IN LOVE WITH THE SPORT

Justifications are varied, and resistance to a serious appraisal of the problem is commonplace, even though all competitors are required to sign the following declaration: "I understand and appreciate that participation in sport carries a risk to me of serious injury including permanent paralysis or death. I voluntarily and knowingly accept and assume this risk." When one boxer was asked if she ever thought she might get punch-drunk, she laughed, and said, "I'm daft already!" Another boxer claimed that the risk of being hurt is minimal, and then went on to say that being the center of attention in the ring is hugely appealing. Other boxers simply disregard the chronic (long-term) effects of boxing and argue that if they are well trained, they can avoid being hit.

The deep feelings of pleasure and empowerment experienced are linked to a denial of danger. It is in particular because "women are taught *not* to be physical," one of the boxers explained, "that it feels good to be in a context where it is *acceptable* to be physical and to discover a side of ourselves we never knew we had. Getting rid of aggression in a physical way is really liberating and attractive."

Women fighters are excited as well about overcoming personal fear, both fear of being hit and fear of hitting someone else. Perversely, they actually enjoy the sense of vulnerability, it "sends up the adrenaline and releases power."

Few of the fighters find problems with their own sense of femaleness. They just want to push their own limits, and in contradiction to popular conceptions of femininity, they claim that they possess an "innate fighting talent."

Their attitudes to their sport are therefore linked at a deep level to the physiological, psychological and emotional sensations experienced during training and fighting. The relation between the physical and the intellectual and between the inner and the outer self is, for them, part of a process of embodiment and self-identity.

Another element of the love of boxing is precisely that it is seen to have a "feminine side," like ballet in that it requires skill, speed, lightness, grace and coordination. This is reflected in the following description of a successful competition fighter:

> People just naturally expect an Amazon when they find out Angel Rodriguez is a boxer. Massive muscles. A few broken teeth. A bashed nose. Maybe a cauliflower ear or so.... That's why the petite, slender body and unlined face are such a surprise. At 5 feet 4 and 107 pounds, it is the body of a ballet dancer, not the top flyweight boxer that Angel Rodriguez actually is.... With her quiet self-assurance, fine-tuned body and angelic features, she's most certainly the best advertisement there could be for the sport. (Krieg, n.d.)

In general, promoters and boxers alike want to present an essentially feminine, "clean, tidy sporting image." They oppose women who take a radical feminist position, who argue that boxing makes them more sensuous, or who wear khaki shorts and shirts and "look like blokes." Deirdre

Women boxing. Courtesy Tacoma Public Library.

Gogarty expresses the fear that most boxers have. "I'm always afraid people think I'm butch," she says. "That's my main fear. I used to hang a
punch bag in the cupboard and bang away at it when no-one was around,
so nobody would know I was doing it because I was afraid people would
think I was weird and unfeminine" (Channel 4 Television, 1994).

The potential radicalization of the female body in sport is contradicted
by the ever-present expression of compulsory heterosexuality and the
attempt to justify female boxing because it has an authentic feminine element. Ian Wooldridge rejects the idea that boxing can be feminized:

> Boxing is about vehement aggression as much as ringcraft and self-
> defence....Do not for a moment fall for the delusion that if two women
> were released into the same ring with a gold medal at stake we would wit-
> ness some choreographed balletic performance with mild sporting under-
> tones. It would be bloody. As bloody awful, in fact, as those few disgraceful
> occasions when women have been lawfully sanctioned to fight one another
> on a professional bill. (Wooldridge, 1994: 61)

At the end of a 1994 contest between Gogarty and Stacey Prestige of the
United States, although the American was the victor on points, she fought

the last rounds with a bruised and battered face, and a bleeding, broken nose. Although there is no justification for moral arguments for boxing to be gendered, the deep desire that some women have to enter a sport which highlights aggression and abuse can be viewed as a confusingly reactionary trend rather than a radical reconstruction of the feminine.

Research carried out at the University of Michigan and at the U.S. Center for Media and Public Affairs suggests that there have been an increasing number of aggressive female role models on television. Examples include *The Avengers, Thelma and Louise, Charlie's Angels,* and *Wonderwoman* (Whitehorn, 1996: 6). It is argued that women seem to be more aggressive now and that when aggressive acts carried out by media heroines are portrayed positively, girls learn to accept this behavior. Boxing could be seen as one element of this trend.

Coinciding with the rising numbers of women in boxing are rising numbers of women taking part in other traditional male contact and combat sports. There is no similar movement of men into "feminine appropriate" sports.

THE SEEDY SIDE

As middle class women move into boxerobics, boxing training, and competitive fighting, working class women continue to play traditional boxing roles having organic links to "Bruising Peg" and her associates. Although serious boxing is gradually replacing explicitly sexualized women's events, it is still the case that many aspiring women fighters wind up on the seedy "tough girls" circuit (popularized in the American South and Midwest). Here, they provide sadistic spectacles for crowds of jeering men and women. They are peepshow fighters, kick-boxers, and wrestlers, often topless, shrieking, kicking, biting, and yanking each other round the ring by the hair while splattering themselves with hidden blood capsules that burst on impact (Hennessy, 1990: 18). Pseudo-serious topless boxing and foxy boxing (which originated in singles bars in California and involves bikini-clad women wearing huge foam gloves and prancing about for male voyeurs) are regular events associated with working-class venues, pubs, bars, night clubs, boxing gyms, smoke and booze, low life, and sleaze.

Descriptions of these contests, usually accompanied by photographs, appear in men's magazines. They provide a titillating mixture of the languages of boxing and sexuality: "Round 1. The girls were unaware of each other's skills, so they feinted around for the first few seconds. Then Zan-abe landed a nice punch to Geraldine's breasts and that got Geraldine going. She concentrated on her younger black opponent's beautifully developed tits, hitting them again and again" (Laird, 1993: 12). In November 1999, a four-round (e.g., preliminary) fighter named Mia St. John combined many of these themes by appearing semi-nude in *Playboy*.

Topless boxing is one tiny element of a huge structure of gender relations of power. Sexualized images of female boxers are part of the general bombardment of sexualized images of the female body, and in this context, the message that female sexuality is more important than boxing ability is clear. This is further consolidated by other female roles in the broader boxing context. For example, traditionally, women have been accoutrements to, or provided sideshows for, men in the game—as spectators, hostesses, show openers, or by holding up counter-boards between rounds. These women are "displayed" as stereotyped (hetero) sexualized commodities in swimsuits, high-heeled shoes, Lycra tights, and black silk stockings. In boxing films, women are usually stereotyped as the gangster's broad or the greedy woman who uses the fighter just for his money, and some are virtually devoid of female characters. Nonetheless, following the success of *Raging Bull* (a fictionalized biography of boxer Jake LaMotta), the boxer's ex-wife Vicki was subsequently invited to appear semi-nude, which she did in the November 1981 *Playboy*.

This severing of women from the "real" sport also happens in advertising and in sports photography. Women wearing boxing gloves has become a popular sporting image in advertisements that use sexual imagery to promote the sales of products—whether or not they have anything to do with sport. Through the convention of commercial sexuality, women's real involvement in sport is again trivialized. Boxing is used simply as a channel for the commodification of the female body in order to encourage clients to spend money on hair products, deodorants, sports shoes, or vitamins.

Boxing photography has also become part of the mass market in pornography. Boxing gloves are potent symbols of masculinity and when topless Page 3 girls wear them a provocative sexual message is produced that "real" sports are for men and that women are there simply to provide excitement and arousal. It is as if women's bodies are part of the equipment—"apparatuses for male 'sporting' pleasure, or playthings for men" (Hargreaves, 1994: 167). Because boxing is commonly believed to be a distinctly masculine sport, to mix it with images that exaggerate the insignia of female sexuality produces a provocative illusion (ibid.).

CONTRADICTIONS

Novelist Joyce Carol Oates explicitly rejects the idea that female boxing could be a subversive activity when she declares, "The female boxer...cannot be taken seriously. She is parody, she is cartoon, she is monstrous" (Oates, 1994: 73). However, the increasing numbers of female boxers from different social backgrounds is a lived example of the way in which women construct a sense of self in relation to their personal bodies, and they, in turn, reject Oates's polemic. The body is the most important signifier of meanings, and in the case of women and boxing and associated activities, these are constantly contested and are changing according to the broader contexts of boxing discourse and gender relations of power. Although strength and muscularity in boxing have symbolically been a source of physical capital for men, the diversities and complexities of representations of the female body in boxing make it difficult to assess the extent to which the sport is a subversive activity for women or an essentially assimilative process with a radical facade. Female boxing in all its different forms links the physical body with the social body and the inner self with the outer self in ways that are riddled with complexities and contradictory cultural values.

FREEING THE AFRIKAN MIND: THE ROLE OF MARTIAL ARTS IN CONTEMPORARY AFRICAN AMERICAN CULTURAL NATIONALISM

Thomas A. Green

INTRODUCTION: CULTURAL NATIONALISM

> Franz [*sic*] Fanon studied, understood, and wrote about the state of the Afrikan mind in the present condition of mental servitude and submission to the European plunderers. He observed that we are the wretched of the earth because we have lost our Afrikan essence. We have allowed our enemies and enslavers to capture our souls; we continue to deny our Afrikan foundation and buy into Eurocentrism. A return to our [Afrikan] essence is our only hope [for freeing the Afrikan mind]. (Afrikan Echoes, 2002; see also Fanon, 1952/1986; Fanon, 1961/1967; Poulos, 1997)

There is remarkable similarity between the previous statement and the following:

> [Our people] have been degraded by mingling with others; they have sacrificed their natural disposition in protracted...servitude; and...imitated a tyrannical prototype for a long time, they are, among all the nations...the least true to themselves. (Halsall, 1998)

However, the author of the second passage was not a Black Nationalist, but the Prussian philosopher Johann Gottfried von Herder (1744–1803). Herder was a pioneer of anthropology, hermeneutics, and linguistics. His theory was that people belong to bounded and defined groups known as "nations." Each nation had a unique and legitimate claim for sovereignty

Novell Bell and Liang Peng practicing *baguazhang* in China. Courtesy Novell G. Bell.

based on its common history, language, and tradition (Forster, 2001; Halsall, 1998).

In Herder's opinion, there were two main ways that a nation established its cultural boundaries, its Manifest Destiny. One required people to pledge loyalty to the state. Thus, the United States introduced a Pledge of Allegiance in 1892, in which students were required to shout, "One Country! One Language! One Flag!" (Bigelow, 2001-2002) This method leads to the destruction of local customs, regional languages, and so on. The other method (and the one advanced by Herder) said that a nation was linguistic and cultural rather than political. Thus, in Herder's case, speaking German was an important marker of ethnicity (Halsall, 2001).

Because Herder's method perpetuates local customs and regional languages, non-German nationalists soon adopted similar agendas. For example, eighteenth-century Scottish and Welsh intellectuals responded to English cultural imperialism by recovering a Gaelic heritage that was built on the partially invented oral traditions of the non-Anglo-Saxon cultures of the British Isles (Trumpener, 1997).

Nineteenth-century Irish efforts aimed at achieving political independence from England also included linguistic and cultural revivals (Chastain, 1997). For example, in July 1893, Douglas Hyde (1860–1949) founded the

Gaelic League. Hyde was a poet, linguist, and folklorist, and he agreed with Herder that language held a nation together. Consequently, the goals of the League included restoring the Gaelic language to Ireland (Hyde, 1998/2000; Quinn, 2001).

A problem with this plan was that only about 14 percent of the Irish population spoke Gaelic, and for many of those people, it was a second language (Embassy of Ireland, 2002; Wholewheatloaf, 2001). Therefore, to reach English-speaking Irish intellectuals, the League also patronized English-language literature by Irish authors. (Indeed, Hyde's own work in folk literature is credited with having inspired the Irish literary renaissance) (Hyde, 1998/2000). Meanwhile, to reach Irish working people, the League looked to sport and dance. Thus, the Gaelic Athletic Association (GAA), established in 1884, was associated with the Irish Republican Brotherhood. Thus, while its stated goals mostly involved encouraging Irish games such as hurling, its unstated goals included encouraging Irish nationalism (Baker, 1983: 63; O'Farrell, 1989).

When historical traditions were unavailable, then they were invented. Eric Hobsbawm and Terence Ranger advanced the notion of invented tradition in 1983 (Introduction). They characterized invented traditions as "instant formulations of new traditions," ranging from ritual and ceremony to costume and genealogy, and added that the purpose of such inventions was to address the immediate social needs of the group.

Perhaps the most notorious Gaelic invention was the epic poem "Ossian, the Son of Fingal." In 1761, during a period of rising nationalism in Scotland, James Macpherson (1736–1796) published "Ossian," an epic poem about a third-century Scottish king, and in 1763, he published a similar poem called "Temora." Macpherson said that these poems came from an ancient manuscript he found while traveling in the Scottish Highlands. Because he would not show anyone the manuscript, suspicions were aroused, and eventually it was conclusively determined that these were forgeries. Irish nationalists were outraged, as in the process, Macpherson had indiscriminately mixed Fenian and Ulster folklore. Moreover, he had said that various Irish cultural heroes were originally Caledonian rather than Hibernian (DeGategno, 1989; Irish Heroes, 2000; University of Delaware Library, 1999).

All of this is to say that using (and sometimes inventing) cultural artifacts to marshal ethnically based nationalism is a common strategy. Consequently, when African American nationalists of the 1960s decided to abandon their slave names, it is hardly surprising that some turned to pan-African culture, and took up the study of African languages such as Swahili.

AFRIKAN CULTURAL NATIONALISM

[African American] cultural nationalism was founded on the belief that blacks and whites have separate values, histories, intellectual traditions and lifestyles and therefore that in reality, there are two separate Americas. (Hiltz and Sell, 1998)

The term most relevant to the definition provided in the previous quote is *Afrikan,* a Swahili loan word that alludes to the principle of a separate African cultural identity in North America.

This usage apparently developed during the Black Governmental Conference held in Detroit, Michigan in March 1968. The participants, who included Betty Shabazz, Amiri Baraka, Queen Mother Moore, Oseijeman Adefunmi, and Maulana Ron Karenga, expressed a desire "to build a new society based on the best of our traditional Afrikan values" (Alisogbo, 1996).

Music, art, and martial art played prominent roles in the new Afrikan worldview. In the words of Karenga, the founder of Kwanzaa, "Let our art remind us of our distaste for the enemy, our love for each other, and our commitment to the revolutionary struggle that will be fought with the rhythmic reality of a permanent revolution" (quoted in Hiltz and Sell, 1998).[1]

ESTABLISHING AN AFRIKAN IDENTITY THROUGH MARTIAL ARTS AND COMBATIVE SPORTS

Early Attempts

Long before anyone thought of Afrikan nationalism, some African Americans tried to establish a positive African American identity through participation in martial arts and combative sports. Although their excellence rarely received appropriate reward, these black fighters had a surprising impact on European and Euro-American popular culture.

Throughout colonial times, African Americans wrestled, "knocked and kicked," and played traditional stick-fighting games. (For details, see "Surviving the Middle Passage" elsewhere in this volume.) In Europe during the early 1800s, a few black men became talented fencers. Examples included Chevalier de Sainte Georges, Soubise, and Jean-Louis. After the American Civil War, some blacks also went into professional wrestling. Viro Small, for example, was a professional wrestler in New York City in 1869, and around 1890, Abdullah Jeffery and "Alix the Negro" were wrestling professionally in France.

Jack Johnson, after getting out of Leavenworth Penitentiary in 1921. Johnson's crime was transporting a white woman (his girlfriend, and future wife) across state lines. While in prison, Johnson fought several exhibitions. By Janet Bradley.

However, African American men enjoyed their greatest professional success in boxing. African American cultural nationalists such as Dennis Newsome, citing Hausa *dambe* boxing as an example, say that this is because boxing is a traditional African activity (personal communication, September 2002). Meanwhile, sociologists say that this is because boxing is a method for members of the economic and ethnic underclass to attain a measure of dignity and short-term economic success (Wacquant, 1994; Wacquant, 1995; Wacquant, 2001; Weinberg and Arond, 1952). A third possibility is that boxing, a naturally percussive activity, corresponds well with African and African American esthetics. Percussive music is an almost universal element of African and African-descended combat arts, and throughout the nineteenth and twentieth centuries, percussive musicals (tap dancing, extended drum solos, and *Stomp!* are examples) have been popular.[2] As Jack Johnson's biographer Randy Roberts wrote (1983: 22–23):

Boxing, like music, is a rhythm activity. Even its exercises—jumping rope, punching the speed bag, shadow boxing, sit-ups—are in essence rhythm. Every great fighter has his own rhythm and style. Some move in jitterbug bebops; some shuffle to an internal slow-drag blues. [Jack] Johnson shuffled; he boxed the way [Jelly Roll] Morton played the piano, with an emphasis on style and grace, not speed and power.

In any event, African American participation in European boxing began early in the settlement of the Americas. Given the circumstances, black fighters made an impressive showing.

Bill Richmond, who was born on Staten Island in 1763, first came to the attention of the British general, Hugh, Earl Percy, by beating three of Percy's soldiers during a brawl in 1777. Percy took Richmond to England with him in 1778, and Richmond took up prizefighting in 1791. After retiring from the ring to become a publican, Richmond trained boxers. Black fighters he trained included Tom Molineaux of Virginia, Sam Robinson of New York, Joseph Stephenson of Maryland, plus others known only as Sutton, Massa Kendricks, Bristow, and Johnson (Ashe, 1988: 17–21; Gorn, 1986: 35–36; Mee, 2001: 60).

Tom Molineux was born around 1784 in Georgetown, South Carolina. Later nicknamed "the Virginia Slave," he reportedly gained his freedom through his pugilistic ability. He subsequently traveled to England where legend claims he was "discovered" by Bill Richmond (Mee, 2001: 62). In England, Molineux established a career, even fighting for the English championship, between 1810 and 1815. Unfortunately, drink brought on fatal liver disease, and in 1818, he died at the age of 34 (Gorn, 1986: 19–22; Mee, 2001: 66).

Historian Thomas Desch-Obi argues that a reason for the success of these early African American fighters was that they had a distinctive style called "cutting." According to Desch-Obi, cutting combined elements of British bare-knuckle pugilism, the hand techniques of *kadenka* (an African style of slap-boxing), head-butts and kicks, and the throws of African wrestling (1995; 2000: 163). Although this interesting contention requires further research, the British photographer Eadweard Muybridge (Edward James Muggeridge, 1830–1904) spent three years during the mid-1880s documenting the motion of animals and humans. One of his series of images shows an African American boxer using an unconventional clubbing style (Treffner, 2002). The style depicted may be Desch-Obi's cutting.

North American pugilistic venues available to blacks often bore more resemblance to brawls than fights under Broughton's, London Prize Ring, or Queensberry Rules. For example, during the late nineteenth and early twentieth centuries, "Battles Royal" involving African American fighters was reportedly popular (CyberBoxingZone, 2002a). These fights were unsanctioned, unregulated, and usually held in remote locations. Groups of fighters fought in the ring, and the last man standing collected a "purse" made up of donations from the spectators. Competitors ranged from locals to fighters of the caliber of Joe Gans (1874–1910) and Jack Johnson (1878–1946) (Coughlin, 1997).

First-rate black boxers hailed from both hemispheres. For example, Peter Jackson (1861–1901) came from St. Croix, in the British West Indies. Among the best heavyweights ever, he was a serious threat to reigning champion John L. Sullivan. However, the two never fought because Sullivan refused to risk his championship to a black man. Similarly, Sam Langford (1883–1956) was born in Weymouth Falls, Nova Scotia. Langford boxed in every class from lightweight to heavyweight, and he is considered one of the best boxers never to have participated in a world championship fight. In 1922, the Senegalese boxer Louis Phal, who fought as "Battling Siki," defeated Georges Carpentier, and in the process became French Africa's first black boxing champion. During the 1930s, Toronto's Larry Gains became a British Empire champion, and more recently, the Biafran Richard Ihetu (who fought as Dick Tiger) and the Ghanaian Azumah Nelson gained considerable international renown.

In 1908, Arthur "Jack" Johnson became the first black boxer to beat a white (Tommy Burns, a.k.a. Noah Brusso) for the world heavyweight championship. Yet, just seven years earlier, Johnson was jailed for a month in Galveston, Texas, for participating in a mixed-race prizefight (Cogswell, 2002; Roberts, July 1983).[3] Thus, Johnson's reign as heavyweight champion was controversial. Johnson didn't help matters with his flamboyant personality and lifestyle. Among other things, he liked fast cars and white women, and he flashed his famous golden grin whenever he beat a white opponent. Consequently, throughout the 1920s and early 1930s, Jim Crow kept African Americans out of title fights.

During the 1930s, Joe Louis (Joseph Louis Barrow, 1914–1981) was allowed to fight for the championships that his talent merited. Nevertheless, Louis's handlers heeded Johnson's lesson and therefore ordered Louis to "never have your picture taken with a white woman" and "never smile when you beat a white opponent" (Coughlin, 1997; Louis with Rust and Rust, 1989).

The relevance of Louis in the present context is not his making black athletes acceptable to a race-conscious white public, but his powerful

Joe Louis, 1935. On May 14, 1935, one day after his twenty-first birthday, Louis signed a contract that specified that 75 percent of his gross earnings from all sources went to his handlers, while he paid all taxes and training expenses. Thus, the more fights he won, the poorer he got. On the other hand, the deal gave Louis the chance to face white boxers in title fights, and Louis's victory over Max Schmeling on June 22, 1938, represents a turning point in American race relations. By Janet Bradley.

symbolization of African American potential. It was not coincidental that calypso singers in Trinidad immortalized Louis's fights with the German Max Schmeling (a loss to Schmeling in 1936, followed by a win in 1938) in songs (Hill, 1998). Such popular bonding with an athletic hero was important, and perhaps necessary, for a program of African American cultural nationalism to succeed.

Recent Attempts

From its inception in Detroit in 1930 until February 1964, the African American religious group called Nation of Islam[4] generally discouraged its members from participating in sports. Explained the Messenger, the Honorable Elijah Muhammad, sports and play caused "delinquency, murder, theft, and other forms of wicked and immoral crimes" (quoted in M. Smith, 2001: 54).

Then, in February 1964, Cassius Clay, who had recently converted to Nation of Islam, defeated Sonny Liston for the world heavyweight boxing title. This unexpected success caused the Messenger to reconsider, and in March 1964, he said, "I'm so glad that Cassius Clay admits he is a Muslim" (M. Smith, 2001: 57). A month later, the Messenger even allowed a photo of Clay (who was now beginning to be called Muhammad Ali) to appear on the cover of a Nation of Islam newspaper. Consequently, after the spring of 1964, young Black Muslims began looking to combative sports as a method of emulating their hero Ali. However, to avoid the taint of gambling associated with boxing, many turned to Asian martial arts instead.[5]

For example, Silis Muhammad, Chief Executive Officer of the Lost-Found Nation of Islam in Chicago, trained bodyguards for the Nation of Islam leader the Honorable Elijah Muhammad (Lost-Found Nation of Islam, 2002). Similarly, New York's Moses Powell "spent innumerable hours conditioning and training members of the Community Mosque security team" (Winston Salem Community Mosque, 2002). And throughout the early 1960s, James Cheatham taught Shito-ryu karate in Newark, New Jersey. Cheatham died in 1966, but his student Shaha Maasi (William Nichols) recalled, "He was very political about power for black people. Very much so. In fact all of his black top guns, the black black belts were affiliated with the Nation of Islam" (Hinton and Rahming, 1994, 51; see also Colling, 2002).[6]

Of course, some African Americans who belonged to Nation of Islam defense cadres pursued martial art careers that were not overtly political. For example, in 1964, Dawud Muhammad began his martial training with the Fruit of Islam. After serving in the Marine Corps and pursuing additional training outside the Nation of Islam, he established a career as professional martial arts instructor in Philadelphia (Muhammad's Martial Arts Academy, 2002).

In any event, the Nation of Islam's military arm remains active today and even provides security services for high-profile events in the African American community. For example, in August 2001, Nation of Islam provided special security for a hip-hop music award show held in Miami

Beach, Florida. Reportedly, the Black Muslims kept order using only "stone cold stares and martial arts training" (Johnson, 2001).

Nation of Islam is not the only African American religious group to include martial arts in its community outreach programs. In Hampton, Virginia, Reverend Franklin Hargrove leads a racially integrated Protestant (African Methodist Episcopal and Southern Baptist) organization called "Karate for Christ." Hargrove began studying Shorin-ryu karate while serving in the Air Force on Okinawa (Holy Temple Community Church, 2002). In Lanham, Maryland, Dr. Lee P. Washington, an African Methodist Episcopal minister, uses Reid Temple as headquarters for a broad-based community outreach program that includes academic, cultural, and "Christian martial art" components (Reid Temple African Methodist Episcopal Church, 2002). Similarly, St. James African Methodist Episcopal Church of Erie, Pennsylvania, offers classes in martial arts that are said to provide empowerment in an African American context (St. James African Methodist Episcopal Church, 2002).

In short, a combination of religion, cultural nationalism, and martial arts is a common thread in late twentieth- and early twenty-first-century African American social programs.[7]

Another Reason Why

By the early 1970s, Muhammad Ali had a rival for the affections of black youth.

An early scene in Berry Gordy's *The Last Dragon* (1985) shows a mostly black audience watching *Enter the Dragon* (1973). The audience greets a screen image with exuberant cheers. However, the object of this adulation is not the black character played by Jim Kelly, but the Chinese American star, Bruce Lee. Like any good spoof, *The Last Dragon* provides a funhouse mirror distortion of reality. Nonetheless, Bruce Lee really was an icon for a generation of African Americans.

For instance, during the 1990s, Wu Tang Clan was an influential Staten Island rap group whose name came from vintage Hong Kong martial arts movies. Its members, who belonged to the Nation of Islam offshoot known as the Five Percent, made pilgrimages to China to study Shaolin boxing, and their lyrics sometimes referred to a Brooklyn street fighting system called the 52s.[8]

In *Ghost Dog—The Way of the Samurai* (1999), Forest Whitaker plays an African American hit man. His roadmap to life is an eighteenth-century Japanese text *(Hagakure)* whose most famous line is "The way of the samurai

Muhammad Ali in Chicago, March 1974. The occasion was a speech by Nation of Islam leader Elijah Muhammad. National Archives and Records Administration, ARC identifier 556247.

is found in death." Wu Tang Clan provides the soundtrack, and the leader of the band, RZA (Robert Diggs), makes a guest appearance (Fuchs, 2000).

Even more recently, the Brothers of Wudang, an association of African Americans practicing Chinese martial arts in New York City, established an Internet presence that links to both hip-hop and Afrikan nationalism (Bell, 2002).

Put another way, African Americans have boxed for over 200 years. The U.S. military has been teaching martial arts to African Americans for over 60 years. The Black Muslims have been teaching martial arts to African Americans for at least 35 years. Nonetheless, African American youth owes much its late twentieth-century interest in the Asian martial arts to one man: Bruce Lee.

AFRIKAN MARTIAL ARTS

Although Bruce Lee was enormously popular with young black men, he was hardly the proper role model for an African American nationalist. True, from an objective standpoint, it shouldn't matter if the martial art is Western, Asian, African, or Martian. After all, the important thing is theoretically the role that the training fulfils within the community. In other words, Afrikan is as Afrikan does.

Of course, theory is one thing and reality is another. "As a youth in the 1950's," writes Ron Van Clief (1996: 11):

> I was first introduced to the martial arts at the St. Johns Community Center. There I met Grandmasters Moses Powell and Ronald Duncan. They were my role models. Until then, I only had non black role models to emulate. They gave me pride in myself and being black. From them, I learned how awesome the black man is.

Adds Dennis Newsome (personal correspondence, October 17, 2002):

> It is significantly more important and even paramount to learn a martial art of African ingenuity than from someone else's culture from an African centered perspective. The whole point is to know thyself instead of other cultures as your center focal point and to honor your own people's collective ingenuity. As a last resort, you use whatever is available to try to reach your goals.

Therefore, a goal of Afrikanist martial arts is to develop a cadre of black instructors capable of teaching Afro-centric martial arts. Consequently, in the following section, we look at how Afrikanists use traditional arts such as capoeira. After that, we examine two modern martial arts, namely the eclectic Kupigana Ngumi and the clandestine Jailhouse Rock. Next, we take a brief look at the revisionist histories that often accompany these Afrikan systems. Finally, we conclude with a discussion of the African American martial esthetic.

Traditional African American Arts

Traditional African American martial arts developed organically in customary cultural settings such as festivals. In the context of Afrikan cultural nationalism, these arts advance social goals such as improved group solidarity and identification with a cultural past.

Sometimes the creation of an Afrikan identity involves reverse discrimination. Thus, although capoeira is probably the most racially inclusive version of the African American martial arts, some U.S. capoeira Angola organizations exclude, or at least discourage, nonblack members (Sansone, 1999).

An example is the curriculum developed by Dennis Newsome (Mestre Preto Velho) of Sao Bento Grande Capoeira Angola in San Diego, California.[9] According to Newsome, this training, when combined with training in dance and other ethnic traditions, "reconnects the youth to their

African Cultural past, modifying thought processes and recapturing their African sense of morals, ethics and artistic Aesthetics" (World Beat Center, 2002a). Newsome characterizes the adult portions of the program as an "entity" conceived to train African Americans, who in turn will train others. He adds, "The motivation behind this program is to restore and maintain the moral and cultural heritage and strength of African American communities through the practice of Capoeira Angola Sao Bento Grande" (World Beat Center, 2002b). This represents a significant example of cultural nationalism in the martial arts.

Besides capoeira, Newsome teaches a Caribbean stick fighting system (kalinda) and an African system (testa: Italian, "head"; Portuguese, "forehead") that he says that he learned from an Ethiopian sailor. His instruction caters to a primarily African American clientele (Planet Capoeira, 2002; Dennis Newsome, personal communication, September 2002).

Like most North American capoeira Angola teachers, Newsome teaches a history that minimizes links to Brazil and maximizes links to Africa. Thus, his instruction includes the other traditional partners of African and African American martial arts, namely dance and religion (Capoeira Angola Sao Bento Grande, 2002a; Dennis Newsome, personal communication, September 2002).

In Newsome's case, the religion is the Yoruba-based Brazilian religion of candomblé. Explaining the role of such cultural artifacts, he writes (with specific reference to stick fighting):

It is paramount that we continue the practice of Kalenda because every time an African tradition stops being practiced by us a little bit more of our national and international African soul dies. A little bit more of our identity, history and dignity dies. (Capoeira Angola, 2002b)

Newsome is hardly alone in using capoeira to foster African identity in the Americas. For example, the International Capoeira Angola Foundation (ICAF), with headquarters in Washington, D.C., seeks to promote capoeira Angola as a cultural artifact and to promote positive feelings about African heritage. ICAF, however, maintains a policy of racial nondiscrimination (International Capoeira Angola Federation, 2002). Nonetheless, Newsome exemplifies community-based efforts to perpetuate an authentic African American system and to revitalize it for purposes of community empowerment. In fact, in 2000, the Alliance for California Traditional Arts awarded him a grant to teach capoeira, kalinda, and their musical traditions to three apprentices (Alliance for California Traditional Arts, 2000).

Kupigana Ngumi

Some Afrikan martial arts are simply eclectic martial arts used to promote pan-African sentiment. One of these is Kupigana Ngumi, founded by Nganga Tolo-Naa (Ray Cooper) and Shaha Maasi during the 1960s.[10]

Although Tolo-Naa was born in Chicago, his early role models included James Cheatham. Tolo-Naa followed Cheatham's career through a magazine called *Judo Digest,* and in 1963, he started studying karate under John Keehan (a.k.a. Count Dante).

In 1964, Tolo-Naa entered an open tournament in Washington, D.C. Tolo-Naa's first opponent was Shimabuku Tatsuo. Shimabuku was the founder of Isshin-ryu karate and reportedly able to kill any man with just a flick of a wrist ("Expert on Karate," 1966/2002). Whether this is true is unknown. However, in point fighting, he lost to Tolo-Naa. The head judge, a Mormon kenpo teacher named Ed Parker, refused to award the victory to Tolo-Naa.[11] Episodes such as this caused Tolo-Naa to become more political. He joined the Black Muslims, and later he was discharged from the Army for refusing to serve in Vietnam (Hinton and Rahming, 1994: 97–100).

Tolo-Naa met Maasi around 1966 or 1967. From New Jersey, Maasi had begun training in karate while serving in the Marine Corps between 1959 and 1962. Following his discharge, he started training with James Cheatham in Newark. When Tolo-Naa met him, Maasi was working as a bodyguard for Amiri Baraka (Leroy Jones), a socialist playwright who performed benefits for the Black Panthers and other radical groups (Academy of American Poets, 2002). In this role, Maasi frequently heard Baraka speak "about Egypt and the contributions of the Ethiopians. It just dawned on me that if we were here first, then we should have made some contributions that we should know about" (Hinton and Rahming, 1994: 92).

After meeting, Tolo-Naa and Maasi decided to give karate an African twist. Toward this end, Maasi proposed the name *ya ngumi,* which means "the way of the fist" in Swahili. Tolo-Naa responded with *kupigana ngumi* ("fist-fighting"), and it was the latter that was chosen (Hinton and Rahming, 1994: 94).[12]

Structurally, Kupigana Ngumi has many Asian influences. Besides karate, these include the *taijiquan* of Tolo-Naa's teacher Hou Chi Kwang, the *qigong* of Maasi's "kung-fu/wu su" teacher Alan Lee, and the bando of Maung Gyi's American Bando Association (Chinese Kung-fu Wu-Su Association, 2002; Hinton and Rahming, 1994: 90–91, 108). That said, Kupigana Ngumi's emphasis on questioning authority ("do your research" is a common refrain) and learning through learning principles rather than rote is *not* standard Asian pedagogy (Hinton and Rahming, 1994: 94).

Publicly, Kupigana Ngumi teachers no longer advocate any radical political positions. However, they continue to stress the importance of education, especially in African languages and African American history. Toward this end, they have been helped through a SciFi Channel animated series, *Maatkara* (2001–), in which a young woman descended from ancient Egyptians uses Kupigana Ngumi techniques to save the world of 9002 c.e. (Okorafor, 2001; SciFi.com, 2002).

Jailhouse Rock

Jailhouse Rock is an African American street system that Dennis Newsome first brought to national attention during the 1980s. Ironically, given his Afrikanist stance, this prominence is owed mostly to Newsome's work with the white film star Mel Gibson (O'Neill, 1987).[13]

Newsome asserts that the roots of Jailhouse Rock are in the fighting systems that slaves brought with them to the Western Hemisphere during the colonial era (Capoeira Angola Sao Bento Grande, 2002c; Dempsy, 1999).[14] He claims that these systems survived into the present due to their being taught in prisons (Planet Capoeira, 2002). They are necessary survivals, he adds, because racist courts and penal laws have created a system of de facto slavery. In his words, the "politics and racism that continue to influence the penal system in the U.S. make this prison combat system thrive as a functional necessity of modern African Americans" (Capoeira Angola Sao Bento Grande, 2002c).[15]

Throughout the 1990s, martial arts practitioners argued about whether Jailhouse Rock existed outside Newsome's imagination. Critics pointed out that prison guards discourage inmates from training in martial arts. Moreover, prison fights tend to be gang fights rather than esthetic marvels (Stickgrappler's Martial Arts Archives, 2002a).

At the same time, however, popular artistic expression routinely alluded to some kind of emerging street system. For example, the lyrics of the hip-hop group Wu Tang Clan made frequent reference to an urban fighting system called "52s" or "52 Hand Blocks." Similarly, the hip-hop dance style known as "up rocking" supposedly owed something to an African American urban fighting system. Finally, some saw connections between Jailhouse Rock and the ring strategies of professional boxing champions Floyd Patterson and Mike Tyson, both of whom had been in juvenile detention before entering the ring (Century, 1999: 79–80; Darling and Per-

A Jailhouse Rock combination. After locking a right hook with his left arm, New-some twists, steps, and (a) strikes Erick under the jaw using an inverted right elbow. Newsome then (b) pulls the right side of Erick's jaw into a left hook, which in turn flows into (c) a left elbow to the head. At normal speed, elapsed time for this series is under two-fifths of a second. Courtesy Dennis Newsome.

ryman, 1974: 21; Dennis Newsome, personal communication, September 2002; Stickgrappler's Martial Arts Archives, 2002b).

The debate was finally resolved in 1999, when journalist Doug Century published an account of gangs, crime, and hip-hop culture in Brooklyn called *Street Kingdom: Five Years inside the Franklin Avenue Posse.* In this book, in a subsequent article in *Details* magazine (August 2001), and in e-mail dialogs, Century clearly documented the existence of a Brooklyn *street* version of Jailhouse Rock known as the 52s.[16]

Century, who is white, paints a more pragmatic and less political image of Jailhouse Rock. He says that the main reason Jailhouse Rock is little known in the white community is that whites rarely interact freely with Brooklyn gangster society. Nonetheless, Century established sufficient credibility to be shown techniques and was even allowed to photograph them.[17]

Century says that Jailhouse Rock has such a distinctive body movement style that whites really cannot master it. "Once you've seen it," he says, "you'll know that it could only be a 'black' style" (Stickgrappler's Martial Arts Archives, 2002b). When called on the unconscious racism of this observation, Century replied that he assumes movement styles develop through habit rather than ethnicity (Stickgrappler's Martial Arts Archives, 2002b).

According to Daniel Marks, who trains in 52 Hand Blocks (personal correspondence, August 2002):

The 52 Hand Blocks is from Brooklyn. At best, it's like a dance. Break dancing pulled some of its diss moves. (Diss is when you show up another dancer.)[18] The hard rocks (gangsters) used to slap box in the streets. (Slap boxing is a form of sparring.) As far as the prisons go, most cats just consider their skill as being nice with their hands.

During the 60s, it was a war tactic [of the Nation of Islam and its Five Percent offshoot], and used to combat racism. Later, once the youth had no direction, they became gangs. This was quite nasty if you were not down with their "Mathematics" (e.g., knowledge of self), which at that time was simple: the original black man is God and the white man is the Devil. Of course, we know now that any man can be a devil.

Anyway, this is what led to 52 Hand Blocks. Only if you were down with the crew (gang) could you learn. Meanwhile, in prison, you became either a Muslim or a Five Percenter, as this was the only protection from Bubba.

Jailhouse Rock was never taught as a martial art, just as a way of fighting. Cats would say, "You don't want none of this," referring to hand skills, but what made it sick (good) was the deceptive hand parries, elbow and knee strikes, and head butts. The main object is to hit, and hit often; thus the [alternative] name, "bum rush."

Today, the 52 is all about style, using the movements but calling them by slick names like "shooting joints" for throwing punches, "shampooing your hair" for throwing elbows, and "getting low" for attacking the legs. "Switching the L" refers to the triangle block, as well as using hammer fist strikes. This is how you pound on a cat, and when your arms look like tree trunks you can get off a serious beat down. The "kiss move" is when you clap your forearms together to trap a jab; the top arm can release easily to block the other punch.

By the way, the up rocking movement is a modified box step in Filipino martial arts. As well, there is the *ginga* [the fundamental standing movement of capoeira]. There is also the 2-step and the 6-step. The 6-step can be seen in break-dancing, but the 2-step is walking like a penguin. You rock side to side and enter with elbows flying.

Every skill in Jailhouse Rock is earned through sparring, which is why it's creative. You have to be creative to hit without being hit.

Revisionist Histories

Revisionist histories often support Afrikanist martial endeavors. Much of the revisionism is valid. For example, the origin stories of most martial arts are replete with nonsense. Furthermore, capoeira is the not the only African martial art, even if it sometimes appears that way in books on martial art history (Corcoran and Farkas, 1988). Finally, the illustrations of wrestlers at the Egyptian tombs at Beni Hassan are among the oldest depictions of martial arts in the world (Carroll, 1988).

On the other hand, some revisionist claims are controversial. For example, J. D. Jackson (2000), citing Nijel Binns (BPG, 1999/2000),[19] claims that the Asian martial arts (and even the word "karate") are of African origin. S. E. Suzar (1992/2002: 10) covers much of the same territory as Jackson and Binns, then concludes that "warrior scientists" of African Egypt "laid the foundation for all martial arts systems, including Kung Fu and Judo."

To accomplish such connections, Afrikanist authors mix oral tradition, the written record, and speculation. Therefore, from a historiographical standpoint, the bond in their stories is more genuine than is their bonding agent. However, from an anthropological standpoint, the accuracy of the story is not really the issue. Instead, the important thing is to observe the steps the storytellers are taking toward the creation of an Afrikan cultural identity.

The African American Esthetic

Based on the evidence presented in the foregoing accounts of Afrikanist martial arts, it seems safe to conclude that there is an African American martial esthetic. Therefore, what are some of its features?[20]

1. *A distinct movement style.* This style incorporates percussive, polyrhythmic beats. Whether this beat comes from berimbau or boom box is irrel-

evant. Admittedly, close links between martial art, music, and dance are not unique to Africans or African Americans. Indonesian *silat,* for example, has always blurred the lines between martial art and theatre. Nonetheless, urban African Americans have their own esthetic, and their fighting styles reflect this.

2. *Prefight rituals involving boasting, derision, and challenge.* Jack Johnson flashed his golden grin. Muhammad Ali spouted outrageous poetry. The Jailhouse Rocker taunts his opponent. Thus, part of the esthetic includes verbal challenges and derisive remarks. Admittedly, verbal dueling is not uniquely African or African American. Indeed, it is documented in cultures as diverse as Turkish, Scandinavian, and Native Alaskan. Nonetheless, the African American rituals resemble patterns seen in both African and African-descended New World forms.

3. *Emphasis on improvisation.* Asian martial arts typically stress robotlike precision. Only after decades of rote is a practitioner allowed to improvise, and even then, only within narrow parameters. On the other hand, African American martial arts stress improvisation, and teachers such as Shaha Maasi say, "We have to go beyond learning by rote. We see it, we memorize it, we imitate it, but don't know what principle it's based upon" (Hinton and Rahming, 1994: 86).

4. *Appearances matter.* As an African American prison guard who had ample opportunities to watch inmates fighting in the Texas prisons at Huntsville observed, "The most important thing to them [the inmates] is looking good" (H.C., personal communication, 1991).[21] Century agreed, saying, "The 52 Blocks is all about looking slick and artistic while you fight" (Stickgrappler's Martial Arts Archives, 2002b).

Because coincidence is not causality, it would be inappropriate to claim that this esthetic represents a direct continuity between Jailhouse Rock and historical African systems. It would be equally wrong to argue that this martial esthetic is uniquely African American. After all, even the Victorian English said that it wasn't whether you won or lost, but how you played the game. Nonetheless, whether festival dancer or Jailhouse Rocker, the African American man of action "acts with style, and he considers that everything he does is being watched and comports himself accordingly" (Abrahams, 1983: 125).

CONCLUSION

Martial arts are among the methods by which African American males have historically sought empowerment. For example, during colonial times, African Americans played martial games such as knocking and kicking, *kalinda,* and flip wrestling (Desch-Obi, 2000; Rath, 2000; Wiggins, 1977). More recently, African Americans have found heroes in boxers such as Jack Johnson, Joe Louis, and Muhammad Ali.

Since the 1950s, Black Nationalists have sometimes turned to non-European martial arts and combat sports for inspiration. For example, during the 1960s, the Detroit-born Nation of Islam, having already adopted a non-European religion, encouraged its members to train in Asian martial arts. At the same time, African Americans who were not Black Muslims began systematically exploring African-descended belief systems such as *santería, candomblé,* or *vodun,* and in some cases practicing martial arts rooted in these belief systems. Because the Afrikan nationalists sought to counter a historically eurocentric system, the strategy employed is logical.

Over time, adaptations occurred. For example, karate and taekwondo work well for self-defense. However, both karate and taekwondo tend to be linear and rigid. Moreover, their social structure is committed to preserving the status quo. Therefore, many African Americans found that they preferred softer, rounder Chinese arts (available in U.S. urban centers since the mid-1960s) or less regimented African-descended arts such as capoeira (available in U.S. urban centers since the mid-1970s).

During the last half of the twentieth century, some African Americans sought to minimize any connection whatsoever to European American culture. The idea was to show dissatisfaction with a government and legal system that perpetuated African American enslavement through Black Codes, Jim Crow, and the prison-industrial complex. Motifs used by these people included adopting and systematizing the outlaw systems of street gangs and prison fighters. Jailhouse Rock is a generic term describing such styles.

Derived arts such as Kupigana Ngumi combine these two trends. That is, they (re)construct African martial arts from the raw materials that characteristically accompany and develop martial skill (dance, music, percussion, improvisation, and so forth), and then use them to serve the ends of African American cultural nationalism.

Whether evolved, reinterpreted, or derived, African American martial arts have social agendas and share a common esthetic (Abrahams, 1983; Rath, 2000; Szwed, 1971; Thompson, 1992). Therefore, whether their individual focus is utilitarian, political, religious, or cultural, their teachers pursue an African American essence, and by so doing, seek to free the Afrikan mind.

ACTION DESIGN: NEW DIRECTIONS IN FIGHT CHOREOGRAPHY

Tony Wolf

> But everywhere he looked he saw signs of war....out of the East, Men were moving endlessly: swordsmen, spearmen, bowmen...all the power of the Dark Lord was in motion. (Tolkien, 1954/1994: 391)

Between 1998 and 2002, J. R. R. Tolkien's *Lord of the Rings* saga was produced as a trilogy of feature films. This undertaking involved an army of actors, stunt people, and other production personnel: a massive creative effort culminating in the release of the first film, *The Fellowship of the Ring,* at the end of 2001.

Director Peter Jackson believed that each of the various cultures represented in the film—Elves, Uruk-hai, Gondorians, and others—should be unique to the world that he was creating. Therefore, during the preproduction phase, he asked me to design a series of culturally specific fighting styles and to train performers in their application.[1] These styles were subsequently used as templates by the fight and stunt coordinators, digital effects department, and so on.

Jackson's vision was novel, as the traditional approach to staging action sequences in fantasy projects is to employ generic fight choreography, which means selecting spectacular combat tricks drawn from an eclectic pool of techniques.

The art of devising and performing fight sequences is often glossed as *stage combat* or *theatrical combat.* These terms are specific to theatre, and

Orc vs. Elf. By Janet Bradley.

do not include fights for movies, TV, or digital effect applications. There-fore, I prefer the more inclusive term *performance combat*. In this essay, I draw from my experiences with the *Rings* project to discuss some recent trends in what I refer to as *action design*—the creative process of fight choreography for theatre, film, and television projects.

These trends include the following:

- The concept of universal movement and performance principles as the basis for combat choreography
- The creation of performance combat representations of existing real world and historical fighting styles
- The idea of individuated performance combat style as the result of a creative design process
- The integration of physical fight choreography and digital special effects techniques

WITH AND *FOR*

Aristotle observed that conflict is the essence of drama. In performance combat this essential conflict is physical and immediate. Every choice of action and reaction should make sense for *this* character, in *this* situation, within *this* story.

Bear in mind that performance combat is an art of illusion, much closer to dance than to fighting. The paradigms are *with* and *for*. Actors and stunt people move safely *with* each other, *for* the entertainment of an audience. That is their priority and perspective. The martial arts/combat sport paradigm is, excepting special cases such as aikido, *against*. Martial art practitioners compete *against* opponents in sparring, or fight *against* enemies during real combat. There is some common ground here; martial art practitioners in training also work with their partners safely, practicing prearranged routines that are, in a sense, forms of fight choreography. Examples would include the paired form and step-sparring exercises of many Asian disciplines, the etudes of classical fencing, and so on.

For reasons of safety, available rehearsal time, and esthetics, a fight director must choreograph a representation of physical conflict between fictional characters, rather than presenting actual fighting techniques. The technical choreography is only one aspect of this dramatic illusion, which is subject to a range of other artistic decisions.

Martial art practitioners can become frustrated when they see their art represented in a dramatic context, rather than being presented as it would be in an educational demonstration or a sparring match, or even in a street-fight or battle. Similarly, people with any area of specialized interest will tend to notice, and often object, when their area becomes subject to creative license. The divisions of perspective between cooperation and competition, realism and reality, performance and demonstration, representation and presentation are the difference between the movie *Gladiator* (2000) and the actual Roman arena.

Modern action designers undertaking historically inspired projects can aim for significantly high levels of both realism and accuracy. The challenge lies in making artistically mature choices, thereby balancing historical accuracy and combat realism with the requirements of safety, story, and character.

UNIVERSAL PRINCIPLES

One emerging trend in performance combat involves research and analysis of real world fighting styles. The idea is to develop safe, dramatically effective performance representations of these styles.

The resulting representational style is built on a foundation of neutral, universal movement and staging principles. These principles provide a conceptual and practical foundation for learning techniques. These are the physical actions of the fight sequence—the kicks, leaps, cuts, dodges, and so on. These techniques are chosen and performed according to a particular combination of styles. *Technique,* then, can be understood as the confluence of principle and style, as performed by a particular character in response to a specific situation.

My own system of performance combat encompasses six foundational principles:

- *Synergy.* Tactile sensitivity and communication, moving safely in close contact with another performer
- *Articulation.* Cycles of visible preparation, action, and reaction
- *Deception.* Cycles of visual misdirection, concealment, and misrepresentation
- *Alignment.* Triangulation of stance and posture for stability, and the use of skeletal structure and body weight to counterbalance another performer's weight during lifts, throws, catches, and drags
- *Extension.* Projecting the kinetic energy of a striking, thrusting, or cutting attack safely away from the performance partner
- *Sequential flow.* Safely absorbing or deflecting the momentum of a fall

All of these principles are universal in application. The performance combat versions of a Shotokan karate punch, a rapier thrust, a savate kick, and a double-handed sword cut will all be articulated, extended, and performed in alignment. Likewise, a pro wrestling throw, an *aikijujutsu* takedown, and a catch-as-can arm-drag will all be articulated, synergized, and aligned, and end with the partner employing sequential flow. Because performance combat is an illusionary art, the principle of deception is inherent to all of the others. These principles interlock in the performance application of literally any fighting technique.

These same principles apply during actual combat. However, during real fights, the goal is to deceive the opponent rather than the audience. A fighter might use synergy to sense and defeat an adversary's movements[2] or extend a thrust into (rather than away from) the opponent.

A DIVERSITY OF STYLES

If we define ourselves by doing, then style is doubly definitive, because style describes the doing (Robbins, 1971).

During Hollywood's silent film boom period, fight sequences were frequently used to embellish historical dramas. Notably, Douglas Fairbanks—arguably the cinema's first superstar—was a great fight and stunt enthusiast, and his trademark acrobatic style thrilled audiences in epics including *Robin Hood* (1922), *The Black Pirate* (1926), and others. Fairbanks almost single-handedly invented the Hollywood swashbuckler, laying many of the foundations for the development of the action genre.

The early studios spared no expense in hiring the some of the best fencing maestros of their day as fight doubles, advisors, and trainers to the stars. However, the actual fight choreography was often a collaborative effort between the director, fencing master, and actors. The maestros brought their extensive ability and knowledge of competitive fencing to the task of creating exciting screen sword fights.

According to pioneer silent movie fencing choreographer Fred Cavens:

> For the screen, in order to be well photographed and also grasped by the audience, all swordplay should be so telegraphed with an emphasis that the audience will see what is coming. All movements—instead of being as small as possible, as in competitive fencing—must be large, but nevertheless correct. Magnified, is the word. The routine—there must be a routine, and so well learned the actor executes it subconsciously—should contain the most spectacular attacks and parries it is possible to execute while remaining logical to the situation. In other words, the duel should be a fight and not a fencing exhibition, and should disregard at times classically correct guards and lunges. The attitudes arising naturally out of fighting instinct should predominate. When this occurs the whole performance will leave an impression of strength, skill and manly grace. (Quoted in Behlmer, 1965/1997; emphasis in original)

During the 1910s and 1920s, there was little easily accessible information on historical fencing styles that used rapier and dagger or the European two-handed sword. Contemporary choreographic philosophy therefore pre-supposed that the action depended upon the techniques of competitive fencing with the foil, épée, and especially the sabre. This was consistent with early Hollywood's approach to history, in which accurate period detail was routinely sacrificed in favor of flamboyant, romantic storytelling.

As the movie industry matured and diversified, some directors began to experiment with increasing levels of period accuracy and combative realism. However, not until Ridley Scott's groundbreaking Napoleonic War drama *The Duellists* (1977) did cinematic swordplay truly begin to reflect serious historical research. Scott's fight director, William Hobbs, was among the first action choreographers to have come from a theatrical rather than purely athletic background, and to bring a knowledge of historical fighting techniques to bear on his work. Consequently, by moving sharply away from the swashbuckling style, Scott's production is generally acknowledged to have broken new artistic ground.[3]

Most modern fight directors would agree with Fred Cavens regarding a degree of magnification, the necessity of a well-learned routine, and that a screen duel should resemble a fight rather than a sporting exhibition. However, a vastly wider range of fighting style models is available to the new school of action designers. These include martial arts and combat sports from a diverse range of cultural traditions, as well as those that have become obsolete and are presently undergoing revival, such as various historical European systems.

Verisimilitude is another important issue in modern action design. Although not appropriate for every production, truly realistic fight choreography must mimic the qualities of broken rhythm, interceptive movement, imbalance, misalignment, and other features of spontaneous combat. It is certainly challenging to create a safe, convincing fight between characters who are not always poised to perform excellent technique, fighters who make mistakes and must sometimes scramble to recover the advantage, or to save themselves. The increasingly sophisticated use of camera angles and editing techniques helps to convey the kinetic, high-impact energy and flow of close combat. Although intended to make the viewing experience as exciting and visceral as possible, the rapid-fire, in-your-face shooting style can be a source of frustration for martial art–oriented viewers who are looking for technical details.

The phenomenal popularity of Bruce Lee's martial art films of the 1970s introduced the stylized gymnastic choreography of the Hong Kong action cinema to an international audience. Representing a development of the Beijing and Cantonese Opera tradition, the Asian school of action design has become an increasingly important stylistic influence for English-language productions.

By working from a stylistically neutral base of efficient movement and staging principles, extant or revived styles can be adapted or combined, or customized to create unique performance combat styles. Alternatively, as with the *Lord of the Rings* project, they can serve as inspirational models for new systems that exist only in the realm of fantasy.

DIGITAL WARRIORS

Another important trend in cinematic action design involves the integration of digital special effects with live-action performance. In general terms, most computer-generated imagery application in fight sequencing can be classified as either key-framing or motion capture. In the former, as in more traditional forms of animation, a computer artist creates the illusion of movement by linking together a sequence of static poses ("key frames"). Unlike traditional animation, however, the key-framed action is three dimensional and almost infinitely malleable.

The *Lord of the Rings* digital effects department made extensive use of motion capture, which is a form of live-action-based animation used extensively in combat-oriented video games. A motion capture performer wears a black costume covered with photoreflective markers, and performs in a studio equipped with a series of cameras connected to a computer system. As the cameras record the pattern of reflections, the computer encodes a moving, three-dimensional, human-shaped constellation of stars. This pattern can then be "dressed" by artists to create a digital stunt double for an actor, multiplied to create an army, or distorted or enhanced in any number of ways. Motion captured data can even be used to help "train" digital warriors who fight and move independently, making their own decisions and reacting to their virtual environment without any human direction.

DESIGNING STYLES FOR MIDDLE EARTH

Serving as the Cultural Fighting Styles Designer, I became responsible for the fighting styles of the Orcs, Rohirrim, Uruk-hai, Gondorians, Elves, Goblins, and Easterlings. Each race or culture had its own substyles as well, based on different weapon combinations—Rohan axe and shield, Elf swordplay, Goblin spear fighting, and so on. Because all three movies were shot simultaneously, the fighting styles for each one were largely designed during the preproduction phase.

The level of detail on costumes and weapons produced as props that would never be seen in close-up inspired me. My ideal was that audiences would be able to tell the character types apart, even if they were seen in the far distance or in silhouette, purely by the way they moved and used their weapons. I also wanted each fighting style to be unique to the Middle Earth culture that produced it, not just a pastiche of moves from disparate real-life sources.

RESEARCH AND CHARACTER-BASED PROCESS

The research phase for each style began by studying a particular culture: costumes, armor, weapons, background stories, biomechanics, physical capabilities, and limitations. We developed two primary referents: Tolkien's novels, and the interpretation of Middle Earth that was being collectively "imagineered" by the growing army of creative personnel attached to the film project.

The key was to start from an intimate understanding of the characters, then to determine which outside influences could be seamlessly combined to create something that made sense for our story. We examined animal predation and defense techniques, combat tactics, locomotion dynamics, dance and movement styles, and many different martial arts traditions. It was a character-based process, in contrast with the more traditional, technique-based approach.

Although we used the term "fighting style," we meant something more than a style in the formal martial arts sense. The Orcs, for example, were imagined as stupid, brutal, chaotic creatures, and it would be out of character for them to exhibit disciplined or refined technique. Also, from a practical standpoint, the Orcs had 108 different types of weapons and it would have been impractical to create a formal fighting style for each. Because the Orcs were so diverse, their style was more tactical than technical—a combination of specific body language parameters and combat strategies. Orcs took techniques from other races in the same way that they cannibalized weapons and armor. Thus, their method was efficient but ugly, a grotesque parody of skilled combat techniques suggesting baboons or hyenas that have learned to use swords and spears.

By contrast, the Elves were beautiful, magical beings, and their martial arts were exquisitely formal. Elvish swordplay reflected a cultural tradition that had been refined over thousands of years.

In short, each Middle Earth culture imposed its own discipline and had to be approached on its own terms.

DEVELOPMENT

The development phase included a great deal of full-contact sparring using padded weapons and body armor. For example, we would pit an Uruk-trained sword-and-shield fighter against a Rohan-trained spear fighter. Special training systems and safety equipment were developed, allowing performers to safely improvise fighting, moving and reacting in character. These bouts were videotaped and extensively analyzed. The styles had to function believably as battlefield-worthy fighting skills before they could be transformed into performance vehicles.

Peter Jackson's motto was, "We're not making fantasy movies, these are historical epics set in Middle Earth." This suggested a serious approach to the fantastic, contrasted with the more traditional (and lazier) approach, "We're making it all up, so who's to say *this* can't happen?"

As a designer, I wanted the discipline of knowing exactly what was right for each character, down to the detail. Which elements of fifteenth-century German longsword fencing will work for the Gondorian style? Can an Orc straighten its arms? Can Elves hear attacks they can't see? How strong is an Uruk's helmet? All of these questions, and many more, had to be answered to ensure continuity and realism. Simultaneously, however, we had to deconstruct the fighting styles into key points so that each different production department could modify them according to its own needs.

QUATRAINS

Because many *Lord of the Rings* characters have abilities that humans do not possess, fight choreography was another major aspect of the design phase. Uruk-hai, for example, were strong enough to use powerful edge blocks with their machete-like swords, and human performers could not safely mimic that action in sparring. Likewise, Elves possessed a variety of superhuman abilities that we could only simulate through prearranged choreography. Therefore, we developed hundreds, perhaps thousands of "quatrains," which were brief choreographed routines that demonstrated different aspects of the styles.

Quatrains were situational acting exercises as well as *kata*-like choreographic sets. They were also used to communicate the styles to different departments within the production, including many people who were completely unfamiliar with fighting, stunt work, or martial arts.

One quatrain demonstrated a Goblin archer, for example, scuttling backward while firing several arrows at an enemy. Another showed an Elf swordsman calmly awaiting an onslaught of Orcs, then slicing and dicing several at once. We created quatrains for mounted fighters, such as the warriors of Rohan, demonstrating spearing and lancing techniques from horseback. I also developed "twists," varying individual quatrains by changing one important action so that a slightly different result would develop, demonstrating how the various quatrains and styles interlocked.

The quatrains modeled an approach to training and demonstration that followed the old adage, "Give them a fish, they are fed for a day; teach them to fish, and they are fed for a lifetime." Under these circumstances, the more traditional, technical drill approach was not appropriate. Instead, I encouraged the performers to focus on the fundamentals of posture, movement dynamics, combat tactics, and character. The quatrains emphasized all of these equally and served as conceptual models. Individual performers, choreographers, and production departments were then able to extrapolate and adapt the styles for their own purposes.

This was important because during the preproduction stage, we didn't know exactly what the characters would be required to do. Thus, the fighting styles had to be flexible enough to cover a whole range of possibilities, yet simultaneously maintain specific key points and details for the sake of continuity.

Once I was happy with the design, Peter Jackson approved or amended it. The final phase involved developing a curriculum for teaching it to the stunt team, and recording a series of sample quatrains on video and in written format for reference by other production departments.

A CONCEPTUAL PROCESS

Although we made extensive reference to real world fighting styles, I did not necessarily give them any more weight than dance styles, or even influences from sports. At the R&D level, I was looking for nuances of movement, and I felt that if I were to start imposing specific techniques from outside sources, I would have become false to the Middle Earth cultures. Everything proceeded from the character and the culture, toward a congruity of weapon and armor function, body language, dynamics, and tactics. Once those were determined, then the techniques essentially created themselves.

After the fact, it is possible to deconstruct a given style and see how individual techniques resemble those of real-world systems such as aikido, Maori *taiaha* combat, medieval *Ringen am Schwerdt* (sword grappling), and a matador dancing with a bull. However, it is important to stress that during the design process, we borrowed concepts rather than techniques.

As an example of this conceptual approach, the following is quoted from the *Fighting Styles Guidebook* that I wrote for continuity reference (Wolf, 1999):

> The Elves are graceful and fluid beings whose every action is poised, neither stiff nor heavy. Their breathing is centered in the lower abdomen. They are grounded from the waist down, yet light and free from the waist up. As holistic fighters, all of the Elves' senses are fully engaged in combat. Their movements are circular, fluid, evasive and deceptive, employing spiraling deflections that flow into lightning-fast slicing attacks. There is a magical, sleight-of-hand quality to their fighting techniques. They do not always look directly at their enemies in combat, seeming almost to be engaged in a kind of moving meditation.

PERFORMER TRAINING

Regarding the performer training process, I offer a quote from theatre practitioner and performance studies researcher Richard Schechner. "Rehearsal is a way of setting an exact sequence of events. Preparations are a constant state of training so that when a situation arises one will be ready to 'do something appropriate.' Preparations are what a good athletic team does" (Schechner, 1976: 222).

Because the *Lord of the Rings* stunt performers were training during pre-production, often weeks or months before any specific fight sequence was to be rehearsed, my work with them emphasized preparation. I believe that it is important for stunt people to be actors who can imaginatively inhabit the characters they are playing. That way, they should be able to do something appropriate when they begin rehearsing specific action sequences.

In preparing the stunt team to perform the Uruk-hai styles, we began by discussing the Uruk-hai as living beings, introducing a precis of all the research done to date. Because breath informs the posture, the first practical exercise involved breathing techniques. Uruks breathe harshly and deeply, and they are enormously strong, tense creatures, top-heavy juggernauts, with massive chest, neck, shoulder, and jaw development. I thought of them as "gorilla-bulldogs."

Next, although the stunt performers would be wearing prosthetic masks and helmets during shooting, I encouraged them to act with their faces. Uruks snarl and grimace, as if they are in constant pain and their only relief lies in violence.

In addition, we moved around the training room as Uruks. As soon as they were spawned, Uruks were locked into heavy plate armor. Thus, there was a feeling of crushing weight and momentum to their stride. They had difficulty turning quickly. An Uruk's gait was like walking uphill on railroad tracks.

I also taught the stunt people a few words of Black Speech[4] and had them grunt orders and curses at each other. The resulting exercise involved a platoon of stunt people lurching, roaring, and shoving-interacting as Uruk-hai.

Now we used quatrains to explore how Uruk soldiers used their weapons and moved in combat situations. This included a variety of scenarios we anticipated would be required during production. We experimented with one-on-one fighting techniques and melee tactics for use on the battlefield.

We knew that the Uruk-hai of our story had limited, if any, formal training (perhaps some basic drill work). However, they were lethal instinctive fighters, much more dangerous than the Orcs. They used their cleaverlike swords and spiked shields interchangeably, smashing, and bashing. Their defenses were power blocks—no finesse, no deflections, just brutal chops that could bounce an attacking weapon straight back the way it came. Sometimes they didn't even bother to defend themselves; they'd just rely on their armor and move straight in to the attack. They would hammer and chop, and occasionally flip their swords around and use the back-spike to pinion an enemy, or gut them with the prongs on their shields.

The final training phase involved getting the stunt people to choreograph their own quatrains. If they were able to work creatively within the style, it meant that they had internalized it—it had become "their thing." The ultimate test is to be able to improvise in character.

CONCLUSION

In the nineteenth-century theatrical tradition, fight sequences for each new production were created by rearranging a predetermined corpus of routines. The term *fight arranging,* which implies simply a compilation of preexisting elements, exemplifies the traditional approach.

Action design is different from fight arranging, and is still evolving as a creative field in its own right. Defining the research and development, performer training, and choreography process as a creative design task is, in itself, a novel perspective. Increasingly, modern professionals have to customize their talents for specific productions. Thus, they must be able to prepare, rehearse, and portray everything from highly realistic domestic violence to fantasy battles, from historically accurate swordplay to slapstick tumbling. Specialization in a given style is increasingly perceived as a limitation.

Today, an action designer may use research techniques drawn from cultural anthropology and download fifteenth-century combat manuals from the Internet. She or he may develop choreography through improvisation using padded weapons and body armor, collaborating with performers rather than imposing a set routine. The resulting fight sequence may be recorded not onto film, but into computer software. As digital technologies become increasingly sophisticated, it is also possible that action designers will become consultants, devising, and demonstrating action to be performed by virtual actors or "synthespians."

Cinematic action design represents a confluence of ancient tradition and cutting-edge technology. The challenge is to strike a balance, to move fluidly between styles and genres in representing Aristotle's "essential drama."

MARTIAL ARTS MEET THE NEW AGE: COMBATIVES IN THE EARLY TWENTY-FIRST-CENTURY AMERICAN MILITARY

Joseph R. Svinth

INTRODUCTION

During the early 1990s, in the aftermath of the Gulf War and the collapse of the Soviet Union, the U.S. military began devoting significant resources to planning and conducting "military operations other than war" (MOOTW). "Although MOOTW and war may often seem similar in action, . . . MOOTW are more sensitive to political considerations and often the military may not be the primary player." Additionally, military personnel had to "understand the political objective and the potential impact of inappropriate actions" (Joint Chiefs of Staff, 1995: vii). In other words, early twenty-first-century warfare would take place under the gaze of both spy satellites and television cameras.

At the same time, futurists predicted that in the coming years, the "jewel in the military's crown" would be special operations forces trained to perform both "international housekeeping and wet-work." These special operations forces would be "capable of precisely applying technologically superior weapons" and engaging in hand-to-hand combat (Szafranski, 1995: 81).

Accordingly, both the U.S. Army Rangers and the U.S. Marine Corps began looking into upgrading existing training in close-quarter battle and hand-to-hand fighting.[1]

FIRST EARTH BATTALION

In 1979, the U.S. Army War College published a futurist document entitled "First Earth Battalion." The tone of the document is hyperbolic and

THE WARRIOR MONK

Chinese Monks were often attacked by robbers. They developed a new fighting system based on using the force of the attacker against him. Likewise the soldiers of the FIRST EARTH will learn martial arts with the same ethical basis. NO EARTH soldier shall be denied the kingdom of heaven because they are used as an instrument of indiscriminate war. The conscience will be developed together with the ability to neutralize the opponent.

First Earth Battalion: The Warrior Monk. "Chinese monks were often attacked by robbers. They developed a new fighting system based on using the force of the attacker against him. Likewise the soldiers of the FIRST EARTH will learn martial arts with the same ethical basis. No EARTH soldier shall ever be denied the kingdom of heaven because they are used as an instrument of indiscriminate war. The conscience will be developed together with the ability to neutralize the opponent." From Jim Channon, *The First Earth Battalion: Ideas and Ideals for Soldiers Everywhere*, 1979. Courtesy Jim Channon.

imbued with New Age jargon. On the other hand, it did predict the role that the Internet and cable news networks would play during the coming decades. Therefore, despite the hyperbole and New Age jargon, author Jim Channon's crystal ball proved clearer than cynics expected (Channon, 1979/2000; see also Dare, 1998; Chevalier, 2001).

Among Channon's suggestions was that future soldiers practice "battle tuning," which he described (in so many words), as a combination of yogic stretches, karate kata, paced primal rock, and Belgian waffles (Channon, 1979/2000). Although "battle tuning" was a bit esoteric for most soldiers, in 1985, the Army hired former Marines Jack Cirie and Richard Strozzi Heckler to provide several dozen Special Forces soldiers with training in aikido, biofeedback, and "mind-body psychology." (Aikido was chosen because the project's purpose was not to train barehanded killers, but to research increases in awareness.) After six months, the soldiers were not aikido masters. Nonetheless, most claimed greater self-awareness, and they were on average 75 percent fitter than when they started (Heckler, 1992). Navy SEALs received an abbreviated version of this course in 1988.

As a rule, however, the U.S. military of the 1980s neglected training in close-quarter battle and hand-to-hand fighting (Wood and Michaelson, 2000: 107). Firstly, the American leadership envisioned a nuclear war with the Soviet Union, and in a nuclear war, skill in hand-to-hand combat is inconsequential. Consequently, commanders did not devote resources to training in hand-to-hand combat. "In no way did the Army or Marines of the 1980s provide purpose, motivation, and direction for their combatives programs," said Matt Larsen (personal communication, July 2002), who was the primary author of Field Manual 3-25-150, *Combatives* (U.S. Army 2002). "The missing element was any sort of plan other than 'Commanders should dedicate more time.'"

Secondly, science, in the guise of "nonlethal" technologies, was supposed to solve the problem of military operations in areas filled with hostile civilians that it was impolitic to forcibly relocate or shoot. Sample nonlethal technologies included chemical sprays, electronic stun guns, sticky foam, net guns, rope sprays, blinding lasers, and acoustic weapons (Alexander, 1999; Wright, 1998).

Thirdly, martial arts (at least as taught by Heckler) were believed to develop soldiers who knew how to "maintain their stand, coordinate with multiple opponents and maintain their dignity" (Krawchuk, 2000).[2] Yet, as a former Special Forces officer named Alan Farrell (1994), put it, the leaders of a nuclear military did not really want self-actualized soldiers. Instead, the ideal soldier of the nuclear-armed military was rigid, conforming, inhibited, and totally obedient. (See also Heckler, 1992: 153.)

Then came the unexpected collapse of the Soviet Union and a series of messy peacekeeping operations in Liberia, Haiti, Somalia, and Bosnia. During these latter operations, soldiers and Marines whose average age was under 23 years were exposed to violent situations in which the use of firearms was not authorized. Meanwhile, the new nonlethal weapons proved "less lethal" rather than "nonlethal." Nonetheless, they still required soldiers and Marines to use (and equally importantly, *not* use) them. Consequently, during the mid-1990s, U.S. military leaders started paying new attention to close-quarter battle and unarmed combatives. In the Army, the impetus involved midlevel officers and NCOs, whereas in the Marine Corps, the driving force was the commandant himself. Thus, two entirely different programs emerged.

THE U.S. ARMY ADOPTS GRACIE JIU-JITSU

During late 1994 or early 1995, then-Lieutenant Colonel Stanley A. McChrystal, the new commander of the 2nd Ranger Battalion at Fort Lewis, Washington, decided to reinvigorate hand-to-hand combat training in his unit. "We got out the FM 21-150," said then–Staff Sergeant Matt Larsen, "and started doing just what it said to do. After about two or three months we went back to the commander and told him that it was a waste of our training time. He told us that it if was a waste of time, then there must be a reason, and told us to come up with a better answer" (personal communication, July 2002).

There was no money to create a Ranger-specific system, so the program had to be reasonably off-the-shelf. Toward determining the best system, the battalion organized a committee of experienced martial arts practitioners. "Our criteria for success was simple," said Larsen (personal communication, July 2002). "The average soldier in the Army had to know what the literature said he should know, and the system should produce its own experts independently of continuing outside instruction."

The style that the Ranger Battalion eventually decided to adopt was Gracie Jiu-Jitsu. It wasn't because other systems were less valid, or that the battalion wanted its soldiers rolling around on the ground with armed enemies. Indeed, Larsen (personal communication, July 2002) readily admitted that a "weakness of Gracie Jiu-Jitsu is its focus on unarmed, one-on-one arena fighting." On the other hand, it "fit the realities of the world" (Larsen, personal communication, July 2002.)

First, Gracie Jiu-Jitsu was reasonably easy to learn and use. Thus, within the few hours per week that commanders were willing to dedicate to combatives training, individual soldiers could become quantifiably more proficient than they were when they started. Additionally, associated injuries were usually no more serious than a black eye or split lip, and fitting it into existing conditioning programs did not put new demands on already-crowded training schedules.

Second, Gracie Jiu-Jitsu allowed competition. This allowed both individuals and units to compete among themselves, thereby building morale and encouraging improvement. "Competition," said Larsen (personal communication, July 2002). "is a key element to the implementation of a successful combatives program. If you can be the unit champion, then there is a reason to excel."

Third, during the years that this program was being designed, the Gracies were winning Ultimate Fighting Championships. Consequently, it was easy

At Fort Dix, New Jersey, Staff Sergeant Ralph Price instructs a recruit during the Combative Ground Fighting Techniques class. U.S. Army photograph by Sargeant Noreen L. Feeney.

to show skeptics that Gracie Jiu-Jitsu worked. Finally, said Larsen (personal communication, July 2002), "The lesson that the Gracies had to teach was that a realistic training plan is necessary if you expect results. The guys they fought in the early Ultimate Fighting Championships had unrealistic training plans, whereas the Gracies had a training plan specifically geared toward that sort of competition."

Therefore, for a variety of reasons, Rangers took to practicing Gracie Jiu-Jitsu without unreasonable pressure from supervisors, or too much complaining from trainees. Subsequently, former Rangers spread the Gracie Jiu-Jitsu gospel to other commands, and in January 2002, Gracie Jiu-Jitsu became the cornerstone of the U.S. Army's combatives program. "Soldiers have a surprising degree of skill retention from one month to the next," said an Army National Guard sergeant who started training his men in these methods later that year. "I think the fact that they actually enjoy the training contributes greatly to that!" (Jeff Cook, personal communication, July 2002).

THE MARINE CORPS MARTIAL ARTS PROGRAM

Like the Army's combatives program, the Marine Corps Martial Arts Program (MCMAP) began because a new commander decided that he wanted his unit to train in combatives. However, in this case, the commander was not a lieutenant colonel, but the commandant of the Marine Corps. Thus, the Marine Corps program was custom designed rather than off-the-shelf, and it became doctrinal within two years.

Shortly after taking office on July 1, 1999, General James L. Jones, the 32nd Commandant of the Marine Corps, initiated a study designed to determine the feasibility of having all Marines study a martial art such as taekwondo or aikido. First, Jones believed that martial arts training (and discipline) might prove useful during operations other than war. Second, as a company commander in Vietnam, Jones had been impressed by Korean Marines going through their taekwondo exercises. Years later, as a battalion commander in California, Jones noticed that junior enlisted personnel who participated in martial arts training had higher morale and fewer discipline problems than did other Marines. Finally, during the mid-1990s, he met (and was impressed by) Richard Strozzi Heckler, who had written a book about teaching aikido to Special Forces.

The Marine Corps study took place at Camp Pendleton, California, during the spring of 2000. Its first year budget was about $173,000 (U.S. Marine Corps, 2002a). To ensure objectivity, two separate programs ran concurrently. Lieutenant Colonel George Bristol ran the control group. Bristol was a reconnaissance Marine with extensive experience in Japanese martial arts. His motto was "One Mind, Any Weapon," and his trainees went through graded combative performance tests (fighting with pugil sticks, hitting and throwing one another, etc.) following forced marches, river crossings, patrols, and assault exercises. In between, they heard lectures about Zulus and Spartans. According to an article in the *Wall Street Journal*, Bristol's goal was "to give the Marines a sense of the fear—and pain—of combat, so they can surmount it" (Jaffe, 2000).

Richard Strozzi Heckler ran the other group. During his instruction, Heckler stressed personal accountability. "During combatives," said Heckler (2002), "accountability became a living concept in regards to how, where, why and with whom one trains to be combat ready." This accountability applied equally on liberty, in garrison, or in combat. In Heckler's world, combatives were part of the force option continuum of a Marine rather than "simply something to do if his rifle malfunctions." Nonetheless, practical hand-to-hand and bayonet skills were necessary. For Heckler, the hand-to-hand techniques that a Marine needed to know included knee strikes, elbow strikes, and neck wrestling. At first, these techniques were done slowly. Later, they were combined with the "aiki principles" of "correct body placement, dynamic relaxation, extension, balance, centering, reading your opponent, entering, fluidity of motion, blending, and power," and done at full speed.

After reading the after-action reports, the commandant directed the establishment of MCMAP. The program officially started in October 2000, and in February 2001, Marines began graduating from its instructor training courses. Full implementation throughout the Corps was expected by September 2002.

MCMAP included elements from both Bristol's and Heckler's programs. Thus, training included "warrior studies" as well as tests of physical skills conducted in simulated combat environments. Of course, since Bristol was program director, his ideas (and those of his chief enlisted man, Master Gunnery Sergeant Cardo Urso) predominated. Well, at least they did until Bristol and Urso were reassigned. Said an observer of an instructor training course conducted during the summer of 2002, "Urso is gone. So is Bristol. Some of the crazy stuff they did is gone too. And it is not uncommon for one of the instructors to say 'the Colonel ain't here anymore' or 'Master Guns isn't running this' when explaining why something has changed" (D.T., personal communication, July 2002; see also U.S. Marine Corps, 2002c).

CONCLUSION

As of this writing (September 2002), both the Army and Marine Corps combatives programs are still evolving. Because both programs are new, it is impossible to predict how they will do in the future. Nevertheless, continuing doctrinal emphasis on "operations other than war" and smaller (but better-trained) special operations forces suggests that combatives are likely to play an increasingly important role in U.S. military training.

At least until the next time doctrine changes.

EPILOGUE:
WHERE WE GO FROM HERE

Joseph R. Svinth

During the last four decades of the twentieth century, martial arts became a growth industry. Probably the most important reason was increased leisure. The decade following World War II was hard, but by the 1960s, first North Americans and then Europeans and Japanese began having the time and money to devote to recreational pursuits.

The commercialization of fantasy played a role, too. Thus, just as movies starring Jack Dempsey introduced boxing into Asia during the 1920s, films featuring Bruce Lee introduced Asian martial arts into late twentieth-century America and Europe.

Commercial fantasies affected martial arts in other ways, too. For example, during the early 1990s, some *Star Trek* fans began practicing Klingon martial arts. Of greater importance to the consumer economy, however, during the 1980s, cable networks began showing kickboxing, professional wrestling, and eventually Ultimate Fighting Championships. This in turn led to the spread of Gracie Jiu-Jitsu and the development of Mixed Martial Arts. In addition, the development of inexpensive video technology meant that businessmen began selling exercise programs and promotions via videotape.

Of course, film was not the only commercial medium to contribute to the spread of martial arts during the late twentieth century. For example, thousands of new books, scores of mass-market periodicals, and an untold number of self-published newsletters and Internet sites appeared. Some were excellent, most were not, but either way, significantly more information became available.

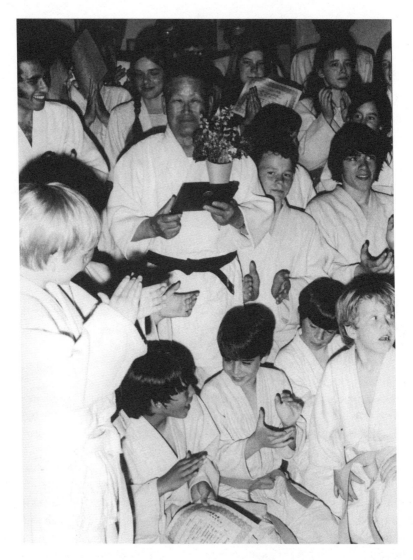

Washington State judo pioneer Ryoichi Iwakiri celebrating his seventy-fifth birthday at the Tacoma Dojo, April 1974. Courtesy Joseph Svinth.

Nationalism remained important, too. For example, Japanese and Korean nationalists got judo and taekwondo introduced into the Olympics, which in turn increased their national medal counts. Not to be outdone, Americans (both North and South) and Europeans began paying more attention to their own heritage arts. Examples of non-Asian heritage arts rejuvenated during the late twentieth century include British backhold wrestling, capoeira Angola, and assorted renaissance swordplay systems.

Other factors involved in the late twentieth-century globalization of the martial arts included the following:

- *Improved transportation.* Until the late 1950s, overseas travel usually involved travel by ship. Then, with the advent of jet airliners, travel to far-away places started taking hours instead of days. Moreover, prices dropped. Thus, students began going to foreign teachers, and vice versa.

- *Changed immigration laws.* During the late twentieth century, North American and European policies changed to allow increased immigration from Africa, Asia, South America, and the former Warsaw Pact countries. Consequently, ethnic martial arts previously unseen outside their home countries have become available worldwide.

- *College clubs.* During the 1960s, a counterculture movement led to the establishment of martial arts clubs on campuses throughout the world. To give an example, in May 1966, a group of fantasy writers and college students established a group that would become the Society of Creative Anachronism, or SCA. The original purpose of the SCA was to recreate life in medieval times. (Selectively, of course, as no SCA members wanted to recreate plagues or the lack of indoor plumbing.) This spurred research into medieval and renaissance martial arts, which in turn became a growth industry of the 1990s.

- *Military martial art programs.* During World War II, the British and U.S. militaries taught hand-to-hand fighting to soldiers, and to this day, combatives programs developed during that era have many followers. Additionally, from 1949 until the early 1970s, the U.S. military actively patronized Japanese and Korean martial arts. Other countries' militaries followed suit. The Soviets, for example, patronized a form of jacket wrestling called sambo, the South Koreans patronized taekwondo, and the Israelis developed krav maga. During the 1980s, many of these U.S. military programs went into decline, but during the early 2000s, both the U.S. Army and Marines reintroduced large-scale military martial arts programs. The long-term impact of these latter programs has yet to be determined.

- *Normalization of relations with the People's Republic of China, the collapse of the Soviet Union, and the end of the Cold War.* Until Richard Nixon went to China in 1972, Chinese martial arts in the West were essentially limited to what was available in Taiwan and Hong Kong. However, with the normalization of relations, the entire gamut of Chinese martial arts became available. Similar things happened with the fall of the Soviet Union in 1991—suddenly, previously obscure Russian, Slavic, and Central Asian martial arts became available to anyone with money.

- *The War on Crime.* Although metropolitan police forces provided officers with training as early as the late nineteenth century, contemporary police training programs date to the mid-1960s and Lyndon Johnson's "War on Crime." Physicians, psychologists, shooters, and martial arts teachers vied for a piece of the comparatively enormous new budgets, and a multi-billion-dollar industry developed. By the 1970s, newly formed SWAT teams had equipment and training previously available only to national police forces, and by the 1990s, contractors offered even the smallest department training in everything from "verbal judo" to "defensive tactics." Similar training was also made available to the well-heeled civilian.

In short, there are many reasons for the increased popularity of martial arts in the late twentieth century, and with the exception of increased leisure, none is necessarily more important than the others. That said, there is no doubt that the way that martial arts were packaged and marketed significantly changed during the last half of the twentieth century. Consequently, styles and systems have become more geographically and culturally dispersed than before. Technically and esthetically, however, there is little evidence to suggest that martial arts have changed significantly. A punch is still a punch, people are still people, and tribalism, ego, and the taste for fantasy (both romantic and violent) remain as strongly entrenched in the human psyche as ever.

APPENDIX:
DEFINITIONS OF TERMS

The following are some technical terms used (or at least implied) in the text whose usage may be unfamiliar to non-specialist readers, or whose use may be contentious to specialist readers.

Combative sports: Physically aggressive athletic games. Individual combative sports such as boxing, wrestling, and fencing essentially mimic dueling while team combative sports such as football, ice hockey, and lacrosse essentially mimic small unit warfare.

Creative anachronism: The perpetuation or reinvention of archaic techniques. Common motivations include the intrinsic pleasure of the activity itself, preserving traditions, learning how things were done in the past, developing personality traits believed to have been more common in earlier times, and building group solidarity. Because their teachers often require students to dress in period costumes, adhere to archaic social codes, and rehearse mayhem using weapons rarely seen outside museums, all traditional martial art classes contain at least a degree of creative anachronism.

Fixing: Athletic jargon for games whose outcome has been arranged so as to guarantee the winner. Motivations include promoting political agendas, pleasing the hometown crowd, and fleecing bettors.

Games: Competitive activities combining varying degrees of luck, skill, and strategy. Although participation can provide intrinsic pleasure, people also use

Adapted from Joseph R. Svinth, *Getting a Grip: Judo in the Nikkei Communities of the Pacific Northwest, 1900–1950,* in press. Used by permission.

games as conflict resolution models and for teaching methods of trickery, deception, and divination not otherwise taught in school.

Martial art: Although "martial art" is a reasonably literal translation of the Japanese *bujutsu* and the Chinese *wushu,* and a term used in English since the Middle Ages, the phrase sends a mixed message. For example, if the emphasis is on the martial, then the term surely includes military strategy. After all, both Sun Tzu and Machiavelli did write books called *The Art of War.* On the other hand, if the emphasis is on the artistic, then the term just as surely includes Dürer's knights and Sousa's marches. Yet neither of these does justice to the flying sidekicks and 7-year-old black belts that most people think of when you say "martial art." Consequently, it is preferable to use more narrowly defined terms whenever possible, especially when discussing pre-modern systems. Nevertheless, that is not always possible. When "martial art" is used in the text, it is intended in the widest possible context.

Military combatives: Military or paramilitary training in hand-to-hand fighting. For police, the emphasis is usually on restraining the opponent while for armies the emphasis is usually on increasing soldiers' self-confidence and physical aggressiveness. Because militaries are nationalistic organizations, such training typically extols the efficacy of "national" methods, often at the expense of actual tactical advantage.

Muscular (or martial) theater: A popular entertainment whose chief feature is visually exciting mayhem. Plots are simplistic, characters are stereotyped, and complete enjoyment requires audiences to suspend disbelief. Examples include kung fu movies, professional wrestling matches, and the evening news.

Non-lethal: Methods designed and used to physically control or restrain people that are unlikely to cause permanent injury or death. Near synonyms that are more literally accurate but less politically correct include "less lethal." When used without any particular malice against reasonably healthy teenagers and adults, most unarmed combative techniques fall into this category.

Play: Recreational activities that provide pleasurable excitement. These activities may be mental, physical, or both, and the player can participate in them as an actor, a spectator, or both. Play becomes work once money, public recognition, a sense of obligation, or other external rewards assume greater importance than the activity itself.

Shooting: Professional wrestling jargon describing wrestling matches in which both wrestlers try to win using every legal technique they know. What constitutes legal? In practice, anything the referee or the crowd doesn't stop is legal.

Sports: Athletic games. The word comes from the Old French *desporter,* and it originally referred to frolics that distracted people from work, school, religion, and similar "serious" pursuits.

Working: Professional wrestling jargon for matches whose results have been determined in advance. Sometimes the purpose of working is to fleece bettors. ("How the Fake Wrestling or 'Big Stores' Game is Worked," was the name of a story in the *Seattle Times* on October 8, 1909.) Usually, though, working is more benign. For example, it can be used to attract students to a club, to entertain paying audiences, or to teach techniques that would be dangerous if done at full speed against fully resistant opponents. Young champions falling easily for an elderly but venerated teacher is related, as is all *kata* (forms) practice with partners.

NOTES

MARTIAL ARTS IN THE MODERN WORLD

1. I am indebted to Joseph Svinth, my coeditor, for this particularly apt turn of phrase. He in turn was inspired by Benz (1998).

SENSE IN NONSENSE

1. Given the degree of loyalty to systems and superiors that many martial art teachers require and expect, anything less than uncritical acceptance of the folk history is intolerable.

2. At best, these traditions are reasonably accurate transmittals passed down (*not* unaltered, however) through the "family line." At worst, they are gleaned from popular literature that was itself borrowed from oral sources or imagination and then sensationalized.

3. Martial art narratives commonly suggest the elite status acquired through study of a particular system, and students often reminisce (or more accurately, gloat) in personal experience narratives about former students who couldn't handle the curriculum or its demands on their time or bodies.

THE MARTIAL ARTS IN CHINESE PHYSICAL CULTURE, 1865–1965

1. Published under the pseudonym "Master of the Studio of Self Respect," this work was probably a secret society publication; certainly it was written by more than one individual. The text itself suggests a *hongquan* boxing manual.

2. During the war with Japan, the name changed to the Liberated Areas.

3. This chapter has not attempted to describe the martial arts of overseas Chinese or China's ethnic minorities. Instead, it focuses on the majority Han Chinese. Note, however, that the Hui (Muslim) minority has played a particularly prominent role in Chinese martial arts over the centuries. Emperor Qianlong himself (reigned from 1736–1795) is said to have commented on the Hui propensity to practice martial arts and produce military leaders (Ma, 2000: 127).

THE SPIRIT OF MANLINESS

1. Names appear as *Japan Times* spelled them. This includes the Korean names. Therefore, Kin is Kim, Jo is Cho, and Boku is probably Park.

2. In 1927, Miller remembered the date as November 1908, and the Japanese as Omato Yujiro (*The Ring,* September 1927: 12). For a third account by Miller of the same event, see *The Ring,* December 1943: 43.

3. Rufe Turner, an African American boxer active in Stockton in the early 1900s, and in Manila during the 1910s.

4. These bouts took place in, respectively, McAlester, Oklahoma (July 4, 1911) and Fort Smith, Arkansas (February 26, 1912 and August 15, 1913).

5. To belong to the association, gym owners first paid an association fee of ¥20,000 (about U.S.$5,000) (*Japan Times,* May 8, 1933: 8). To recover their investment, gym owners had to develop or manage boxers that crowds were willing to pay money to see. This meant a definite preference for Japanese rather than foreign boxers. Whenever possible, Japanese managers also found it advantageous to indenture boxers, apparently in much the same way as brothel owners indentured prostitutes. The fighters, meanwhile, received salaries. In 1933, a preliminary boxer's salary was between ¥25 and ¥50 per month (*Japan Times,* May 8, 1933: 8; *Japan Times,* June 5, 1933: 1). Inasmuch as Korean day laborers earned about ¥1 per day (exchange rates varied, but that equals between U.S.$.25 and U.S.$.47), the sum probably struck many working-class youths as a reasonable wage. Moreover, salaried boxers could always dream of becoming champions earning a princely ¥300 per month. Unfortunately, there is reason to believe that promoters expected boxers to pay their own living and training expenses and reimburse the promoters for indenturing fees. If so, then many, perhaps most, boxers would have been deep in debt upon reaching the end of their careers.

6. Nobuo Kobayashi died following a professional bout on August 29, 1930, and Ryu Kiei died following an amateur bout on November 13, 1940.

7. For example, in October 1933, a Keijo boxing team defeated two Japanese collegiate teams and tied a third. In September 1935, another Keijo team fought a mostly Russian team at Dairen. According to *Japan Times,* the Manchurian fans considered the Koreans, who included the Korean bantamweight champion Ko Zaiko, to be clean fighters, and much better sportsmen than the average Japanese professional (*Japan Times,* September 8, 1935: 5). Additionally, in November

1939, another Keijo team met a team from California's San Jose State University. The result was a victory for the Koreans.

8. According to Leslie Nakashima (*Honolulu Star-Bulletin,* February 22, 1937: 10), "The Filipino won a clean cut decision before 25,000 fans but the supporters of Horiguchi, who had been hoping for a draw if not victory...hurled cushions and the ring and put the place in an uproar. So the Fuji Boxing Club, with which Horiguchi is connected...issued a statement yesterday that the vote of the judges and the referee were two to one in favor of Horiguchi, therefore the Japanese boy won....They also made public the copy of an apology written by the announcer, Hachiro Kawada, for having raised Eagle's hand in token of victory." Following this fight, Eagle gained weight, tanked several more fights, and subsequently became one of Japan's most successful fight promoters.

PROFESSOR YAMASHITA GOES TO WASHINGTON

1. Yamashita's personal name can be transliterated as Yoshitsugu, Yoshiaki, or Yoshikazu. Although "List or Manifest" shows that he used Yoshitsugu on his passport, I used Yoshiaki because that is what commonly appears in English-language texts.

2. *Dan* means step, grade, or degree, and refers to ranks in judo and other Japanese combative sports. In the modern *dan* grades, one is low and ten is high.

3. Between 1881 and 1906, 16 Japanese attended the Naval Academy. However, Kitagaki was not among them. The reason was that in 1906 Congress passed laws that prohibited the Academy from accepting foreign students.

THE CIRCLE AND THE OCTAGON

1. What is the difference between judo and jujutsu? Jujutsu is a generic term describing unarmed (or minimally armed) methods of hand-to-hand combat. Therefore it is not a system per se, but instead a name for the techniques taught by a specific school or teacher. Judo, on the other hand, is a system (and philosophy) devised by Kano Jigoro and subsequently modified by various Japanese and international regulatory bodies. As for the difference between jujitsu, jujutsu, and jiu-jitsu, that is simply different orthographic conventions. Gracie Jiu-Jitsu, however, is a registered trademark.

2. Despite what one sometimes hears, there is no known evidence to suggest that Kano Jigoro had anything to do with Tomita going to the United States, except perhaps wishing Tomita luck on his foreign adventures.

3. This was presumably Miguel Enrique Araujo, who was president from March 1, 1911, until his assassination on February 8, 1913.

4. Hélio Gracie claims that Maeda taught his brother Carlos jiu-jitsu rather than judo (Nishi, 2002). Of course, in those days, the two words were used interchangeably.

5. If one insists on presenting an argument in this direction, then a more plausible (but equally hypothetical) explanation is that Gracie only trained with Maeda from sometime in early 1920 until sometime in 1921. As a rule, it takes 6 to 12 months to train someone to reasonable proficiency at groundwork, and 3 to 5 years to train that same person to equal proficiency at standing wrestling. Thus, if Maeda knew that he had only a few months to work with Gracie, then he probably would have concentrated on teaching groundwork rather than standing throws.

6. Kosen (*koto senmon gakko,* senior high school/technical university) is an acronym describing a Japanese intercollegiate judo style in which the contest rules encouraged *newaza,* or groundwork, rather than *tachiwaza,* or standing throws. The style flourished in Kyoto from 1914 to 1940 (Kojima, 2000).

THE MYTH OF ZEN IN THE ART OF ARCHERY

1. For example, in 1923, Ohira Zenzo assumed the pseudonym Shabutsu (Shooting Buddha), founded the Dainippon Shagakuin (Greater Japan Institute for Awakened Archery), and proclaimed the doctrine of "seeing true nature through the Zen of shooting" *(shazen kensho).*

2. *Translator's Note:* The translation of many of these technical terms is speculative.

3. *Translator's Note:* When Herrigel discusses the "Great Doctrine" in *Zen in the Art of Archery* (1953: 19, 20, 27, etc.), the actual referent is Awa's Daishadokyo, not Zen. The name Daishadokyo translates more literally as the "Doctrine of the Great Way of Shooting," but I have decided to follow the form found in the English language version of *Zen in the Art of Archery.*

4. *Translator's Note:* In his original essay, Yamada cited only Japanese translations of Herrigel's works. In preparing this version, I added references to the English-language translations of Herrigel's works where available.

5. *New Note for this Translation:* Recent research (Yamada, 2002) has revealed that before his journey to Japan, Herrigel acquired knowledge of Zen from Shuei Ohazama and Kita Reikichi, who were exchange students studying at Heidelberg University.

6. *Translator's Note:* The statement on page 31 of the 1953 English-language translation of *Zen in the Art of Archery* that Herrigel taught at the University of Tokyo is incorrect.

7. *New Note for the English Translation:* Recent research has revealed that Herrigel's retirement was in 1948.

8. *Translator's Note:* Yamada cites the Japanese translation of Die ritterliche Kunst des Bogenschiessens [The chivalrous art of archery (1936); Japanese translation (1941), Rev. ed., 1982]. Because that work is not available in English, I have quoted the English-language translation of *Zen in the Art of Archery,* which contains an identical passage. Subsequent cases of this practice are not noted, but should be obvious from the publication dates of the works cited. Regarding D. T.

Suzuki's influence on Herrigel, a footnote on page 22 of the English translation of *Zen in the Art of Archery* gives the following publication dates for Suzuki's *Essays in Zen Buddhism:* First Series 1927, Second Series 1950, Third Series 1953. Actually, the dates of first publication were 1927, 1933, and 1934, and all three sets of essays appeared in time for Herrigel to read them before writing his first account of Japanese archery.

9. *Translator's Note:* "The target in darkness" *(ancho no mato)* is the title of the eighth chapter (pp. 96–110) of the Japanese-language edition (1956) of *Zen in the Art of Archery.* The English-language translation (1953) is divided into a different number of untitled chapters, and this section corresponds to pages 79–88.

10. *Translator's Note:* Herrigel's foreword was not included in the 1953 English-language translation of *Zen in the Art of Archery.*

11. As we have already seen, the use of the bow and arrow in Japanese archery differs depending on the objective, whether it is foot archery, equestrian archery, or temple archery; and the practice of equestrian archery died out for a period during the Muromachi period while the practice of temple archery has disappeared in modern times.

"THE LION OF THE PUNJAB"

1. The area that in 1910 was British India is today divided into India, Pakistan, Bangladesh, Sri Lanka, Myanmar (Burma), and the disputed area of Kashmir. References to "India" and "Indians" are therefore geographical and historical rather than political. At this point, the author also wishes to acknowledge the inspiration provided by the writings of Joseph Alter, and the assistance and contributions of Nadeem S. Haroon, Mark Hewitt, Balbir Singh Kanwal, Michael Murphy, Joe Roark, Robert W. Smith, John Spokes, and Joseph Svinth.

2. Alter (1995:3) describes *yakhi* as a "boiled down glutinous extract of bones, joints, and tendons, which is regarded by many Muslim wrestlers as being a source of great strength, and being particularly good for the development of knees, ankles, and other joints."

3 Depending on exchange rates and how you calculate purchasing power, in 2002 it required about £58 to equal the purchasing power of a 1910 pound sterling. Thus, £5 represented a significant amount of money for English working men, and a fortune for Indian laborers.

4. A sovereign was a gold coin valued at 20 shillings (e.g., £5). In 2002, the numismatic value of a 1910 sovereign in very fine condition was approximately £60.

THE LITTLE DRAGON

1. Because this article began life as a newspaper article, it is not annotated in standard academic fashion. For additional reading, see Corcoran and Farkas,

1988; Crowley, 2001; DeMile, 2002; Ellsworth, 2002; Eng, 1997; Gong, 2001; and Seven, 1998.

2. *Editor's note:* The cinematic stereotyping of Asian Americans persists into the twenty-first century. See, for example, Media, 2002; and Sandata, 1997.

SURVIVING THE MIDDLE PASSAGE

1. Before the mid–nineteenth century, most people viewed sports as amusing diversions rather than a way of promoting middle class morality, demonstrating national prowess, or increasing sales of newspapers, train tickets, and beer. For more detailed analysis, see (for example) Baker, 1983; Gorn and Goldstein, 1993; Guttmann, 1995; Mandell, 1984; Newsome, 1961; Radford, 2001; and Young, 1984.

2. In 1902, an editorial in Baltimore's *Afro-American Ledger* complained that professional boxer Joe Gans "gets more space in the white papers than all the respectable colored people in the state." This was not to take anything away from Gans, but to wonder why illiterate prizefighters should be more influential role models than "respectable colored people" such as Booker T. Washington or W. E. B. DuBois (Ashe, 1988: 16). See also C. Smith, 2001.

3. Powe argues that the similarity among these martial activities attest to their baNtu origin. This is a significant argument in light of the unmistakable baNtu influence in the martial systems of African America.

4. Powe (2002a: 50) notes, however, that this is not usually done. "While a Hausa combatant would typically praise himself and insult his adversary, the *capoeirista* praises both his teacher and his opponent." The reason is that capoeira is not a fight between enemies, but a game between friends.

5. In 1741, the English pugilist Jack Broughton began developing rules that he hoped would make the prize ring safer. In general use for about 90 years, Broughton's Rules prohibited hitting below the waist or after the opponent was down, specified rest periods, and designated starting marks. In 1838, London Prize Ring rules replaced Broughton's Rules. London Prize Ring Rules introduced a 24-foot-square roped ring (it kept the crowd from interfering), prohibited hip throws and boots with spiked toes, and stated that seconds could no longer help a semiconscious fighter toe his mark at the beginning of a round.

6. See Szwed (1971) and Thompson (1990) for a discussion of how baton twirling went from Kongo to U.S. football half-time shows.

7. Capoeira Angola is famous for acknowledging its African roots, while capoeira Regional maintains closer allegiance to a Brazilian identity. As Powe (2002a: 24) puts it, "An appropriate metaphor would be to liken Capoeira Angola to pure coffee; Capoeira Regional to coffee with cream." That emphasis notwithstanding, both *Mestres* Bimba and Pastinha received their initial instruction in capoeira from Angolans: Bimba from Nosinho Bento and Pastinha from *Mestre* Benedito (Dawson, 1993: 16–17).

8. Such martial magic is reminiscent of the *dambe* boxer's use of protective medicines and the boxers of the African Indian Ocean touching the earth for spiritual blessing (Powe, 1994, 2001).

9. Hollywood movies such as *Lethal Weapon* (1987), *Brenda Starr* (1992), and *Mission Impossible II* (2000) have featured capoeira, and *Only the Strong* (1993) used it as its central focus.

KENDO IN NORTH AMERICA, 1885–1955

1. The Dai Nippon Butokukai was a martial arts organization headquartered in Kyoto that served as a licensing body for kendo, judo, bayonet fencing, and other modern martial arts that were not directly tied to existing traditional lines.

2. Second-generation Japanese American.

3. See also *Japanese-American Courier,* October 1, 1932: 3, where Seattle's Welly Shibata described a group of children in Stockton, California, playing with yo-yos before taking their turns "at head-klonking—or Japanese fencing lessons, as it is more familiarly known."

4. Before World War II, North American kendo and judo clubs often closed during the summer, so that their members could work at jobs in agricultural or fisheries.

5. In postwar kendo associations, *renshi, hanshi,* and *kyoshi* are generally part of a parallel licensing system *(shogo)* that is not directly dependent on *dan* grade. That is, one can be ranked seventh *dan* without also being a *renshi* or *kyoshi.* Additionally, postwar associations usually impose time-in-grade requirements. For example, one postwar association specifies that you cannot test for *renshi* until you have been sixth *dan* for a year, *kyoshi* until you have been a seventh *dan renshi* for two years, or *hanshi* until you have been an eighth *dan kyoshi* for eight years.

6. Emphasis is put on "mainland," because in Hawaii, there was no wholesale relocation, and the civilian government had recently reasserted its authority over military rule. Therefore, in September 1945, Shuji Mikami resumed teaching kendo in Honolulu, and in 1947, he helped establish a territorial kendo federation (Hawaii Kendo Federation, 2002).

7. More precisely, reestablished the club, as in 1940, an exchange student named Kono Hiromasu started a kendo club at Berkeley (*Japan Times,* February 6, 1940: 3).

OLYMPIC GAMES AND JAPAN

1. The names of Japanese people mentioned in this chapter appear in Western name order. The reason is that is how Kano wrote them.

2. Kano referred to the Far Eastern Championship Games, to which he was opposed.

THE EVOLUTION OF TAEKWONDO FROM JAPANESE KARATE

I wish to express my appreciation to Matthew Benuska, Ben Brumback, Dakin Burdick, Shannon Burton, Harry Cook, Robert Dohrenwend, Andrew Jennings, Brian Kennedy, Jim Kuhn, Harvey Kurland, Kurosaka Hiroshi, Moo Yong Lee, Eileen Madis, Ron Marchini, Matsumoto Hiroshi, Patrick McCarthy, Dennis McHenry, Tom Militello, Nagashima Toshi-ichi, Graham Noble, Jim Palais, Ken Robinson, Bruce Sims, Michael Shintaku, Kim Sol, Robert W. Smith, Joseph Svinth, and Takaku Kozi.

1. During 1923 and 1924, Funakoshi Gichin conducted karate classes in the kendo dojo of Nakayama Hakudo (1859–1958). Nakayama was the sixteenth headmaster of Muso Jikiden Eishin Ryu (Shimomura branch), and at the time, he was arguably Japan's best-known living swordsman.

2. Early names for karate acknowledged its origins in southern Shaolin *quanfa.* Examples include *Ryukyu kenpo* (Okinawan *quanfa*), *toudi* (China hand), and *karate-jutsu* (China hand method) (Funakoshi, 1922/1997; McCarthy and McCarthy, 2001: 22, 27, 69). However, Japanese nationalists objected to students training in a martial art with a foreign name. Therefore, in 1935, Funakoshi changed to ideograms that were pronounced *karate-do* (empty hand way), but that alluded to Rinzai Zen Buddhism instead of China (Funakoshi, 1935/1973; Guttmann and Thompson, 2001; 147; McCarthy and McCarthy, 2001: 22, 27; Redmond, 2000). In Korean, the ideograms meaning "China hand way" are pronounced "*tangsoodo,*" while the ideograms for "empty hand way" are pronounced "*kongsoodo.*"

3. According to Lee Chong-woo (2002), a direct student of Yun Kwei-byung and Chun Sang-sup, Chun studied karate while attending a Japanese university called *Dong-yang Chuk-sik.* According to Jim Palais (personal communication, September 2, 2002), and Ken Robinson (personal communication, October 3, 2002), *Dong-yang* is a Korean pronunciation of *Toyo,* and *Chuk-sik* is probably a Korean pronunciation of *Takushoku. Toyo* and *Takushoku* are different universities located in Tokyo. The *Toyo* karate program was taught by Motobu Choki until 1939, and after 1939 by Mabuni Kenwa (Moledzki, 2002). *Takushoku* had a Shotokan karate program administered by Funakoshi Gichin (Funakoshi, 1973: 11).

4. In North America, *Jidokwan* is sometimes transliterated Chidokwan. This latter romanization was popularized by S. Henry Cho, a student of Yun and a major proponent of the style in the United States (Burdick, 1997/1999; Cho, 1968: 1).

5. Yun's Japanese friends and students usually called him Yun Gekka (Hwang, 1995: 39–40; Marchini and Hansen, 1998; Nakamura, 2000; Takaku Kozi, personal communication, October 12, 2000).

6. Chaoyang is in northeastern China, about 250 miles northeast of Beijing. (The precise location is 41.55° N, 120.42° E.) From 1932 until 1945, it was part of Japanese-controlled Manchukuo, but today it is in China's Liaoning Province.

7. Although Warrener claims this film dates to 1924, Harry Cook (2001: 303), Patrick McCarthy (McCarthy and McCarthy, 2001: 131), and Graham Noble (personal communication, July 2000) state that it is early 1930s. Their evidence includes text in the background that describes the emperor as Showa (1926–1989) rather than Taisho (1912–1926).

8. About this text, John Della Pia (1994: 70) writes, "In a book of nearly three hundred pages, only sixteen deal with empty-hand fighting and most of the quoted sources in this section are Chinese. With the exception of Hwang Kee's modern interpretations…none of the martial arts taught as 'Korean' today can show a direct connection to this book."

9. Kim's tactics reportedly included bribery of international sports officials and fight fixing (Jennings, 1996: chap. 10; "S. Korea's sports chief," 2002).

FREEING THE AFRIKAN MIND

I wish to acknowledge the assistance of Joseph Svinth in the preparation of this chapter. His suggestions on productive lines of argument, command of research sources, and insights into combat sports proved indispensable at all stages of the work.

1. Such coupling of festive events, art, music, dance (including martial dance), and ethnic pride to advance social and political agendas is a firmly established pattern among African cultures in the New World (Liverpool, 2001).

2. The syncopated rhythms of folk music also accompany *muay Thai,* or Thai boxing. The musicians typically include a piper, two drummers, and a cymbal player. The piper controls the percussionists, and changes his tunes according to the tempo of the fight and the mood of the crowd (Marre and Charlton, 1985: 208–212).

3. Mixed-race fights were illegal in Texas until 1953. However, because prize-fighting was illegal in Texas until 1933, even fighters of the same race were subject to some persecution (Miletich, 1994: 147–168.)

4. For an introduction to Nation of Islam beliefs, see Dodoo, 2001.

5. Judging from published autobiographies, Nation of Islam members generally preferred striking arts such as karate, taekwondo, and *quanfa* to wrestling arts such as judo. That said, many African Americans did study judo, and some achieved considerable athletic success. For example, Warren Lewis, 2-*dan,* participated in a Los Angeles judo tournament attended by Kano Jigoro (*Great Northern Daily News,* October 27, 1936: 8). In March 1943, Arvin Ghazlo taught judo and bayonet fighting to black Marines at Montford Point, North Carolina (Library of Congress, n.d.). Finally, in 1964, Air Force Sergeant George Harris was a member of the U.S. Olympic judo team ("George Harris," 1997).

6. Cheatham's seniors included Karreem Allah, Prentiss Newton, and Ibretheem Shariff. Although a Methodist rather than a Muslim, the future New Jersey boxing commissioner, Larry Hazzard Sr., also trained at Cheatham's school, achieving black belt ranking in 1968 (Colling, 2002; Clary, 1992; Hinton

and Rahming, 1994: 51; New Jersey State Athletic Control Board, 2002). Kevin "Lil KA" Thompson's Shakil's School of Martial Arts is descended from Kareem Allah's lineage (Ayoob, 1976).

7. Secular organizations such as Oakland, California's New Afrikan Nation also incorporate martial art training into their programs. New Afrikan Nation's goal is the establishment of the separate Afrikan nation of Kush. However, acknowledging the superior military power of the U.S. government, New Afrikan Nation's immediate goals include establishing a network of men and woman dedicated to the defense of the New Afrikan community (Front for the Liberation of the New Afrikan Nation, 2002).

8. The name may allude to Five Percent beliefs, as in Five Percent numerology, seven (5 + 2) signifies male perfection. See Swedenburg, 1997.

9. Although this style is labeled "Angola" to distinguish it from capoeira Regional and emphasize its African roots, it developed as a lineage distinct from the Bahian capoeira Angola of Mestre Pastinha (Dennis Newsome, personal communication, September 2002).

10. Although exemplars, these two styles are not unique. For example, other martial arts with African American cultural agendas include Kiungo Cha Mkono (Shackle Hand Style), created by Nganga Tolo-Naa (Martial Science Institute International, 2002); Mshindi Vita Saana ("Champion [or Victor's] war art"), created by Changa Mshindi and Umeme Maharibi (Africam Village, 2002); and Ta-Merrian ("Egyptian"), created by Kilindi Iyi. In addition, some African American martial art teachers imbue their modern eclectic styles with African names, terminology, and philosophies. Examples include Chaka Zulu's Zujitsu and Darrell Sarjeant's Kamau Njia. Finally, there are people with Afrikanist sentiments teaching traditional styles. As the Web site of one of the latter people (Novell Bell) puts it: "Let it be understood we are not racist. We have a lot of European associates, friends and students. But were [sic] also quite proud of who and what we are. So if you attack us on that level we're going to give it back on that level and more. The difference is were [sic] not going to sugarcoat it" (Bell, 2002).

11. The story is reminiscent of the story told by Seattle kendo practitioner Jim Akutsu (Joseph Svinth, personal correspondence, January 13, 1998): "By the time I got *dan* [senior] rank, I could beat most of them [the instructors]. But beating them was no big deal since they taught kendo as mental discipline rather than military training or sport."

12. Other teachers associated with Kupigana Ngumi include Tayari Casel, Hassan Kamau Salim, and Watani Tyehimba.

13. Newsome was a fight choreographer for Gibson's 1987 film *Lethal Weapon*.

14. This is possible. Solid evidence exists for North American pugilistic traditions known as Knocking and Kicking (Bibb, 1850/1969; Gwaltney, 1981) or Pushing and Dancing (Rath, 2000), and Newsome's description of "trip and flip" sounds like the African American wrestling style that Desch-Obi labeled "side-

hold." In addition, E. R. Spuriell of Norfolk, Virginia, claimed to have knowledge of an African American family system called the "pyramid fighting method" (Daniel Marks, personal correspondence, August 2002).

15. There is substance to Newsome's allegations of politics. For example, since Lyndon Johnson declared war on crime in the mid-1960s, the prison industry has become big business (Schlosser, 1998). Meanwhile, some prisons really are plantations. See, for example, Tabolt's description of Angola Prison in Louisiana (Tabolt, 2000).

16. *Street* is emphasized because, as Jailhouse Rock practitioner Daniel Marks put it (personal communication, August 2002), "The real OGs (gangsters) are doing life bids. That's why it seems that it [Jailhouse Rock] never left the prison system. A brother would be locked up, learn to survive, and see a young blood to pass on the skill to. The young blood rolls out on the streets, beats down a cat or two, and says, 'I got this up state.' His rep grows, and so does his legend. Meanwhile, we were being shown bits and pieces of the art form all our lives. It took a place like jail to bring that diamond out of the rough. Sad, but true."

17. As support for Century's thesis, note that in July 1974, Miguel "Mikey" Pinero, a Puerto Rican from New York, demonstrated a prison style in *Black Belt* magazine (Darling and Perryman, 1974). Newsome has appeared in photos published in martial art magazines, and in 1987, *Fighting Arts International* published photos of Mel Gibson in Jailhouse Rock poses (O'Neill, 1987).

18. Both Century and Newsome state categorically that there are organic ties between Jailhouse Rock and the modern dance style known as up-rocking. Nonetheless, credits for the film *Rooftops* (1989), which is frequently cited as a showcase for up-rocking, list New York City capoeira pioneer Jelon Viera as choreographer. Moreover, the arrival of Viera and Loremil Machado in New York City in 1975 precedes the development of up-rocking and b-boyin'. (Both are generally dated to the late 1970s.) Consequently, Freddy Correa ("Furacao" of Abada-Capoeira) stated that up-rock came from the *ginga,* which is the basic upright movement of capoeira (Delgado, 2000; c.f. Dempsy, 1999; Planet Capoeira, 2002; Stickgrappler's Martial Arts Archives, 2002b). However, other researchers say that Rock Steady Crew and High Times Crew were responsible for popularizing b-boyin' during the late 1970s, without any influence from capoeira (George, 1992: 18; Mr. Wiggle's Hip-hop, 2002). Meanwhile, there were contemporary (but essentially unrelated) developments in California (Pabon, 1999). Finally, some breakers cite kung fu movies as a source of inspiration (Delgado, 2000). Thus, based on the available evidence, it seems likely that there was considerable cross-fertilization between dance and other expressive physical activities.

19. In 2002, Binns was using the name Nijel BPG.

20. For detailed examinations of the African esthetic in the New World, see the works of Roger D. Abrahams and Robert Farris Thompson. Meanwhile, for a discussion of boasting in a West African setting, see Powe, 1994: 30–37.

21. The same guard noted that the unorthodox style of the African American inmates used flurries of wheeling and clubbing punches (compare to Treffner, 2002) to drive opponents literally to the ground.

ACTION DESIGN

I wish to acknowledge the assistance of Deborah Klens-Bigman in formulating the questions that led to the writing of this chapter.

1. The official title was "Cultural Fighting Styles Designer."

2. Examples include the *chi sau* (Pinyin: *tui chou*) of wing chun (Pinyin: *yongchun*) and the *sentiment de fer* (sense of the blade) of classical fencing.

3. The swashbuckling style still has its place, but not at the head of the table. Today, it is usually used during deliberate homage to the classic swashbucklers, as a style in its own right, when that suits the mood and genre of a particular story.

4. Black Speech is the language created by Tolkien for his Orc characters.

MARTIAL ARTS MEET THE NEW AGE

1. According to a serving member (S.C., personal communication, August 1, 2002), Army Special Forces Groups did not have standardized programs in close-quarter battle and hand-to-hand combatives. Instead, each Group had its own individual program. Because of the frequency of troop deployments, Special Forces support personnel often received more training in hand-to-hand fighting than did team members.

2. Wood and Michaelson (2000: 107) describe this process as "fear inoculation."

REFERENCES

BOOKS, MAGAZINE ARTICLES, AND WEB SITES

All Web sites listed were valid on September 9, 2002.

Abe Ikuo, Kiyohara Yasuharu, and Nakajima Ken. (2000). Sport and physical education under fascistization in Japan (rev. ed.). *InYo,* http://ejmas.com/jalt/jaltart_abe_0600.htm. (Original work published 1990)

Abrahams, Roger D. (1983). *The man of words in the West Indies: Performance and the emergence of creole culture.* Baltimore: Johns Hopkins.

Academy of American Poets. (2002) Amiri Baraka, http://www.poets.org/poets/poets.cfm?prmID=458&CFID=7204221&CFTOKEN=57534356.

Africam Village. (2002). Mshindi vita saana [Champion's (or victor's) war art], http://www.africamvillage.com/lib/africamvillage/VS-Introduction.htm.

Afrikan Echoes. (2002). Afrikan Echoes' mission statement, http://66.149.36.177/ae_mission.html.

A-KATO (American Karate and Tae Kwon Do Organization). (2002). The forms for American Nam Seo Kwan Tae Kwon Do, http://www.a-kato.org/forms.html.

Alexander, John. (1999). *Future war: Non-lethal weapons in twenty-first century warfare.* New York: St. Martin's Press.

Alisogbo, Vodunsi. (1996). What's in a name? Identity and cultural self-determination, http://www.geocities.com/BourbonStreet/7614/identity.html.

All China traditional sports festival. (n.d.). Hong Kong.

Alliance for California Traditional Arts, California Arts Council. (2000). Traditional folk arts program, grants recipients, 2000, http://www.actaonline.org/funding_resources/CAC_2000_grantees.htm.

Alter, Joseph. (1995, October). Gama the world champion: Wrestling and physical culture in colonial India. *Iron Game History* (pp. 3–9).

American Psychological Association. (1994). *Publication Manual of the American Psychological Association* (4th ed.). Washington, DC: American Psychological Association.

Asawa, George. (1962, January). The one-legged swordsman. *Black Belt,* http://www.blackbeltmag.com/archives/blackbelt/1962/jan62/onelegged/onelegged swordsman.html.

Ashe, Arthur R., Jr. (1988). *A hard road to glory: A history of the African-American athlete 1619–1918.* New York: Warner Books.

Ayoob, Massad. (1976, August). Little "Karriem Allah" 95 pound karate machine. *Black Belt,* http://blackbeltmag.com/archives/blackbelt/1976/aug76/karriem/karriem.html.

Azuma, Eiichiro. (2000). Social history of kendo and sumo in Japanese America. In Brian Niiya (Ed.), *More than a game: Sport in the Japanese American community* (pp. 78–91). Los Angeles: Japanese American National Museum.

Baker, William J. (1983, Spring). The state of British sport history. *Journal of Sport History, 10,* (1), 53–66.

Barbosa de Medeiros, Rildo Heros. (2002). The history of judo: The arrival to Brazil: Count Koma, http://www.judobrasil.com.br/komtr.htm.

Barnes, John G. (1952, October). International Judo Federation and European Judo Union. *Budokwai Quarterly Bulletin* (pp. 13–19).

Behlmer, Rudy. (1997). Swordplay on the screen, http://www.mdle.com/Classic Films/Guest/rb1a.htm. (Original work published 1965)

Bell, Novell G. (2002). Brothers of Wudang, http://www.blacktaoist.com/Intropage .html.

Bernett, Hajo. (1980). Das Scheitern der olympischen Spiele von 1940 [The failure of the Olympic games of 1940]. *Stadion, 6,* 251–290.

"Best Olympic Games ever" over. (2000, August 30). *Houston Chronicle,* http://www.chron.com/content/chronicle/sports/oly/00.

Bibb, Henry. (1969). *Narrative of the life and adventures of Henry Bibb, an American slave, written by himself* (Introduction by Lucius C. Matlack). Miami, FL: Mnemosyne Publishing. (Original work published 1850)

Bigelow, Bill. (2001-2002, Winter). One country! One language! One flag! *Rethinking Schools Online,* http://www.rethinkingschools.org/sept11/16_02/hist162 .htm.

Bishop, Joseph Bucklin (Ed.). (1919). *Theodore Roosevelt's letters to his children.* New York: Charles Scribner's Sons.

Bishop, Mark. (1989). *Okinawan karate.* London: A. & C. Black.

Boliard, Greg A. (1989). *Korean martial arts student's manual.* Brandon, FL: World Moo Duk Kwan Tang Soo Do Federation.

Bordo, Susan. (1990). Reading the slender body. In Mary Jacobus, Evelyn Fox Keller, and Sally Shuttleworth (Eds.), *Body/politics: Women and the discourse of science.* London: Routledge.

Bortole, Carlos. (1997): Muda a História. Após Longa Pesquisa, o Amazonense Rildo Heros Descobre a Verdadeira Versão Sobre a Chegada do Judô no Brasil. *Judo Ippon 1* (12), 10–11.

Bourdieu, Pierre. (1984). *Distinction: A social critique of the judgement of taste.* London: Routledge.

Bourdieu, Pierre. (1986). The forms of capital. In John G. Richardson (Ed.), *Handbook of theory and research for the sociology of education.* New York: Greenwood Press.

Bourdieu, Pierre. (1995). *Sociology in question.* London: Sage Publications.

BPG, Nijel (a.k.a. Nijel Binns). (2000, July 1). Nuba Wrestling™: The African origin of the martial arts revealed, http://www.motherofhumanity.com/Nijart%20Webs/archives%20article%202.htm. (Rev. ed.; original work published 1999)

Breen, Michael. (1998). *The Koreans: who they are, what they want, where their future lies.* New York: Thomas Dunne/St. Martin's Press.

Bristol, George H. (2001, July). Integrated fighting system: The Marine Corps Martial Arts Program. *Marine Corps Gazette, 85,* (7), 38–39.

British girl amazes Dallas with ring skill. (1955, May 29). *Dallas Morning News.*

British Medical Association. (1993). *The boxing debate.* London: Chameleon Press.

Brooks, Peter. (1993). *Body Work: Objects of Desire in Modern Narrative.* Cambridge, Mass: Harvard University Press.

Brown, Nancy Marie. (2002). The rainforest: A special report, http://www.rps.psu.edu/edchoice/rainforest4.html.

Burdick, Dakin. (1999). People and events of t'aekwondo's formative years, http://www.indiana.edu/~iutkd/history/tkdhist.html. (Original work published 1997)

Capener, Steven D. (1995, Winter). Problems in the identity and philosophy of t'aegwondo and their historical causes. *Korea Journal,* student forum, http://www.bstkd.com/capener.1.htm.

Capener, Steven, and Herb Perez. (1998, July). State of taekwondo: Historical arguments should be objective. *Black Belt,* http://www.advanced-taekwondo.net/state_of_taekwondo.htm.

Capoeira Angola Sao Bento Grande. (2002a). Os malandros de Mestre Touro [The tough guys of Master Bull], http://www.malandros-touro.com/generic.html; $sessionid$HZETEZQAABCAIP5MFMKZPQR53QVSNPX0?pid = 5.

Capoeira Angola Sao Bento Grande. (2002c). Jail house rock, http://www.osmalandrosdemestretouro.bigstep.com/generic.html;$sessionid$QFT5L1QAADQWOP5MFMLZPQR53QVSNPX0?pid = 2.

Carroll, Scott T. (1988, Summer). Wrestling in ancient Nubia. *Journal of Sport History, 15,* (2), http://www.aafla.com/SportsLibrary/JSH/JSH1988/JSH1502/jsh1502b.pdf.

Century, Douglas. (1999). *Street kingdom: Five years inside the Franklin Avenue posse.* New York: Warner Books.

Century, Douglas. (2001, August). Ghetto blasters: Born in prison, raised in the 'hood, the deadly art of 52 Blocks is Brooklyn's baddest secret. *Details, 19,* (9), 77–79.

Channel 4 Television. (1994, May 9). *Champions: Hard hitting women.* London: Channel 4 Television.

Channon, James B. (2000). The First Earth Battalion: Ideas and ideals for soldiers everywhere. *Journal of Non-lethal Combatives,* http://ejmas.com/jnc/jncart_channon_0200.htm. (Original work published 1979)

Chastain, James. (1997). Young Ireland, http://www.ohiou.edu/~Chastain/rz/youngire.htm.

Chengdu Tiyu Xueyuan Tiyushi Yanjiushi [Chengdu Physical Culture Institute, Physical Culture History Research Office]. (Ed.). (1981). *Zhongguo jindai tiyushi jianbian* [A concise modern history of Chinese physical culture]. Beijing: Renmin Tiyu Chubanshe.

Chevalier, Remy. (2001). The Hollywood roots of First Earth Battalion. *Journal of Non-lethal Combatives,* http://ejmas.com/jnc/jncart_Chevalier_0901.htm.

Chin Hee-gwan. (2001, Summer). Divided by fate: The integration of overseas Koreans in Japan. *East Asian Review, 13,* (2), 57–74.

Chinese athletes of Wuchang. (1999). *Journal of Combative Sport,* http://ejmas.com/jcs/jcsart_NChinaHerald_1199.htm. (Original work published May 10, 1924)

Chinese Kung-fu Wu-Su Association. (2002). History of the association, http://users.rcn.com/michaeljf/kungfuwusu/cmp/wuSuTemple.html.

Cho, Sihak Henry. (1968). *Korean karate: Free fighting techniques.* Rutland, VT, and Tokyo: Charles E. Tuttle.

Cho, Soo-Se. (1981). Twenty Centuries of Taekwondo. *Traditional Taekwondo* (winter), 25–29.

Clarke, Joseph I. C. (1920). *Japan at first hand.* New York: Dodd, Mead and Co.

Clary, David W. (1992, June). A conversation with kickboxing pioneer Jeff Smith, http://blackbeltmag.com/archives/blackbelt/1992/jun92/jeffsmith/jeffsmith.html.

Club News. (1948, October). *Budokwai Quarterly Bulletin, 4(3),* 2.

Cobb, Irving. (1976). Dempsey vs. Carpentier. In Red Smith (Ed.), *Press box: Red Smith's favorite short stories* (pp. 60–67). New York: Avon Books.

Coetzee, Marié-Heleen. (2002). Zulu stick fighting: A socio-historical overview. *InYo,* http://ejmas.com/jalt/jaltart_Coetzee_0902.htm.

Cogswell, Don. (2002). Joe Choynski vs. Jim Corbett, http://www.be-hold.com/Content/Article.html.

Cole, Cheryl, and Amy Hribar. (1995). Celebrity feminism: Nike style, post-Fordism, transcendence, and consumer power. *Sociology of Sport Journal* 12:4 (pp. 347–369).

Colling, Michael. (2002). Chitose Tsuyoshi: a bridge through time. *Dragon Times,* http://www.dragon-tsunami.org/Dtimes/Pages/article33.htm.

Cook, Harry. (2001). *Shotokan karate: A precise history.* Haltwhistle, Northumberland, England: Harry Cook.

Corcoran, John, and Emil Farkas. (1988). *Martial arts: Traditions, history, people.* New York: Gallery Books.

Coughlin, John. (1997, April 6). Invisible ring: The role of prizefighting and the battle royal in *Invisible Man,* http://www.oakland.edu/~jcoughli/br.htm.

Courlander, Harold. (1960). *The drum and the hoe: Life and lore of the Haitian people.* Los Angeles: University of California at Los Angeles Press.

Crowley, Walt. (2001, April 9). Chinatown-International District—Thumbnail history, http://www.historylink.org/output.CFM?file_ID = 1058.

Cunningham, Don. (2002, July 3). Belt colors and ranking tradition, http://www.concentric.net/~Budokai/articles/belts.htm.

CyberBoxingZone. (2002a). CBZ black dynamite battle royal, http://www.cyberboxingzone.com/boxing/battleroyal.htm.

Danmyé in Martinique. (2002). French traditions and festivals, http://www.europeanschoolprojects.net/festivals/Martinique/danmye/danmye_e.htm.

Dare, Michael. (1998, August 7–12). Thus spake Lennon. *LA Weekly,* http://www.laweekly.com/ink/98/37/first-dare.shtml.

Darling, Anne, and James Perryman. (1974: July). Karate in prison: Menace, or means of personal survival? *Black Belt* (12), p. 21.

Dawson, C. Daniel. (1993). Capoeira Angola and Mestre João Grande: The saga of a tradition; the development of a master. In *Capoeira Angola,* n.d. (pp. 3–28). Washington, DC: International Capoeira Angola Foundation.

Debien, Gabriel. (1972, April–June). Night-time slave meetings in Saint-Domingue (La Marmelade, 1786) (John Garrigus, Trans.). *Annales historiques de la revolution française, 44,* 273–284, http://www.vancouver.wsu.edu/fac/peabody/voodoo.htm.

DeGategno, Paul J. (1989). *James Macpherson.* Boston: Twayne.

Delgado, Julie. (2000, April 7). Capoeira and break-dancing: At the roots of resistance. *Wiretap,* http://www.wiretapmag.org/story.html?StoryID = 87.

Della Pia, John. (1994). Korea's *Mu Yei Do Bo Tong Ji* [Illustrated manual of martial arts]: A sample of martial arts training in the Yi Dynasty. *Journal of Asian Martial Arts, 3,* (2), 62–69.

DeMile, James W. (2002). Wing chun do International, http://www.wingchundo.com.

Dempsy. (1999). Jailhouse Rock info, http://stickgrappler.tripod.com/ug/jhr1.html.

Desbonnet, Edmond. (1910). *Les rois de la lutte* [The kings of wrestling]. Paris: Berger-Levrault.

Desch-Obi, Thomas J. (1995, May). *The surprising success of early black boxers.* Paper presented at the African Activist Association, University of California at Los Angeles.

Desch-Obi, Thomas J. (2000). *Engolo: Combat traditions in African and African diaspora history.* Unpublished doctoral dissertation, University of California at Los Angeles.

Dodoo, Jan. (2001, May 29). Nation of Islam. For Sociology 452, Sociology of Religious Movements, University of Virginia, http://etext.lib.virginia.edu/~jkh8x/soc257/nrms/Nofislam.html.

Dohrenwend, Robert E. (2002). Informal history of Chung Do Kwan tae kwon do, http://www.sos.mtu.edu/husky/tkdhist.htm.

Donahue, John J. (1993, Winter). The ritual dimension of *karate-do* [empty hand way]. *Journal of Ritual Studies, 7,* (1), 105–124.

Downes, M. (1989, March 9–16). Raging belles. *City Limits* (pp. 14–16).

Draeger, Donn F., and Robert W. Smith. (1969). *Asian fighting arts.* Tokyo: Kodansha International.

Dussault, James, and Sandra Dussault. (1993). Lee Nam Suk: Patriarch of the Chang Moo Kwan. *Inside Tae Kwon Do, 2,* (5), 42–49.

Dyer, K. (1982). *Catching up the men: women in sport.* London: Junction Books.

Eigner, Julius. (1938, January). The ancient art of Chinese boxing. *China Journal, 28,* (1), 11–14.

Ekunfeo, Babalorisha Obalorun Temujin. (1999, December). When was Aborisha, Orisha worship, first practiced by African Americans in the United States? http://www.church-of-the-lukumi.org/temujinhist.htm.

Elkins, Stanley M. (1976). *Slavery: A problem in American institutional and intellectual life.* Chicago: University of Chicago Press. (Original work published 1959)

Ellsworth, Skip. (2002). Bruce Lee, the greatest martial artist who ever lived, http://www.premier1.net/~loghouse/bruceleememorial.html.

Embassy of Ireland. (2002). Gaeilge [Gaelic], http://www.irelandemb.org/gaeilge.html.

Eng, Lily. (1997, March 7). Visitors pay homage at Bruce and Brandon Lee's gravesite. *Seattle Times,* http://archives.seattletimes.nwsource.com/cgi-bin/texis.cgi/web/vortex/display?slug=blee&date=19970307&query=bruce+lee+%22bruce+lee%22.

Enoki Shinkichi. (1991). Herigeru shoden [Herrigel: A brief biographical sketch]. In Herrigel, Eugen (pp. 195–208). Tokyo: Kodansha Gakujutsu Bunko.

Esherick, Joseph W. (1987). *The origins of the Boxer uprising.* Berkeley: University of California Press.

Eskin, L. (1974, August). Complete history of women's boxing. *Boxing Illustrated* (pp. 29–32).

Expert on karate visits local school. (2002). http://www.isshinryu-islife.com/tswaz1.htm. (Original work published 1966)

Fanon, Frantz. (1986). *Black skin, white masks* (Charles Lam Markmann, Trans.). London: Pluto. (Original English translation published 1967; original French work published 1952)

Fanon, Frantz. (1967). *The wretched of the earth,* preface by Jean-Paul Sartre (Constance Farrington, Trans.). Harmondsworth: Penguin. (Original English translation published 1963; original French work published 1961)

Farrell, Alan. (1994, March). The Green Beret: *Schreckfigur* for the New Age. *Vietnam Generation Journal, 5,* 1–4, http://lists.village.virginia.edu/sixties/HTML_docs/Texts/Narrative/Farrell_Schreckfigur.html.

Fayer, Joan M. and Joan F. McMurray. (1999). The Carriacou Mas. *Journal of American Folklore, 112,* 58–73.

Featherstone, Mike. (1991) The body in consumer culture. In Mike Featherstone, Mike Hepworth, and Bryan S. Turner (Eds.), *The body: Social process and cultural theory.* London: Sage Publications. (Original work published 1982)

Fiehrer, Thomas. (1979). Slaves and freedmen in colonial Central America: Rediscovering a forgotten black past. *Journal of Negro History, 64,* (1), 39–57.

Fleischer, Nat. (1933, March). Nat Fleischer says. *The Ring* (p. 20).

Flores, Anthony R. (1960, August 31). Letter to Helen Foos, http://www.bestjudo.com/article18.shtml.

Forster, Michael N. (2001). Johann Gottfried von Herder. *Stanford encyclopedia of philosophy, http://plato.stanford.edu/entries/herder.*

Foucault, Michel. (1979). *Discipline and punishment.* New York: Vintage.

Friday, Karl. (1994, May). Bushido or bull: A medieval historian's perspective on the Imperial Army and the Japanese warrior tradition. *The History Teacher, 27,* (3), 339–349.

Front for the Liberation of the New Afrikan Nation. (2002). National strategy of the Front for the Liberation of the New Afrikan Nation, part IV, http://www.geocities.com/Heartland/Woods/4623/frolinan/frolinan4.html.

Fuchs, Cynthia. (2000). Interview with Forest Whitaker. *PopMatters,* http://www.popmatters.com/film/interviews/whitaker-forest.html.

Funakoshi Gichin. (1973). *Karate-do kyohan [Karate paradigms (literally, teaching empty hand way meanings by example)]: The master text* (Tsutomu Ohshima, Trans.). Tokyo: Kodansha International. (Original work published 1935)

Funakoshi Gichin. (1975). *Karate-do [empty hand way]: My way of life.* Tokyo: Kodansha International.

Funakoshi Gichin. (1997). *To-te jitsu* [Chinese hand techniques]. Hamilton, Ontario, Canada: Masters Publication. (Original work published 1922)

Fushun Xilu Tian Meikuang Shenjing Dang Zongzhi [Fushun Xilu Tian Coal Mine Deep Shaft Party General Branch]. (1976, October–November). Women shi zenma yang bian kuanggongquan de [How we developed mineworker's boxing]. *New Sports,* 65–66.

George, Nelson. (1992). *Buppies, b-boys, baps & bohos: Notes on post-soul black culture.* New York: HarperCollins Publishers.

George Harris 1971 judo sensei award. (1997). *Black Belt,* http://w3.blackbeltmag.com/halloffame/html/29.html.

Giles, Herbert A. (1906). The home of jiu jitsu. *Adversaria Sinica, 5,* 132–138. Shanghai: Kelly & Walsh.

Godia, George. (1989). Sport in Kenya. In Eric A. Wagner (Ed.), *Sport in Asia and Africa: A comparative handbook.* New York: Greenwood.

Gong, Tommy. (2001). Jeet Kune Do. In Green. (pp. 202–209). Santa Barbara, CA: ABC-CLIO.

Gorer, Geoffrey. (1949). *Africa dances: A book about West African Negroes.* London: J. Lehmann. (Original work published 1935)

Gorn, Elliot J. (1986). *The manly art: Bare-knuckle prize fighting in America.* Ithaca: Cornell University Press.

Gorn, Elliot J., and Warren Goldstein. (1993). *A brief history of American sports.* New York: Hill and Wang.

Green, Thomas A. (1997a). *Folklore: An Encyclopedia of Beliefs, Customs, Tales, Music, and Art.* Santa Barbara: ABC-CLIO.

Green, Thomas A. (1997b). Historical narrative in the martial arts: A case study. In Tad Tujela (Ed.), *Usable pasts: Traditions and group expressions in North America* (pp. 156–174). Logan: Utah State University Press.

Gu Liuxin. (1982, January). Yi Tang Hao [Remembering Tang Hao]. *Zhonghua wushu, 1,* 18–20.

Guo Xifen. (1970). *Zhongguo tiyu shi* [History of Chinese physical culture]. Taibei: Taiwan Shangwu Yinshu Guan. (Original work published 1919)

Guttmann, Allen. (1991). *Women's sports.* New York: Columbia University Press.

Guttmann, Allen. (1995). Sports, Eros, and popular culture. *Stanford Humanities Review, 6,* (2), http://www.stanford.edu/group/SHR/6–2/html/guttmann.html.

Guttmann, Allen, and Lee Thompson. (2001). *Japanese sports: A history.* Honolulu: University of Hawai'i Press.

Gwaltney, John. (1981). Drylongso: A self-portrait of black Americans. New York: Random House.

Halsall, Paul. (1998, November). Johann Gottfried von Herder: Materials for the Philosophy of the History of Mankind, 1784. *Internet Modern History Sourcebook,* http://www.fordham.edu/halsall/mod/1784herder-mankind.html.

Halsall, Paul. (2001, May). Nationalism. *Internet Modern History Sourcebook,* http://www.fordham.edu/halsall/mod/modsbook17.html.

Haniff, A. (n.d.). Gama of India. *Mat* 4: 23 (p. 14).

Hargreaves, Jennifer. (1994). *Sporting females: Critical issues in the history and sociology of women's sports.* London: Routledge.

Harries, Meirion, and Susie Harries. (1991). *Soldiers of the sun: the rise and fall of the Imperial Japanese Army.* New York: Random House.

Harrison, E.J. (1910). *Peace or war east of Baikal?* Yokohama: Kelly & Walsh.

Harrison, E.J. (1946, July). Famous judo masters I have known. *Budokwai Quarterly Bulletin* (p. 16).

Harrison, E.J. (1982). *Fighting spirit of Japan.* Woodstock, NY: Overlook Press. (Original work published 1955)

Hartnett, Richard A. (1998). *The saga of Chinese higher education from the Tongzhi Restoration to Tiananmen Square: Revolution and reform.* Lampeter, UK: The Edwin Mellen Press.

Hawaii Kendo Federation. (2002). History, http://www.hawaiikendo.com/history
.html.

Hazard, Benjamin. (1973). Revival of kendo in Northern California. *International
Kendo Federation 2nd world kendo tournament championships souvenir
book*. San Francisco: Kendo Federation of the United States.

Hazard, Benjamin. (2001). *An overview of kendo 1945–2000*. Unpublished manuscript.

Heckler, Richard Strozzi. (1992). *In search of the warrior spirit* (2nd ed.). Berkeley, CA: North Atlantic Press.

Heckler, Richard Strozzi. (2002). Marine Warrior Project, http://www.aiki-
extensions.org/newsletters/doc/aen9.doc

Hennessy, V. (1990). Punching Judy show. *You Magazine (The Mail on Sunday)*
(pp. 16–20).

Henning, Stanley E. (1999, Fall). Academia encounters the Chinese martial arts.
China Review International, 6, (2), 319–332, http://muse.jhu.edu/demo/
cri/6.2henning.pdf.

Henning, Stanley E. (2000). Traditional Korean martial arts. *Journal of Asian
Martial Arts, 9,* (1), 9–15.

Henning, Stanley E., and Thomas A. Green. (2001). Folklore in the martial arts.
In Green. (pp. 123–136). Santa Barbara, CA: ABC-CLIO.

Herrigel, Eugen. (1941). *Nihon no kyujutsu* [Japanese archery; originally, Die ritterliche Kunst des Bogenschiessens] (Shibata Jisaburo, Trans.), with an
essay (1940) by Komachiya Sozo. Tokyo: Iwanami Shoten.

Herrigel, Eugen. (1948). *Zen in der Kunst des Bogenschiessens* [Zen in the art of
archery] Muenchen-Planegg: Otto Wilhelm Barth-Verlag.

Herrigel, Eugen. (1953). *Zen in the art of archery* [originally, *Zen in der Kunst des
Bogenschiessens* (1948)] (Richard F.C. Hull, Trans.), with an introduction
by D.T. Suzuki. New York: Pantheon Books.

Herrigel, Eugen. (1956). *Yumi to Zen* [Bow and Zen; originally, *Zen in der Kunst
des Bogenschiessens,* 1948] (Inatomi Eirjiro and Ueda Takeshi, Trans.).
Tokyo: Kyodo Shuppan.

Herrigel, Eugen. (1958). *Der Zen-Weg* [The way of Zen] (Hermann Tausend,
Compiler). Muenchen-Planegg: Otto Wilhelm Barth-Verlag.

Herrigel, Eugen. (1960). *The method of Zen* [originally, *Der Zen-Weg*] (Richard
F.C. Hull, Trans.). New York: Pantheon Books.

Hill, Donald R. (1998). "I am happy just to be in this sweet land of liberty": The
New York City calypso craze of the 1930s and 1940s. In Ray Allen and Lois
Wilcken (Eds.), *Island sounds in the global city* (pp. 74–92). New York:
Institute for Studies in American Music and the New York Folklore Society.

Hiltz, Virginia, and Mike Sell. (1998). Cultural nationalism. http://www.umich
.edu/~eng499/concepts/nationalism.html.

Hinton, William, and D'Arcy Rahming. (1994). In *Men of steel discipline: The
official oral history of black pioneers in the martial arts,* Jennifer H. Baar-
man (Ed.). Chicago: Modern Bu-jutsu.

Hobsbawm, Eric, and Terence Ranger. (1983). *The invention of tradition.* Cambridge: Cambridge University Press.

Hoff, Feliks F. (1994). Herrigel and the consequences. In *1st international kyudo symposium proceedings* (pp. 25–35). Hamburg: Deutscher Kyudo Bund.

Holloway, Thomas H. (1993). *Policing Rio de Janeiro: Repression and resistance in a nineteenth-century city.* Stanford, CA: Stanford University Press.

Holy Temple Community Church. (2002). Karate for Christ, http://karate.tni.net.

Hosokawa, Bill. (1982). *JACL in Quest of Justice.* New York: William Morrow.

Hsu, Adam. (1986, October). Long fist: The mother of northern kungfu styles. *Black Belt* (24), 64–67, 129–130.

Huang Jiexin (Bonian). (1971). *Xiezhen quanjie jiaofan* [Illustrated boxing and weapons manual]. Taibei: Hualian Chubanshe. (Original work published 1928).

Hudson, Charles. (1966). Folk history and ethnohistory. *Ethnohistory, 13,* 52–70.

Hunt, L. (1996, January). Boxing damages young brains. *Independent* 2:18 (p. 2).

Hwang Kee. (1978). *Tang soo do (soo bahk do).* Springfield, NJ: U.S. Tang Soo Do Moo Duk Kwan Federation.

Hwang Kee. (1995). *The history of Moo Duk Kwan.* Springfield, NJ: U.S. Tang Soo Do Moo Duk Kwan Federation.

Hyde, Douglas. (2000). Ireland's millennia, http://www.rte.ie/millennia/people/hydedouglas.html. (Original work published 1998).

International Capoeira Angola Federation. (2002). Progress through tradition, http://www.capoeira-angola.org.

International Shudokan Karate Association. (2002). History of Toyama Kanken, *http://*www.wkf.org/shudokan.html.

Irish Heroes. (2002). http://www.gods-heros-myth.com/herosireland.html.

Ishida Kakuya. (2000, August 12). I was a Japanese soldier. *Daily Yomiuri,* http://www2.gol.com/users/coynerhm/understanding_japan.htm.

Ito, Kazuo. (1973). *Issei: A history of Japanese immigrants in North America* (Shinichiro Nakamura and Jean S. Gerard, Trans.) Seattle: Japanese Community Service.

Jackson, J.D. (2000, Spring). Roundhouse kick: A brief global and African-centered perspective on the martial arts. *Vulcan Review, 4,* http://www.sbs.uab.edu/history/varticles/martlart.htm.

Jaffe, Greg. (2000). A few good men try the Marine martial art, and take on 2 gurus. *Wall Street Journal,* http://www.mcu.usmc.mil/TbsNew/Pages/Martial_Arts/media_articles/wsjarticle.htm.

Jennings, Andrew. (1996). *The new lords of the rings: Power, money and drugs in the modern Olympics.* London: Pocket Books.

Jensen, Kirsten. (2001). Changing gender roles in sabar performances: A reflection of changing roles for women in Senegal, http://depts.washington.edu/poa/content/paper.html.

Jin Enzhong. (1970). *Guoshu mingren lu* [Record of well-known martial artists]. Taibei: Zhonghua Wushu Chubanshe. (Original work published 1933)

Jing Bai. (1965, April). Taijiquan huodong zhongde caopo bixu qingchu [The chaff must be separated from the *taijiquan* movement]. *New Sports,* 22–23.

Jinsoku Kakan. (1956). Interview with Gogen Yamaguchi about karate-do [empty hand way]. *Tokyo Maiyu.*

Joint Chiefs of Staff. (1995). Joint Pub 3-07. *Joint doctrine for military operations other than war.* Washington, DC: Joint Chiefs of Staff.

Johnson, Akilah. (2001, August 14). Miami Beach prepares for hip-hop awards, downplays chance of problems, *Sun-Sentinel,* http://www.sun-sentinel.com/news/local/miami/search/sfl-dsource14aug14.story?coll=sfla-miami-archives.

Jones, Francis Clifford. (1949) *Manchuria since 1931.* London: Oxford University Press.

J. V. Humphries School. (2002). Community life, http://www.kin.bc.ca/JVH/Programs/JCdn/CommunityLife.html.

Kang Gewu. (1995). *The spring and autumn of Chinese martial arts: 5000 years.* Santa Cruz, CA: Plum Publishing.

Kang Won-sik and Yi Kyong-myong. (1999). *T'aekwondo hyondaesa* [Modern history of taekwondo]. Seoul: Pogyong Munhwasa.

Kemp, P., A. Houston, M. Macleod, and R. Pethybridge. (1995). Cerebral perfusion and psychometric testing in military amateur boxers and controls. *Journal of Neurology, Neurosurgery and Psychiatry* 59 (pp. 368–374).

Kimm He-young. (2000, January). General Choi, Hong Hi: A taekwondo history lesson, *Taekwondo Times* (20), 44–58.

Kim Kyong-ji. (1986, August). T'aekwondo: Its brief history. *Korea Journal, 26,* (8), 20–25.

Koizumi, Gunji. (1947, April). Judo and the Olympic games. *Budokwai Quarterly Bulletin* (pp. 7–8).

Kojima Shimpei. (2000). History of Kyoto University Judo Club (Okumura Koshi, Trans.), http://www.kusu.kyoto-u.ac.jp/~judo/history-e.htm#foundation.

Komachiya Sozo. (1965). Zadankai: Awa Kenzo hakase to sono deshi Oigen Herigeru hakase no koto wo Komachiya hakase ni kiku [Symposium: Professor Komachiya talks about Professor Awa Kenzo and his disciple, Professor Eugen Herrigel]. *Kyudo* 183 (pp. 4–7).

Komachiya Sozo. (1982). Herigeru-kun to yumi [Mr. Herrigel and the bow]. In Eugen Herrigel, *Nihon no kyujutsu* (pp. 69–100). Tokyo: Iwanami Bunko.(Original work published 1940)

Krawchuk, Fred T. (2000, November/December). Developing the capacity for decisive action. *Military Review,* 47–54.

Lai Yiwu. (1982). Guo Shaoyu and his "History of Chinese Physical Culture." *China Sports, 2,* 22–23.

Laird, Donald. (1936, March). Why aren't more women athletes? *Scientific American* 151 (pp. 142–143).

Laird, J. (1993, May). Wrestling and boxing. *Amazons in Action* 62 (pp. 4–15).

Lan Suzhen. (1959). *Mianquan* [Mian boxing]. Beijing: Renmin Tiyu Chubanshe.

Lash, Scott. (1991). Genealogy and the body: Foucault/Deleuze/Nietzsche. In Featherstone, Hepworth, and Turner (Eds.), *The body: Social process and cultural theory.* London: Sage Publications. (Original work published 1984)

Lee Chong-wu. (2002). Interview. *New York University Jidokwan Club,* http://www.geocities.com/aroman21/grandmasterleeinterview.html.

Lee Jeong-kyu. (2002, March 7). Japanese higher education policy in Korea during the colonial period (1910–1945). *Educational Policy Analysis Archives, 10,* (14), http://epaa.asu.edu/epaa/v10n14.html.

Lee Kang-seok. (1997, March). Grandmaster Won Kuk Lee, founder of Chung Do Kwan (interview). *Taekwondo Times* (17), 44–51.

Lee Ki-Baik and Edward W. Wagner. (1984). *A new history of Korea.* Cambridge, MA: Harvard University Press.

Lee Se-ree. (2002). Lee, Chong Woo: Pioneer of TKD, http://www3.nf.sympatico.ca/cot/chongWOOlee.htm.

Lewis, George H. (1987, Winter). From common dullness to fleeting wonder: The manipulation of cultural meaning in the Teenage Mutant Ninja Turtles saga. *Journal of Popular Culture, 20,* (3), http://xroads.virginia.edu/~DRBR/lewis.txt.

Lewis, J. Lowell. (1992). *Ring of liberation: Deceptive discourse in Brazilian capoeira.* Chicago: University of Chicago Press.

Lewis, J. Lowell. (1999, August). Sex and violence in Brazil: Carnaval, capoeira, and the problem of everyday life. *American Ethnologist, 26,* (3), 539–557.

Liedke, Bob. (1990, May). Korea's living legend: Tangsoodo-Moodukwan's Great Grandmaster Hwang Kee (interview). *Taekwondo Times* (10), 38–40.

Lingo, Kaira. (1996). *The politics of race and power in capoeira.* Unpublished honors thesis, Stanford University, Stanford, CA.

Liverpool, Hollis. (2001). *Rituals of power and rebellion: The Carnival tradition in Trinidad and Tobago, 1763–1962.* Chicago: Research Associates School Times Publications.

Longhurst, Percy. (1936). The finest form of self defence. *Superman Magazine* (p. 200).

Losik, Len. (1999, May). The history and evolution of Song Moo Kwan. *Taekwondo Times* (19), 64–67.

Losik, Len. (2001, May). The Jidokwan way of wisdom. *Taekwondo Times* (21), 74–78.

Lost-Found Nation of Islam. (2002). Chief Executive Officer, the Lost-Found Nation of Islam, http://members.aol.com/akankem/Ceo.htm.

Louis, Joe, with Edna Rust and Art Rust, Jr. (1989). *Joe Louis: My life.* New York: Harcourt Brace Jovanovich.

Ma Guoyao. (1995, December). Yi wushujia Xu Zhedong [Remembering martial art practitioner, Xu Zhedong]. *Wu Hun, 90,* 21.

Ma Mingda. (2000). *Shuojian conggao* [Collected articles discussing the sword]. Lanzhou: Lanzhou University Press.

Mandell, Richard D. (1984). *Sport: A cultural history.* New York: Columbia University Press.

Mao Zedong (under the sobriquet "Twenty Eight Stroke Student" or "Ershibahua Sheng" [the number of brush strokes in his name]). (1917). Tiyu zhi yanjiu [Physical culture research]. *Xin Qingnian [New Youth], 3, 2.*

Marchini, Ron, and Hansen, Daniel D. (1998). History of Renbukai, http://www.renbukai-usa.com/history.htm.

Marre, Jeremy, and Hannah Charlton. (1985). *Beats of the heart: Popular music of the world.* London: Pluto Press.

Martial Science Institute International. (2002). Kiungo cha mkono [Shackle hand style], http://www.msii-online.com/african.htm.

Massar, Frank, and Adrian St. Cyrien. (1999, April). Won Kuk Lee, an interview with the true founder of taekwondo. *TKD and Korean Martial Arts,* 14–17.

Matsuda Ryuji. (1984). *Zhongguo wushu shilue* [Short history of Chinese martial arts] (Lu Yan and Yan Hai, Trans.). Chengdu: Sichuan Kexue Jishu Chubanshe.

McCarthy, Patrick, and Yuriko McCarthy. (Trans. and compiled). (1999). *Ancient Okinawan martial arts: koryu uchinadi.* Boston: Tuttle Publishing.

McCarthy, Patrick, and Yuriko McCarthy. (Trans. and compiled). (2001). *Karate-do Tanpenshu: Funakoshi Gichin* [Short stories of karate (empty hand way): Funakoshi Gichin]. Brisbane, Australia: International Ryukyu Karate Research Society.

Media Action Network for Asian Americans. (2002). Restrictive portrayals of Asians in the media and how to balance them, http://www.manaa.org/a_stereotypes.html.

Mee, Bob. (2001). *Bare fists: The history of bare-knuckle prize-fighting.* Woodstock, NY: Overlook Press.

Mende Conny, Beth, compiler. (1993). *Winning women: Quotations on sports, health and fitness.* New York: Peter Pauper Press.

Messner, Michael. (1992). *Power at play: Sports and the problem of masculinity.* Boston: Beacon Press.

Michalon, Josy. (1987). *Le ladjia: Origine et pratiques* [Ladjia: Origins and practice]. Paris: Editions Caribéennes.

Miletich, Leo N. (1994). *Dan Stuart's fistic carnival.* College Station: Texas A&M University Press.

Miller, Heinie. (1922, December). Now *you* tell one! *The Ring,* 5–6.

Minamoto Ryoen. (1995). Budo no shizenkan: Awa Kenzo no baai [The attitude toward nature in martial arts: The case of Awa Kenzo]. In Ito Shuntaro (Ed.), *Nihonjin no shizenkan: Jomon kara gendai kagaku made* [The Japanese attitude toward nature: From the Jomon to modern science]. Tokyo: Kawade Shobo.

Moledzki, Sam. (2002). Sakio Ken, *Karate-do Shito-kai Canada,* http://www.shitoryu.org/bios/sakio/sakio.htm.

Montejo, Esteban. (1968). *The autobiography of a runaway slave* (Miguel Barnet, Ed.; (Jocasta Innes, Trans.). New York: Pantheon.

Mooney, Robert Johnstone. (1923, October). Boxing and wrestling with Roosevelt in the White House. *The Outlook* 24 (p. 311).

Morris, Andrew. (1998). *Cultivating the national body: A history of physical culture in Republican China.* Unpublished doctoral dissertation, University of California, San Diego.

Mr. Wiggle's Hip-hop. (2002). The underground hip-hop timeline, http://www.mrwiggleshiphop.net/timeline.htm.

Muhammad's Martial Arts Academy. (2002). Sensei Dawud Muhammad, http://muhammadsmartialarts.com/about%20us.htm.

Muzumdar, S. (1942). *Strong men over the years: A chronicle of athletes.* Lucknow: B.R. Bhargava.

Nagamine, Shoshin. (2000). *Tales of Okinawa's great masters* (Patrick McCarthy, Trans.). Boston: Tuttle.

Nakamura, Norio. (2000, May). The people (interview). *Karate-do* [Empty hand way]. (Translated from the Japanese)

New Jersey State Athletic Control Board. (2002, July 22). Commissioner Larry Hazzard, Sr., http://www.state.nj.us/lps/sacb/commissioner.html.

Newsome, David. (1961). *Godliness and good learning: Four studies on the Victorian ideal.* London: John Murray.

Nishi Yoshinori. (2002, May 1). Interview with Hélio Gracie (Kondo Yoko, Trans.). *Kakutou Striking Spirit,* http://www.geocities.com/global_training_report/helio.htm.

Nishio Kanji. (1978, April 11). Wakon yokon, mushin [Western spirit, no-mind]. *Nihon keizai shinbun.*

Nishio Kanji. (1982). *Koi suru shisaku* [Meditations on falling in love]. Tokyo: Chuo Koron.

Nixdorf, Jimmie. (1993, January). The beginning forms of taekwondo. *Black Belt* (31), 30–32, 66.

Noble, Graham. (1996b). The first karate books. *Dragon Times, 12,* 27, 36.

Noble, Graham. (2000a). Master Choki Motobu, "A real fighter." *Journal of Combative Sport,* http://ejmas.com/jcs/jcsart_noble1_0200.htm.

O'Neill, Terry. (1987). Terry O'Neill interviews Mel Gibson. *Fighting Arts International,* http://stickgrappler.tripod.com/52/mel1.html.

Oates, Joyce Carol. (1994). *On boxing.* New Jersey: Echo Press.

Okorafor, Nnedimma. (2001, June 8). Maatkara brings ancient Egypt to the Web. *Africana.com,* http://www.africana.com/DailyArticles/index_20010608.htm.

Omori, Sogen. (1982). Zen to kyudo: Herigeru hakase no Yumi to Zen ["The Bow and Zen" by Professor Herrigel]. In Uno Yozaburo (Ed.), *Gendai kyudo koza* [A course on modern kyudo] (pp. 160–170). Tokyo: Yuzankaku.

One-hundred-twelfth IOC Session. (2001). Candidates: Un Yong Kim, http://www.moscow2001.olympic.org/en/president/candidats/kim.html.

Our cultural heritage: A joint venture. (2001). National Archaeological Anthropological Museum of the Netherlands Antilles, http://www.curacao.com/naam/english.html#slaghout.

Ozawa, Takashi. (1965, June). Kendo: Samurai of southern California. *Black Belt,* http://www.blackbeltmag.com/archives/blackbelt/1965/jun65/kendomen/ kendomen.html.

Pabon, Jorge. (1999, September 10–12). Physical graffiti, http://members.tripod .com/~MastaMovementz/articles.html.

Park, R. (1994). From "Genteel Diversions" to "Bruising Peg": Active pastimes, exercise, and sports for females in late 17th and 18th century Europe. In D. Margaret Costa and Sharon R. Guthrie (Eds.), *Women and sport: Interdisciplinary perspectives.* Champaign, IL: Human Kinetics.

Park Yeon-hee, Park Yeon-hwan, and Jon Gerrard. (1989). *Taekwondo: the ultimate reference guide to the world's most popular martial art.* New York: Facts on File.

Pederson, Michael. (2001). Taekyon. In Thomas A. Green, *Martial arts of the world: An encyclopedia* (pp. 603–608). Santa Barbara, CA: ABC-CLIO.

Pedreira, Roberto. (2002). Then came Rorion: How Rorion Gracie revolutionized the way some people think about martial arts training in America and reinvented himself as the Bill Gates of the grappling world in the process, http://www.geocities.com/global_training_report/rorion.htm.

Peng Ming. (1984). *Wusi yundong shi* [May Fourth movement history]. Beijing: Renmin Chuban She.

Philip, R. (1983, April 7). Memoirs of a happy left hooker. *Sport* (p. 39).

Pinckney, Roger. (2000). *Blue roots: African-American folk magic of the Gullah people.* St. Paul, MN: Llewellyn Publications.

Planet Capoeira. (2002). Interview with Contre-Mestre Preto-Velho, http://www .capoeira.com/planetcapoeira/view.jsp?section=Features&viewArticle=116.

Poulos, Jennifer. (1997, April 19). Frantz Fanon, http://www.emory.edu/ENGLISH/ Postcolonial/Fanon.html.

Powe, Edward L. (1994). *Black martial arts: Vol. 1. Combat games of Northern Nigeria.* Madison, WI: Dan Aiki Publications.

Powe, Edward L. (2001). *Black martial arts: Vol. 2. Combat games of the African Indian Ocean (Madagascar, Reunion, Comores).* Madison, WI: Dan Aiki Publications.

Powe, Edward L. (2002a). *Black martial arts: Vol. 3. Capoeira and Congo: Danced martial arts of the Americas, part 1.* Madison, WI: Dan Aiki Publications.

Quinn, Eileen Moore. (2001). Can this language be saved? *Cultural Survival: Ethnosphere,* http://www.cs.org/publications/CSQ/252/quinn.htm.

Radford, Peter. (2001). *The celebrated Captain Barclay: Sport, money and fame in Regency Britain.* London: Headline.

Rath, Richard Cullen. (2000). Drums and power: Ways of creolizing music in coastal South Carolina and Georgia, 1730–1790. In David Buisseret and Steven G. Reinhardt (Eds.), *Creolization in the Americas.* College Station: University of Texas at Arlington Press.

Redmond, Rob. (2000, November 4). Introductory texts, http://www.24fighting chickens.com/shotokan/reviews/01_int.html.

Regulation Sets for Martial Arts Competition. (1960). People's Physical Culture Press.

Reid Temple African Methodist Episcopal Church. (2002). Message from the pastor, http://www.rtamec.org/newreid/pastmsg.htm.

Robbins, Tom. (1971). *Another roadside attraction.* New York: Ballantine.

Roberts, Randy. (1983). *Papa Jack: Jack Johnson and the era of white hopes.* New York: The Free Press.

Roberts, Randy. (1983, July). Galveston's Jack Johnson: Flourishing in the dark. *Southwestern Historical Quarterly, 87,* (1), 37–56.

Rosalia, Rene. (1996). Legal repression of afro-cultural expressions: The cases of the 24th of June (San Juan), kokomakaku and tambu, Curaçao. In E. Ayubi (Ed.), *Papers of the third seminar on Latin-American and Caribbean folklore.* Willemstad, Curaçao: AAINA.

Rules for Martial Arts Competition. (1959). People's Physical Culture Press.

S. Korea's sports chief offers to resign. (2002, February 28). *CNN/SportsIllustrated. com,* http://sportsillustrated.cnn.com/olympics/2002/news/2002/02/28/korea_kim_ap

Sakurai Yasunosuke. (1981). *Awa Kenzo: oi naru sha no michi no oshie* [Awa Kenzo: The teaching of the Great Way of Shooting]. Sendai: Awa Kenzo Sensei Shotan Hyakunensai Jikko Iinkai.

Saltzman, Rachelle H. (1994). Folklore as politics in Great Britain: Working-class critiques of upper-class strike breakers in the 1926 general strike. *Anthropological Quarterly, 67,* (3), 105–121.

Saltzman, Rachelle H. (1995). Public displays, play, and power: The 1926 general strike. *Southern Folklore, 52,* (2), 161–186.

Sandata, Sabrina. (1997). Asian FUCKING Stereotypes, *Stonewall Inn,* http://www.stonewallinn.com/Features/GirlsAsian.html.

Sansone, Livio. (1999). From Africa to Afro: The use and abuse of Africa in Brazil. SEPHIS/CODESIRA Lecture Series. Amsterdam and Dakar: SEPHIS/CODESIRA.

Sawicki, Jana. (1991). *Disciplining Foucault: Feminism, power and the body.* New York: Routledge.

Scannell, Vernon. (1971). *The tiger and the rose.* London: Hamish Hamilton.

Schechner, Richard. (1976). From ritual to theatre and back. In Richard Schechner and Mady Schuman (Eds.), *Ritual, play and performance: Readings in the social sciences/theatre* (pp. 196–222). New York: Seabury Press.

Schlosser, Eric. (1998, December). The prison-industrial complex. *Atlantic Monthly,* http://www.theatlantic.com/issues/98dec/prisons.htm.

Schumpeter, Elizabeth B. (Ed.). (1940). The industrialization of Japan and Manchuko, 1930–1940: Population, raw materials and industry. New York: MacMillan.

SciFi.com. (2002). *Maatkara: Credits,* http://www.scifi.com/maatkara/pages/bios/crewbio_lessanu.html.

Scott, James C. (1985). *Weapons of the weak: Everyday forms of peasant resistance.* New Haven: Yale University Press.

Secretariat of the European Judo Union. (1976). *40 Years: European Judo Union* [pamphlet].

Seven, Richard. (1998, July 12). Bruce Lee is gone but not forgotten, *Seattle Times,* http://archives.seattletimes.nwsource.com/cgi-bin/texis.cgi/web/vortex/display?slug=plee&date=19980712&query=bruce+lee+%22bruce+lee%22+%22taky+kimura%22.

Smith, Chris. (2001). Martinique: Cane fields and city streets. *Musical Traditions,* http://www.mustrad.org.uk/reviews/martiniq.htm.

Smith, Maureen. (2001). *Muhammad Speaks* and Muhammad Ali: Intersections of the Nation of Islam and sport in the 1960s. *International Sports Studies* 21:1 (pp. 54–69), http://www.aafla.org/SportsLibrary/ISS/ISS2201/ISS2201f.pdf#xml=http://www.aafla.org/search/highlight.gtf?nth=2&handle=000002d9.

Smith, Robert W. (1963, Summer). Gama the Lion: Master of the arts. *Black Belt,* http://64.224.111.216/archives/blackbelt/1963/summer63/gamathelion/gamathelion.html.

Smith, Robert W. (1964). *Secrets of Shaolin temple boxing.* Rutland, VT, and Tokyo: Charles E. Tuttle.

Smith, Robert W. (1974). *Chinese boxing: Masters and methods.* Tokyo: Kodansha International.

Spring, Christopher. (1993). *African arms and armor.* Washington, DC: Smithsonian Institution Press.

St. James African Methodist Episcopal Church. (2002). Community involvement today, http://www.stjamesamec.org/community.html.

Stickgrappler's Martial Arts Archives. (2002a). 52 hand blocks, http://stickgrappler.tripod.com/52/52.html.

Stickgrappler's Martial Arts Archives. (2002b). 52 handblocks/jailhouse rock thread started by me, Stickgrappler, http://stickgrappler.tripod.com/52/52jhr.html.

Strenuous athletics in China, including pre-Japanese jiu-jutsu. (1999). *Journal of Non-lethal Combatives,* http://ejmas.com/jnc/jncart_LitDigest_1299.htm. (Original work published May 29, 1920)

Stroud, Robert. (2002). History of Obukan kendo club, 1905–2001, http://www.obukan.com/history.html.

Suzar, S. E. (2002). Blacked out through whitewash, http://www.ibiblio.org/nge/blacked/bl10.html. (Original work published 1992)

Svinth, Joseph R. (2000a). A day to rest and wrestle: Benjamin Franklin Roller, master of angles and feuds (Rev. ed.). *InYo,* http://ejmas.com/jalt/jaltart_svinth_0700.htm. (Original work published 1999)

Svinth, Joseph R. (2000b). Amateur boxing in pre-World War II Japan: The military connection. *Journal of Non-Lethal Combatives,* http://ejmas.com/jnc/jncart_svinth2_0100.htm.

Svinth, Joseph R. (2001a, February). The evolution of women's judo. *InYo,* http://ejmas.com/jalt/jaltart_svinth_0201.htm.

Svinth, Joseph R. (2001b). Fighting spirit: An introductory history of Korean boxing, 1926–1945 (Rev. ed.). *Journal of Combative Sport,* http://ejmas.com/ jcs/jcsart_svinth_0801.htm. (Original work published 1999)

Swedenburg, Ted. (1997, February 19). *Islam in the mix: Lessons of the Five Percent.* Paper presented at the Anthropology Colloquium, University of Arkansas, http://comp.uark.edu/~tsweden/5per.html.

Sweetman, Jack. (1995). *The U.S. Naval Academy: An illustrated history* (2nd ed.) (Rev. by Thomas J. Cutler). Annapolis: U.S. Naval Academy Press.

Szafranski, Richard. (1995, Spring). When waves collide: Future conflict. *Joint Forces Quarterly,* 5:77–84.

Szwed, John. (1971). Introduction. In Arthur Huff Fauset, *Black gods of the metropolis.* Philadelphia: University of Pennsylvania Press.

Tabolt, Nicole. (2000). A close encounter with Angola Farm, http://www.aclu-mass.org/youth/risingtimes/11closeencounterAngola.html.

Tacoma Kendo Club. (2002). TKC history, http://www.tacomakendo.com/ favorite.htm.

Takashima, Shizuye. (1971). *A child in prison camp.* Montreal: Tundra Books.

Thomas, Chris. (1988, October). Did karate's Funakoshi found taekwondo? *Black Belt,* 21:26–30.

Thompson, Robert Farris. (1990). Kongo influences on African-American artistic culture. In Joseph E. Holloway (Ed.), *Africanisms in American culture.* Bloomington: Indiana University Press.

Thompson, Robert Farris. (1992). Introduction. In J. Lowell Lewis, *Ring of Liberation: Deceptive Discourse in Brazilian Capoeira,* xi–xiv. Chicago: University of Illinois Press.

Thornton, John K. (1988, April). The art of war in Angola, 1575–1680. *Comparative Studies in Society and History, 30,* 360–378.

Tolkien, J. R. R. (1994). *The fellowship of the ring.* New York: Houghton Mifflin. (Original work published 1954)

Tomita, Tsuneo. (1962, November). Histoire du judo [History of judo]. *Revue Judo Kodokan, 12,* 5.

Tomlinson, Alan. (1990). Leisure, Labour, and Lifestyles: International Comparisons. In *Proceedings of the Leisure Studies Association Second International Conference.* Eastbourne, UK: LSA Publications.

Training the helpless flapper to fight her own battles. (1927, August 27). *Literary Digest* (p. 47).

Treffner, Paul. (2002). Eadweard Muybridge, pioneer in movement recording, http://www.int.gu.edu.au/~s227447/boxer.html.

Tuhy, John E. (1983). *Sam Hill: The prince of Castle Nowhere.* Beaverton, OR: Timber Press.

Twenty Centuries of Taekwondo. (1981, Winter). *Traditional Taekwondo,* 25–29.

University of Delaware Library, Special Collections Department. (1999). Forging a collection: James Macpherson and the Ossian poems, http://www .lib.udel.edu/ud/spec/exhibits/forgery/ossian.htm.

Urban, Peter. (1967). *The karate dojo: Traditions and tales of a martial art.* Rutland, VT, and Tokyo: Charles E. Tuttle.

U.S. Army. (2002). *Combatives.* Field Manual 3-25-150. Fort Benning, GA: Infantry School.

U.S. Marine Corps. (2002c, May 16). MARADMIN 275/02. Marine Corps Martial Arts Program (MCMAP) Safety Advisory 1–02, http://www.usmc.mil/ maradmins/maradmin2000.nsf/37f49138fc3d9c00852569b9000af6b7/5c0 c4ce0eb213b5a85256bbb006ae51d?OpenDocument.

Van Clief, Ron. (1996). *Black heroes of the martial arts.* Brooklyn, NY: A & B Publishers.

Wacquant, Loïc. (1994, November). The pugilistic point of view: How boxers feel about their trade, http://sociology.berkeley.edu/public_sociology/ Wacquant.pdf.

Wacquant, Loïc. (1995, March 1). Pugs at work: Bodily capital and bodily labour among professional boxers. *Body and Society* 1 (pp. 65–94).

Wacquant, Loïc. (2001, June). The whore, the slave and the stallion. *Le Monde Diplomatique,* http://www.mail-archive.com/brc-news@lists.tao.ca/msg 00465.html.

Wang, George. (2002). History of Gracie Jiu-Jitsu, http://www.geocities.com/ Colosseum/5389/maeda.html.

Warrener, Don. (2001). *Gichin Funakoshi: The original Shotokan karate.* [Videotape]. (Available from Masterline Video Productions, 5 Columbia Dr., Suite #108, Niagara Falls, NY 14305-1275)

Watt, Michael. (1995–2002). Mitsuyo Maeda: The legendary story of "Conde-Koma" Mitsuyo Maeda. *Judo Journal.* This series began with volume 18:4 (July/August 1995) and was still ongoing in volume 26:2 (April/August 2002).

Webster's Ninth New Collegiate Dictionary (1990). Springfield, Mass: Merriam Webster.

Weinberg, S. Kirson, and Henry Arond. (1952, March). The occupational culture of the boxer. *American Journal of Sociology, 57,* (5), 460–469.

Whitehorn, K. (1996, February 2). What little girls are really made of. *Observer* (p. 6).

Wholewheatloaf. (2001). Cultural nationalism in Ireland, http://wholewheatloaf .org/papers/culteire.html.

Wiggins, D. (1977). Good times on the old plantation: Popular recreations of the black slave in antebellum South, 1810–1860. *Journal of Sport History, 4,* (1) 260–284.

Winston Salem Community Mosque. (2002). Community mosque Winston Salem, NC history/accomplishments, http://www.communitymosque.com/abtmos .html.

Wolf, Tony. (1999). *Fighting styles guidebook.* Unpublished manuscript.

Wood, Ray O. III, and Matthew T. Michaelson. (2000, May–June). Close quarters combat and modern warfare. *Military Review,* 8:106–108.

Wooldridge, Ian. (1994, October 26). Keep boxing clear of the gender trap. *Daily Mail* (p. 61).

World Beat Center. (2002a). World Beat Center classes, http://www.world beatcenter.org/classes.shtml.

World Beat Center. (2002b). African reconnection program, http://members .tripod.com/~worldbeat/WorldBeat_Center_African.html.

World Karate Championships (1970, October). *Budo, 6,* 5,22 (program reprinted).

World Taekwondo Federation. (2002a). About taekwondo (history), http:// www.wtf.org/main.htm.

World Taekwondo Federation. (2002b). About taekwondo (*poomsae*) [forms], http://www.wtf.org/main.htm.

Wrestling in the Nuba Mountains: Past and present. (2001, November). *Nuba Vision, 1,* (2), http://www.nubasurvival.com/Nuba%20Vision/Vol%201%20 Issue%202/8%20Wrestling.htm.

Wright, Steve. (1998). *An appraisal of the technologies of political control.* Luxembourg: European Parliament, Directorate General for Research, Directorate B, the STOA Programme, http://www.europarl.eu.int/stoa/publi/ 166499/execsum_en.htm.

Wu Wenzhong. (1967). *Zhongguo jinbainian tiyushi* [A History of Physical Culture in China during the Last 100 Years]. Taibei: Taiwan Shangwu Yinshuguan.

Wu Wenzhong. (1975). Zhongguo wushu fazhan jianshi [A short history of the development of Chinese martial arts]. In *Zhongguo wushu shiliao jikan* [Collection of historical materials on the Chinese martial arts] *2* (pp. 1–10). Taibei: Jiaoyubu Tiyusi.

Wushu: Chinese girl athletes, form and fascination. (2000). *Journal of Combative Sport,* http://ejmas.com/jcs/jcsart_NChinaHerald1_0200.htm. (Original work published May 8, 1920)

Xi Yuntai. (1985). *Zhongguo wushu shi* [Chinese martial arts history]. Beijing: Renmin Tiyu Chubanshe.

Xiang Ling. (1965, May). Fandui guanyu taijiquan de shenmihua guandian [Oppose the mystical view of *taijiquan*]. *New Sports,* 29–30.

Yamada Shoji. (2002, February). Eugen Herrigel no shougai to zen: shinwa to shite no yumi to zen (2) [The life of Eugen Herrigel and Zen: The myth of *Zen in the Art of Archery* (2)]. *Nihon kenyu: Kokusai Nihon bunka kenkyu senta kiyo* [Researching Japan: International Research Center for Japanese Studies symposium proceedings] 24 (pp. 201–226).

Yamamoto Tsunetomo. (1981). *Hagakure* [Hidden among the leaves] (William Scott Wilson, Trans.). New York: Avon Books. (Original work published 1716)

Yang, Jwing-ming. (1999). *Taijiquan-classical Yang style: the complete form and qigong.* Boston, MA: YMAA Publication Center.

Yang, Jwing-ming, and Jeffrey A. Bolt. (1982). *Shaolin long fist kung fu.* Hollywood, CA: Unique Publications.

Yates, Keith D. (1991). A history of Korean karate in America. [Videotape] (Available from A-KaTo, 1218 Cardigan St., Garland, TX 75040, http://www.a-kato.org/books.html)

Yi Jiandong. (1995). Minguo shiqi wushu jingji shulun [Discussion of Republican-era martial arts competition]. *Journal of Chengdu Physical Education Institute, 21,* (3), 7–12.

Young, David C. (1984). *The Olympic myth of Greek amateur athletics.* Chicago: Ares Publishers.

Zhao Renqing. (1965, May). Yong jieji guandian kaocha taijiquan de lishi [Investigating *taijiquan* history from a class viewpoint]. *New Sports,* 30–31.

Zhonggong Hunan Sheng Xinhua Xian E Tang Gongshe Weiyuanhui [Hunan Province Xinhua County E Tang Chinese Communist Party Commune Committee]. (1976, April 26). Take class struggle as the main principle to develop the mass martial arts movement. *Physical Culture News.*

Zhonghua Xin Wushu [New Chinese Martial Arts]. (1917). Commercial Press.

Zi, Etienne. (1971). Pratique des examens militaires en Chine [The practice of military examinations in China]. *Varietes Sinologiques 9.* Taibei: Ch'eng Wen Publishing Company. (Original work published 1896)

Zun Wo Zhai Zhuren [Master of the studio of self-respect]. (1971). *Shaolin quanshu mijue* [Secrets of Shaolin boxing]. Zhonghua Wushu. (Original work published 1915)

ARCHIVAL MATERIAL (UNPUBLISHED)

Chief, Bureau of Navigation. (1905, November 4). Letter to Superintendent, U.S. Naval Academy, in U.S. Naval Academy archives.

City of Richmond Archives. (2002). Steveston Community Society fonds, http://www.city.richmond.bc.ca/archives.

FBI. FBI documents obtained through Freedom of Information request, courtesy the Guy Power collection.

Henry H. Okuda. (n.d.). Accession number 2345, box 1. Manuscripts and University Archives Division. Seattle: University of Washington.

Library of Congress. (n.d.). Image LC-USW3-022983-C [P&P].

List or Manifest of Alien Passengers for the U.S. Immigration Officer at Port of Arrival. SS *Shinano Maru,* October 8, 1903, in M1383, Passenger and Crew Lists of Vessels Arriving at Seattle, Washington, 1890–1957, Roll 2 (Apr. 17, 1900, SS GOODWIN—Jan. 17, 1904, SS TOSA MARU).

Superintendent, U.S. Naval Academy. (1905, November 17). Letter to Y. Yamashita, care Imperial Japanese Legation, Washington, D.C., in U.S. Naval Academy archives.

Superintendent, U.S. Naval Academy. (1906, May 4). Letter to Chief of Bureau of Navigation, Navy Department, in U.S. Naval Academy archives.

EPHEMERA

Cho Scrapbook. (n.d.). Copy of Walter Cho scrapbook in the Paul Lou collection.

Daly, J. (n.d.). Foremothers of boxing. Unidentified clipping in the Jennifer Hargreaves personal collection.

Krieg, J. (n.d.). The angel of the ring. Unidentified clipping in the Jennifer Hargreaves collection.

Toyama, Kanken. (1959). *Karate-do nyumon* [A karate (empty hand-way) primer] (Xerox copy of several pages in Eric Madis collection).

Who Is the Grandmaster? (n.d.). Unidentified clipping in the Eric Madis personal collection.

MINUTES

Minutes of the British Judo Association

ADDITIONAL SOURCES

Almeida, Bira. (1986). *Capoeira: A Brazilian art form.* Berkeley: North Atlantic.

Alter, Joseph. (1992). *The wrestler's body: Identity and ideology in North India.* Berkeley: University of California Press.

Alter, Joseph. (2000, Summer). Gama the Great: Indian nationalism and the world wrestling championships of 1910 and 1928. *Yugantar Punjab,* http://www.yugantar.com/sum00/gama.html.

Bowen, Richard. (2002a). History, http://www.budokwai.org/history.htm.

Bowen, Richard. (2002b). Koizumi Gunji, 1885–1965: Judo master. In Hugh Cortazzi (Ed.), *Britain and Japan: Biographical portraits 4* (pp. 312–322). London: Japan Society.

Bowen, Richard. (in press). Gunji Koizumi. In *Oxford dictionary of national biography.* Oxford: Oxford University Press.

Brownell, Susan. (1995). *Training the body for China: Sports in the moral order of the People's Republic.* Chicago: University of Chicago Press.

Campbell Johnston, Rachel. (1995, February 13). Velvety hands in iron gloves. *Observer,* 29.

Capoeira Angola. (n.d.). Washington, DC: International Capoeira Angola Foundation.

Capoeira Angola Sao Bento Grande. (2002b). Kalenda, http://www.malandrostouro.com/generic.html;$sessionid$ZYFDSOQAAAXG4P5MFMKZPQR53QVSNPX0?pid = 10.

Chen Gongzhe. (2001). *Jingwu hui 50 nian* [Jingwu association: 50 years]. Shenyang: Chunfeng Wenyi Chubanshe.

Chen, Jim. (1997). Masahiko Kimura, the man who defeated Hélio Gracie, http://www.judoinfo.com/kimura.htm.

Cohen, Paul. (1987). *History in three keys.* Stanford, CA: Stanford University Press.

Cohen, Paul. (1992, February). The contested past: The Boxers as history and myth. *Journal of Asian Studies, 51,* (1), 82–113.

CyberBoxingZone. (2002b). Peter Jackson, http://www.cyberboxingzone.com/boxing/jackson.htm.

CyberBoxingZone. (2002c). Sam Langford, http://www.cyberboxingzone.com/boxing/langford.htm.

Donald, B. (1994, January 27). Christie and Suzie slug it out in Vegas. *Guardian* (p. 17).

Eskin, L. (1974, September). Complete history of women's boxing. *Boxing Illustrated* (pp. 25–28).

Foucault, Michel (1980). In *Power/Knowledge,* C. Gordon (Ed.). Brighton: Harvester Press.

Gentry, Clyde III. (2001). *No holds barred: Evolution.* Richardson, TX: Archon Publishing.

Gorsuch, Mark. (2002). Mitsuyo Maeda (Count Koma) biography, http://bjj.org/interviews/maeda.html.

Gracie, Renzo, and Royler Gracie, with Kid Peligro and John Danaher. (2002). *Brazilian jiu-jitsu: Theory & technique.* Montpelier, VT: Invisible Cities Press in association with Editora Gracie.

Green, Thomas A. (Ed.). (2001). *Martial arts of the world: An encyclopedia.* Santa Barbara, CA: ABC-CLIO.

Grix, Arthur E. (1937). *Japans Sport in Bild und Wort* [Japan's sport in pictures and words]. Berlin: Wilhelm Limpert-Verlag.

Guojia Tiwei Wushu Yanjiuyuan [National Physical Culture Commission Martial Arts Research Institute] (Eds.). (1997). *Zhongguo wushu shi* [Chinese martial arts history]. Beijing: Renmin Tiyu Chubanshe.

Guttmann, Allen. (1992). *The Olympics: A history of the modern games.* Urbana: University of Illinois Press.

Herrigel, Eugen. (1936a). Die ritterliche Kunst des Bogenschiessens [The chivalric art of archery]. *Nippon Zeitschrift für Japanologie, 2,* (4), 193–212.

Herrigel, Eugen. (1936b). Kyujutsu ni tsuite [On archery; originally, Die ritterliche Kunst des Bogenschiessens] (Shibata Jisaburo, Trans.). *Bunka, 3,* (9), 1007–1034.

Herrigel, Eugen. (1982). *Nihon no kyujutsu* [Japanese archery; originally, Die ritterliche Kunst des Bogenschiessens (1936)] (Shibata Jisaburo, Trans.), with an essay (1940) by Komachiya Sozo (Rev. ed. with a new afterword by the translator). Tokyo: Iwanami Bunko. (Original work published 1941)

Herrigel, Eugen. (1991). *Zen no michi* [The way of Zen; originally, *Der Zen-Weg*] (Enoki Shinkichi, Trans.). Tokyo: Kodansha Gakujutsu Bunko.

Hill, Sam. (1903, July 21). Letter to Yamashita Yoshiaki in Maryhill Museum of Art collection.

Hwang, Tony, and Grant Jarvie. (2001). Sport, nationalism and the early Chinese Republic 1912–1927. *The Sports Historian,* http://www.umist.ac.uk/sport/SPORTS%20HISTORY/BSSH/The%20Sports%20Historian/TSH%2021–2/Art1-HwangJarvie.htm.

Inatomi Eijiro. (1956). Herigeru sensei no omoide [Memories of Professor Herrigel]. In Herrigel, (pp. 148–65).

Isenberg, Michael T. (1988). *John L. Sullivan and his America.* Urbana: University of Illinois Press.

Ivan, Dan. (1997, March). Bassai dai (comparing Shotokan and Shito-ryu). *Black Belt,* 32–38, 170.

Jennings, Andrew. (2001). Sports, lies and Stasi files: A golden opportunity for the press, http://www.play-the-game.org/articles/jennings/sport_lies_stasi.html.

Jin Renlin. (1996, January). Xu Zhedong tan taijiquan [Xu Zhedong discusses *taijiquan*]. *Wu Hun, 91,* 16–17.

Jordan, Pat. (1989, September). Rorion Gracie interview. *Playboy, 36,* (9), http://bjj.org/interviews/rorion-89–09.html.

Kenney, K. (1982). The realm of sport and the athletic woman, 1850–1900. In Reet Howell (Ed.), *Her story in sport: A historical anthology of women in sports.* New York: Leisure Press.

Kiley, J. (1974, June). For the cause of women boxers. *Boxing Illustrated,* 62.

Kiley, J. (1974, July). For the cause of women boxers. *Boxing Illustrated,* 62.

Kiley, J. (1974, September). For the cause of women boxers. *Boxing Illustrated,* 58.

Kolatch, Jonathan. (1972). *Sports, politics and ideology in China.* Middle Village, NY: Jonathan David.

Korea and Olympism. (1979, February). *Olympic Review, 136,* 99–108), http://www.aafla.org/OlympicInformationCenter/OlympicReview/1979/ore136/ore136u.pdf#xml=http://www.aafla.org/search/highlight.gtf?nth=27&handle=000002ca

Korean Embassy. (2000). Korean history: The independence army. *Asian Info.org,* http://www.asianinfo.org./asianinfo/korea/history/independence_army.htm.

Largey, Michael. (2000). Politics on the pavement: Haitian rara as a traditionalizing process. *Journal of American Folklore, 113,* 239–254.

Lenskyj, Helen. (1986). Fighting women. In Helen Lenskyj (Ed.), *Out of bounds: Women, sport and sexuality* (pp. 115–126). Toronto: Women's Press.

Lewis, Marion. (1933, December). Leather and lingerie. *The Ring,* 40–41.

Lu Xun. (1989). *Lu Xun quan ji* [Complete works of Lu Xun]. (Vol. 1, pp. 309–310; Vol. 8, pp. 81–86). Beijing: Renmin Wenxue Chubanshe.

Marushima, Takao. (1997). *Maeda Mitsuyo: Conte Koma.* Tokyo: Shimazu Shobo.

Meadows, Travis. (2002, May). UA Fighting 2: The gathering. *Ultimate Athlete,* 49–52, 83–84.

Momii, Ikken. (1939). *Hokubei kendo taikan* [An overview of North American kendo]. San Francisco: Hokubei Butokukai.

Murray, Dian H., and Qin Baoqi. (1994). *The origins of the tiandihui: The Chinese Triads in legend and history.* Stanford, CA: Stanford University Press.

Nakamura, Taizaburo, with Guy Power and Takako Funaya. (1998). Thoughts on iaido [Sword drawing way]. *Dragon Times,* http://www.dragon-tsunami .org/Dtimes/Pages/articled2.htm.

Noble, Graham. (1996a). History of Shorin-Ryu karate. *Dragon Times, 12,* 15–17.

Noble, Graham. (2000b). The odyssey of Yukio Tani. *InYo,* http://ejmas.com/jalt/ jaltart_Noble_1000.htm.

Noble, Graham. (2001). The life and death of the Terrible Turk. *Journal of Manly Arts,* http://ejmas.com/jmanly/jmanlyart_noble_0501.htm.

O'Farrell, Patrick. (1989). Review of the book *The Gaelic Athletic Association and Irish nationalist politics 1884–1924. Sporting Traditions, 5,* (2), 238–241, http://www.aafla.org/SportsLibrary/SportingTraditions/1989/st0502/st0502o .pdf

Okazaki, Robert K. (1996). *The Nisei mass evacuation group and P.O.W. Camp "101" Angler, Ontario.* Scarborough, Ontario: Markham Litho.

Ortiz, Fernando. (1985). *Los bailes y el teatro de los Negros en el folklore de Cuba* [The dance and theatre of the blacks in the folklore of Cuba]. Havana: Editorial Letras Cubanas.

Paman, Jose. (1994 September). The Rio story. *Martial Arts Masters,* http:// www.gracie.com/pubs/riostory1.html.

Pieter, Willy. (1994). Notes on the historical development of Korean martial sports: An addendum to Young's history and development of tae kyon. *Journal of Asian Martial Arts, 3,* (1), 82–89.

Powe, Edward L. (2002b). *Black martial arts: Vol. 4. African arts of stick-fighting: Northern Nguni, part 1.* Madison, WI: Dan Aiki Publications.

Schnabel, Jim. (1997). *Remote viewers: The secret history of America's psychic spies.* New York: Dell.

Shibata Jisaburo. (1982a). Kyohan e no yakusha koki kara [From the translator's postscript to the old edition]. In Eugen Herrigel, *Nihon no Kyujutsu* (pp. 101–105). Tokyo: Iwanami Shoten. (Original work published 1941)

Shibata Jisaburo. (1982b). Shinpan e no yakusha koki [Translator's postscript to the new addition]. In Eugen Herrigel, *Nihon no Kyujutsu* (pp. 107–22). Tokyo: Iwanami Shoten. (Original work published 1941)

Svinth, Joseph R. (2001c). Fighting spirit II: Korean American boxers. *Occasional Papers, A Publication of the Korean American Historical Society, 5,* 135–154.

Svinth, Joseph R. (2001d). Karate pioneer Yabu Kentsu, 1866–1937. *Journal of Asian Martial Arts, 10,* (2), 8–17.

Svinth, Joseph R. (2001e). Combatives: military and police martial art training. In Eugen Green, *Martial arts of the modern world: An encyclopedia* (pp. 83–92). Santa Barbara, CA: ABC-CLIO.

Svinth, Joseph R. (2003). *Getting a grip: Judo in the Nikkei communities of the Pacific Northwest, 1900–1950.*

Swift, Joe. (2002). Roots of Shotokan: Funakoshi's original 15 kata (three parts). *Fighting Arts Magazine,* http://www.fightingarts.com/content02/roots_shotokan_1.shtml.

Taekwondo, an Olympic sport for the year 2000. (1994, November). *Olympic Review, 323,* 475–477, http://www.aafla.org/OlympicInformationCenter/OlympicReview/1994/ore323/ORE323o.pdf.

Trumpener, Katie. (1997). *Bardic nationalism: The romantic novel and the British Empire.* Princeton: Princeton University Press.

University of Pennsylvania, Archives. (1999, November). Eadweard Muybridge 1830–1904, http://www.archives.upenn.edu/histy/features/muybridge/muybridge.html.

Van Sertima, Ivan, and Runoko Rashidi (Eds.). (1988). *African presence in early Asia* (Rev. ed.). New Brunswick, NJ: Transaction Books.

Williams, James, and Stanley A. Pranin. (1995, Fall). Interview with Rorion Gracie. *Aikido Journal, 105,* http://www.aikidojournal.com/index.asp ("Interviews").

Williams, James, and Stanley A. Pranin (1996, Winter). Interview with Rorion Gracie. *Aikido Journal, 106,* http://www.aikidojournal.com/index.asp ("Interviews").

Yamada Shoji. (1999). Shinwa to shite no yumi to Zen [The myth of *Zen in the Art of Archery*]. *Nihon kenkyu: Kokusai Nihon bunka kenkyu senta kiyo* [Researching Japan: International Research Center for Japanese Studies symposium proceedings] *19* (pp. 15–34).

Yamashita, Yoshiaki. (1903, August 26). Letter to Sam Hill in Maryhill Museum of Art collection.

INDEX

Sanbo, Amy, 121, 122–24
Sasaki Tokujiro, 37
Satake Shinjiro, 66
Savate, 213–14
Seattle Kendo Kai, 151, 160
Shado, 76–78
Shaolin, Boxing, 21–22, 27, 34;
  Monk, 16–17; Temple, 5–7, 24
Silat, 6, 247
Songmookwan, 194–95
Sports, 131, 284; African American,
  232, 248; China, 15, 18–19, 28,
  30–32, 36; Japan, 42–46, 167–72;
  kendo in North America, 160–62;
  Korea, 203–7
Sultaniwala, Rahim, 97
Sumo, 63
Sun Lutang, 23
Supernatural aid, Africa and
  African America Martial Arts,
  132–33

Taekwondo, 185–207
Taekyon, 185, 189, 202
Taijiquan/T'ai Chi ch'uan, 6, 23, 24,
  25–26, 28–30, 32–34
Taiwan, 28–29
Takahashi Kazuo, 42
Tang Hao, 24–25
Tangsoodo, 193, 201–2
Taro Miyak, 64
Taussig, J. J. "Moose," 40
Tetsuro, "Rubberman" Higami, 64
Tolo-Naa, Nganga, 242
Tomita Tsunejiro, 64–65
Triad Societies, 7
Turner, Rufe, 39, 280
Tyson, Mike, 243

Ueshiba Morihei, 52
Ultimate Fighting Championship, 61,
  63, 70, 271

United States Army Ranger Combatives Program, 266–68
United States Marine Corps Combatives Program, 268–69
United States Military Academy,
  64–65
United States Naval Academy, 56–59,
  281
Uriu Sotokichi, 37

Van Clief, Ron, 240
Verbal Duel, African and African
  American, 135, 247, 284

Wantanabe Yujiro, 37, 39–42, 46
Wing Chun/Yongchun, 6, 115,
  118–19, 125
Women: Boxing, 209–28; China,
  15–16, 17, 28; judo, 52, 66; kendo,
  157–58
Woo, Charlie, 117
Wrestling: "Western," 56–57, 63–64,
  65–67, 99–106, 108; Indian, 93–109
Wu Tang Clan, 238–39, 243
Wudang, 27

Xingyiquan, 23–24, 34
Xu Zen, 25–26

Yabu Kentsu, 188–90
Yamaguchi Gogen, 7–8
Yamashita Yoshiaki, 47–59, 64, 281
Yip Man, 30, 118, 124
Yun Byung-in, 196–97
Yun Kwei-byung, 197–98, 205
Yunmookwan, 195–96

Zen/Chan Buddhism, 71–73, 79–81,
  90, 282
Zhang Sanfeng, 6, 24
Zumbi, 7
Zbyszko, Stanislaus, 102–7

ABOUT THE EDITORS
AND CONTRIBUTORS

RICHARD BOWEN has over fifty years experience in judo. He trained in Japan and was a member of the Kodokan *kenshusei* (teacher training program) for almost four years. He competed in the European and World championships and performed *kata* during the Kodokan New Year's celebration of 1958. He is a former chairman of the British Judo Association Coaching and Technical Subcommittee, a vice-president of the Budokwai, and author of many technical articles. He lives in London, England.

THOMAS A. GREEN is associate professor in anthropology at Texas A&M University. His books include *Folklore: An Encyclopedia of Beliefs, Customs, Tales, Music, and Art* (1997) and *Martial Arts of the World: An Encyclopedia* (2001). He has been training in martial arts since 1972.

JAMES HALPIN is an investigative journalist who lives in Seattle, Washington. In addition to Bruce Lee, he has also profiled Sasquatch and the conservative activist, Alan Gottlieb.

JENNIFER HARGREAVES is professor of the sociology of sport and a co-director of the Centre for Sport Development Research at the Roehampton Institute in London, England. Her books include *Sporting Females: Critical Issues in the History and Sociology of Women's Sports* (1994) and *Heroines of Sport: The Politics of Difference and Identity* (2001).

STANLEY E. HENNING is an independent scholar living in Honolulu, Hawaii. He served twenty-eight years in the U.S. Army in a variety of assignments in the Asia-Pacific region, taught English in Kunming, China, from 1995 to 1996, and is currently employed as an International Relations Specialist. He studied Yang *taijiquan*, Shanxi *xingyiquan*, and several martial art weapons routines in Taiwan during the 1970s.

KANO JIGORO was both the founder of judo and a member of the International Olympics Committee. From 1932 until his death six years later, he was a leader of Japan's bid for the 1940 Olympics.

ERIC MADIS is a recording artist and educator whose professional publications are primarily in the field of ethnomusicology. He has been training in martial arts in 1963 and is an instructor in Tang Soo Do, which he has practiced since 1982.

GRAHAM NOBLE began studying Shotokan karate in 1966, but soon expanded into various self-defense systems. As a martial arts historian and prolific author, he is currently writing a book on early twentieth-century jujutsu and professional wrestling, and plans to write a book on karate history. He has an engineering degree but works as an accountant in a local government office in North Tyneside, England.

JOSEPH R. SVINTH is an editor for the *Electronic Journals of Martial Arts and Science*. A former Marine and a retired soldier, he has practiced martial arts since 1980. His book, *Getting a Grip: Judo in the Nikkei Communities of the Pacific Northwest, 1900-1950* is in press.

TONY WOLF has over twenty years experience in a variety of Asian, Brazilian, and European combat styles. He has an interest in historical European martial arts—particularly obscure folk martial arts. A former professional wrestler and stuntman, he currently works as a fight coordinator and trainer in the New Zealand entertainment industry. His most recent film project was *Lord of the Rings: The Fellowship of the Ring* (2001).

YAMADA SHOJI is an assistant professor at the International Research Center for Japanese Studies in Kyoto, and his publications include various articles on *kyudo* history. He began training in *kyudo* in 1985, and he currently holds a fifth *dan* from the All Nippon Kyudo Federation.